TREASURES FROM PAUL

Ephesians

Ken Chant

TREASURES FROM PAUL
Ephesians

Ken Chant

ISBN 978-1-61529-227-1

Copyright © 2020 by Ken Chant

Revised Edition 2020

Vision Publishing
P.O. Box 1680
Ramona, CA 92065
1 800 9 VISION
www.booksbyvision.org

All rights to this book are reserved worldwide.

No part of this book may be reproduced in any manner without the written permission of Vision Publishing except in brief quotations embodied in critical articles of review.

Table of Contents

What You Will Find Here 7
Section One: Starting Out 11
   One: Called To Be Saints 12
Section Two: In The Heavenlies 23
   Two: Over The Hills and Far Away 24
   Three: Your Provision in The Heavenlies 33
   Four: Your Power In The Heavenlies 47
   Five: Your Position in The Heavenlies 55
   Six: Your Profession in The Heavenlies 61
   Seven: Your Protection in The Heavenlies 67
Section Three: Inheritance and Strength 73
   Eight: A Guaranteed Inheritance 74
   Nine: Beyond Measure 81
   Ten: An Extraordinary Strength 91
   Eleven: An Extraordinary Strength – 2 97
Section Four: Christian Life 105
   Twelve: Forgiveness 106
   Thirteen: Transformation 121
   Fourteen: Meekness 127
Section Five: Throne Rights 143
   Fifteen: Enthroned in the Heavenlies 144
   Sixteen: Bravely Into The Holiest! 157
   Seventeen: Exceeding Abundantly 173
Section Six: Ministry Gifts 185
   Eighteen: Finding Your Place In The Church 186

Nineteen: The Ministry Gifts 197
Section Seven: The Bride of Christ 207
   Twenty: Chosen by The Father................................ 208
   Twenty-one: Betrothal Obligations – The Groom 217
   Twenty-two: Betrothal Obligations – The Bride 227
   Twenty-three: United For Ever 237
Section Eight: War in Heaven 243
   Twenty-four: A Declaration of War...........................244
   Twenty-five: The Armour of God 257
   Twenty-six: Playing Your Part...................................285
   Twenty-seven: The Rules of Combat........................297

A NOTE ON GENDER

It is unfortunate that the English language does not contain an adequate generic pronoun (especially in the singular number) that includes without bias both male and female. So "he, him, his, himself, man, mankind," with their plurals, must often do the work for both sexes. Accordingly, wherever it is appropriate to do so in the following pages, please include the feminine gender in the masculine, and vice versa.

FOOTNOTES

A work once fully referenced will thereafter be noted either by "ibid" (the same) or "op. cit." (the work previously cited).

SCRIPTURE TRANSLATIONS

All scripture translations in these pages are my own, unless otherwise noted.

ABBREVIATIONS

Abbreviations commonly used for the books of the Bible are –

Genesis	Ge	Habakkuk	Hb
Exodus	Ex	Zephaniah	Zp
Leviticus	Le	Haggai	Hg
Numbers	Nu	Zechariah	Zc
Deuteronomy	De	Malachi	Mal
Joshua	Js		
Judges	Jg		
Ruth	Ru	Matthew	Mt
1 Samuel	1 Sa	Mark	Mk
2 Samuel	2 Sa	Luke	Lu
1 Kings	1 Kg	John	Jn
2 Kings	2 Kg	Acts	Ac
1 Chronicles	1 Ch	Romans	Ro
2 Chronicles	2 Ch	1 Corinthians	1 Co
Ezra	Ezr	2 Corinthians	2 Co
Nehemiah	Ne	Galatians	Ga
Esther	Es	Ephesians	Ep
Job	Jb	Philippians	Ph
Psalm	Ps	Colossians	Cl
Proverbs	Pr	1 Thessalonians	1 Th
Ecclesiastes	Ec	2 Thessalonians	2 Th
Song of Songs	Ca *	1 Timothy	1 Ti
Isaiah	Is	2 Timothy	2 Ti
Jeremiah	Je	Titus	Tit

Lamentations	La	Philemon	Phm
Ezekiel	Ez	Hebrews	He
Daniel	Da	James	Ja
Hosea	Ho	1 Peter	1 Pe
Joel	Jl	2 Peter	2 Pe
Amos	Am	1 John	1 Jn
Obadiah	Ob	2 John	2 Jn
Jonah	Jo	3 John	3 Jn
Micah	Mi	Jude	Ju
Nahum	Na	Revelation	Re

* *Ca* is an abbreviation of Canticles, a derivative of the Latin name of the *Song of Solomon*, which is sometimes also called the *Song of Songs*.

What You Will Find Here

The studies that follow make no pretence of providing a full commentary on Paul's *Letter to the Ephesians*. If you want information about background, when and why the letter was written, and the like, you should turn to the internet or to any good Bible dictionary, encyclopaedia, or commentary.

What you will find here is *treasure* – that is, a cluster of ideas taken from *Ephesians* and expounded in various ways, often drawing on many other parts of scripture, and always directed toward successful Christian life and to the enrichment of your mind and spirit.

I should mention here, too, that the sections of this book that comment on Paul's phrase *"in the heavenlies"* are similar to Chapter Two of my book *Throne Rights*. The ideas seemed important enough to warrant a re-statement, especially since not everyone who reads one book will read the other.

As for *Ephesians* itself, it baffles me how anyone can read this letter and then deny the truth of the gospel. [1] Were more wonderful words ever written? Were more extraordinary ideas ever compounded?

This letter contains that rarest of things, a cluster of ideas that no one on earth had ever before imagined! It defies the maxim of old that *"there is nothing new under the sun"* (Ec 1:9-10). This small letter is filled with concepts that here come into the world for the very first time. It is a miracle! Let anyone who wishes to scorn the gospel first explain away the divine mystery of *Ephesians*! How could any man have

---

(1) The same could be said of its companion, Paul's letter to the *Colossians*. Both letters were written at about the same time, circa A.D. 60.

conceived and written such things unless they are simply true?

Yet this becomes even more wonderful when you remember that Paul was a first-century Jew, a devout monotheist, utterly committed to the worship of one God, Yahweh of Israel. He reckoned it foul blasphemy deserving a savage death to call any man divine. Yet suddenly we find him ascribing to Jesus of Nazareth an astonishingly exalted rank. Paul no longer sees Christ as merely human, but as wholly divine, possessing supernal glory and a dazzling magnificence equal to that of Yahweh! Such a transformation is inexplicable apart from a radical conversion – that is, a mind-change based upon a shattering encounter with irrefutable evidence. And that, of course, is just what did happen to Paul on the road to Damascus (Ac 9:1-8; 22:3-10; 26:9-19).

Someone may say that certain scholars doubt that Paul wrote the letter, that in fact it was written by a later disciple of his, possibly as late as 80 A.D. Yet even among those who question Paul's authorship a scholarly consensus remains that *Ephesians* at least echoes his teachings. In any case, we are still left with the same problem – how to account for the incredible ideas in the letter? If they are not true, then they were invented, which seems impossible! [2]

Nevertheless, there are people who do insist that the letter is a piece of fiction, a human invention, an irresponsible fabrication. But why *would* any man of the first century

---

(2) I have no personal doubt about the Pauline authorship of *Ephesians*. The arguments for it are at least as strong as those against it, and I find them stronger. And when I read the critics, I am astonished by their spiritual dullness. Have they ever truly read the letter? Do they have the faintest idea of what it really says? How can they so focus on textual minutiae that they utterly miss the thrilling vistas the letter unfolds, its marvellous promises, its enthralling vision of Christ?

invent the scenario presented in *Ephesians*, and then present it as life-changing truth? And how *could* he do so, when the ideas are so unique, so exalted, so improbable, so dangerous – unless they had come to him as undeniable truth?

Even if *Ephesians* were only a summary of Paul's beliefs, written by a disciple not long after the apostle's death, it still runs counter to all that he had formerly been as a man, a Jew, a scholar, and it remains a miracle of revelation. Here are beliefs that undo many of his previous deepest convictions. He was a fiercely monotheistic Jew for whom even the thought of a man of flesh and blood possessing divinity was foul blasphemy, deserving savage death. Yet now, barely 30 years after the Cross, here is Paul describing Jesus in the most exalted terms. How can such an astonishing shift be understood apart from the reason Paul himself gave – his cataclysmic confrontation with the risen Christ on the road to Damascus?

Indeed, so great was the shake-up wrought in him by that encounter, that whereas he once called it blasphemy to accord divinity to anyone but Yahweh, now he calls it blasphemy to deny that Christ possesses divinity equal to Yahweh! (Ac 26:11)

Furthermore, Paul dared to write such things while thousands of people were still alive who had actually seen Jesus in Palestine, walking and talking, eating and drinking, laughing and weeping, sleeping and waking. To those observers, Jesus was just as human as they were. Paul too, during the years when he furiously persecuted the Church, had thought of Jesus as a man, a blasphemer, if not insane. Yet now we find him, with immense drama and passion, calling Jesus God! And he presents visions of Jesus so supernal they demand that all creation should revere the former Man of Galilee and offer him heartfelt worship.

No explanation of this transformation of Paul the Jew to Paul the Christian is easier to accept than the claim that what he writes is no human coinage, but came to him by divine revelation.

Further, Paul had nothing to gain from inventing a glorious Christ – except what he did gain, floggings, imprisonment, starvation, hardship, and eventual violent death. He expected this. He knew it was inevitable. He had no hope of benefit from his writing unless what he wrote was so ineluctably true that he dared not do otherwise! And to Paul, the evidence truly was unassailable. He *knew* that Jesus was the promised Messiah. He *knew* that Jesus had lived, died, risen from the dead. He *knew* that Jesus had ascended back to the Father's right hand, where he now reigns invincibly until the time of his return. Paul rejoiced in the irrevocable destiny of the Church to share the kingdom with Christ for ever. So, sizzling with joy he wrote his letter to the Christians at Ephesus.

Ephesians exalts Christ in terms that human ears had never before heard. It describes the salvation believers find in Christ in a fashion more dramatic than any playwright has ever conceived. Its ideas are breath-taking, revolutionary, unlike anything ever before written about anybody by anybody. No wonder – they came from God! (2 Co 12:2-4)

Across the centuries since Paul, ten thousand other books have been written about *Ephesians,* but none of them has ever been its equal, nor would ten thousand more exhaust it. The height and depth of its wonders and mysteries, the astonishing and enthralling riches that lie in its pages, are boundless. I can but hope that you will find in my book a map to some of those treasures.

Section One:

Starting Out

One:

Called To Be Saints

"From Paul, by the will of God an apostle of Jesus Christ, to the faithful saints in Christ Jesus who are in Ephesus" (Ep 1:1).

The very first verse of the *Letter to the Ephesians* forces us to confront one of the most vexing problems that trouble Christians – how to understand who we are in Christ. We could call it –

An Identity Crisis

We begin with the extraordinary fact that all who are *justified by faith* are called *"saints"* (Ep 1:1; etc). How can that be? And in any case, what is a "saint"?

Popularly, a *"saint"* is a holy person who becomes a religious hero, famous for a singularly holy life, miracles, or for a martyr's death. Saints, too, are often renowned for harshly ascetic behaviour, or for prodigious sacrifices, or sundry extraordinary exploits. Of course, saints are usually recognised only after their death; moreover, during their life they do not speak of themselves as saints – indeed, people who call themselves "saints" will probably not be called saintly by their neighbours!

Yet scripture calls *every* Christian a "saint" – and we are saints right now, without having done anything! Indeed, the term is used many times in the NT of all believers. Like it or not, we who believe in Christ are *all* classified as *"saints"*.

But at once we have a problem, for we find ourselves each day looking into the mirror at a person who is not all saintly! We don't *look* or *feel* like saints! How peculiar it would sound if I addressed you as "St So-And-So", and even more strange for you to announce yourself by that title. For that reason, and because we feel so uncomfortable with the term, or because it seems quaint and old-fashioned, Christian people nowadays seldom address each other as saints.

So then, can we truly call ourselves and each other *saints*, not in the coming kingdom, but *this very day?* We find the answer in

The Example of Jesus

The preeminent *"saint"* is surely Jesus. So isn't it strange that all the NT leaders are called saints, *except* Jesus? We read about *St John, St Paul, St Matthew*, and so on, but no one ever says *St Jesus*! Yet those other men were at best only pale reflections of his virtue. Likewise, in history, many people have become designated as "saints" (St Aiden; St Christopher; and so on), but again, no one ever says *St Jesus*!

Perhaps that is because in many ways Jesus did not (and does not) match the popular image of what a "saint" should be! But we should make *him* our model, not church tradition nor popular fancies.

Now notice this vital fact – Jesus began as a *natural* man, not as a *supernatural* man (except in his conception). What does that mean? The Church has always maintained both the full *humanity* and the full *deity* of Jesus. That is, normal Christian doctrine claims that Jesus is –

- one person (the *Eternal Logos,* Jn 1:1),
- with two natures (*human* and *divine*, Cl 2:9),
- and probably a single will (that of the *Logos*); but that

- during the years of his incarnation he confined himself to those attributes that are proper to human nature (Ph 2:6-8);[3] that is,
- at no time did he make use of any attribute that is proper only to the Deity (cp. Mt 4:3-4).

How then did he do his mighty works? <u>Answer</u>: he had to do just as we must do: he first had to discover from scripture his true identity in God, and then utilise the resources available to him through prayer, faith, and the Holy Spirit.

Now this means that Jesus, in order to fulfil his mission, had to break through many barriers. Had he not done so, he could not have fulfilled his destiny. In particular, he had to overcome – [4]

The Barrier of Natural Perception

Nothing in his natural perception of himself could have given Jesus knowledge of his divine origin. Although he was conceived by a miracle, and born without sin, from then on his development and birth followed ordinary natural processes. As a baby, Jesus was as helpless and as ignorant as any human infant. He had to learn the same things that all

---

(3) Opinions differ about whether or not Jesus retained the possession and use of all his divine attributes as the Logos. I take it that he did in fact cast off everything except what properly belonged to a natural man – that is, he truly did "empty" himself of all that belonged only to God (Ph 2:7). Others argue that he retained possession of every attribute, human and divine, but voluntarily confined himself only to the human. Whichever is true, the result is the same, he lived as a natural man, and resisted at all times Satan's attempts to get him to step outside his humanity and to resume the powers of God (Mt 4:3-4). The idea is called the kenosis of Christ, based on the Greek word that is translated "empty". This thought is taken up again a page or two below, under "The Barrier of Satanic Opposition".

(4) An outline similar to the four headings given below, but with somewhat different contents, can be found in Chapter Seven of my book *The Authenticity and Authority of the Bible*.

children must learn, and in the same way, sometimes even through pain (He 5:7-8). He had no innate understanding of his divine origins. That knowledge dawned in him (by revelation from the Holy Spirit) only as he daily studied scripture and prayed. (5)

Indeed, Jesus had probably reached manhood before he gained *full* awareness of his true identity, with the final realisation perhaps coming to him only at the time of his baptism by John (Lu 3:22).

But aside from that biblical revelation of his heavenly identity, all the evidence of his natural senses told him that he was just a man like any other, with the same needs and infirmities. When he worked in Joseph's carpentry shop, his muscles ached as fiercely as any man's, his thumb bruised like any thumb when he banged it with a hammer, and he was as thirsty and hungry as any worker after several hours' labour!

This ordinary humanity is shown by the failure of his brothers, his sisters, his neighbours, to notice anything unusual in his life until after he had begun his ministry (cp. Mt 13:55; Mk 3:20-21; 6:2,3; Lu 4:22). Indeed, even then, despite performing amazing miracles, Jesus still mostly lived as an ordinary man – he needed sleep, he could be physically wounded, he had to walk like any other person, he liked a warm fire on a winter's evening, he enjoyed a good dinner with friends, he was sociable and related to people normally.

But a time came when Jesus had to put aside all that evidence of his natural humanity, and instead believe with all his heart everything scripture said about him, no matter how

---

(5) By the time he was 12, Jesus had certainly begun to realise his true identity, but it is improbable that he had reached full understanding at so young an age (Lu 2:49).

impossible it seemed. Yet think how hard it must have been for him, after spending many years as a carpenter's assistant, to apply to himself the staggering words of Isaiah 9:6-7 –

> *A Child will be born for us and to us a Son will be given. All rule and authority will belong to him. And he will be called the Wonderful Counsellor, the Mighty God, the Everlasting Father, and the Prince of Peace. His dominion will never stop expanding and his peace will be eternal.*

When did Jesus first realise that *he* was the Child, *he* was the Son? We don't know. But there must have come a certain day when, reading those words, he realised that they spoke about *him* – that, impossible as it might seem, he was truly the prophesied Counsellor, God, Father, and Prince, destined to reign for ever!

Nothing that his eye could see, nothing that his hand could feel, nothing in the world around him, gave the slightest indication that those words could be even partly true. Yet that was what scripture said, and the Holy Spirit kept showing him that he was indeed the predicted Messiah. So he faced a choice – to *believe* or to *reject* the testimony.

He chose to believe – and it was upon that foundation of an *inner revelation* of the word of God that all his subsequent ministry was built.

Likewise, we too have to break through the contrary message of our natural perception, the witness of our physical senses, and believe what the scriptures say about us, no matter how incredible their statements may seem, or how unrelated to what we observe on earth. And scripture says that we who have come into union with Christ through faith, are all *saints*, able to be and to do all that lies in the Father's incredible purpose for us. Break through the barrier of your natural state and grip the supernatural identity that God has given you in Christ. The truly *real* thing is not what your eye sees but what scripture says!

The Barrier of Peer-Group Pressure

Remember that Jesus' family thought he was mad, and several times the crowds tried to stone him to death (Mk 3:21; Jn 7:5; 10:20; Lu 4:28-29; Jn 8:59). Do you suppose that it was easy for him to withstand the grief of being called insane by people he loved, or to resist the violent scorn of the ravening mob? Was it trivial for him to stand up in that Capernaum synagogue, facing a congregation made up of his friends, neighbours, cousins, siblings, aunts, uncles, yet knowing that he was about to deeply offend them? Was it painless for him to make a speech that he *knew* would sound wickedly blasphemous and stir them to an anger so furious that they – his own dear friends and relatives –wished to kill him? (Lu 4:28-29)

Of course not. Christ was well aware of the terrible effect his words would have. He could have preached the same sermon almost anywhere else with less hurt. But he chose the Capernaum synagogue. Perhaps he did so just because it *was* the hardest place on earth for him to call himself the promised Messiah. If he could press his claim there, among those fond and familiar people, he could press it anywhere!

So Jesus allowed nothing, not even the bitterest social pain, to turn him aside from scripture, or from affirming all that the prophets had said about him.

Likewise, we too must affirm our sainthood, and our call and authority in Christ, by steeling ourselves against the face of man and clinging to the promises of God with unshakeable confidence.

The Barrier of His Natural Desire

In the Garden of Gethsemane Jesus struggled so awfully in prayer that blood was wrung out of his veins and mingled with his sweat as it fell into the dust (Lu 22:44). Why was he in such agony? Certainly not because he feared death, nor even the dire torment of crucifixion. Many Christian martyrs bravely, even joyfully, endured worse and more prolonged physical torture, and died a more terrible death. Crucifixion was an ugly and agonising way to die, yet the sufferings of Jesus were ended within a few hours. But many martyrs were tortured in every imaginable way for days on end before death released them. Yet they bore it bravely, even singing as they perished. Christ was scarcely less courageous than they.

No, the cup from which he shrank was not the gall of dying horribly, but the bitter poison of sin. He the righteous one had to be made a sinner so that we who were sinners might be made righteous (2 Co 5:21). From that cup everything in his holy being shrank in horror, and he begged the Father to find another way. But there was no other way. If the Father's purpose were to be fulfilled, then drink that cup Jesus must, and drink it all, to the last foul and rancid dregs.

Before he could do this, Jesus had to suppress his natural wants (*"Please don't ask me to drink this cup"*) and entirely submit to the dictate of heaven (*"Nevertheless, not my will, Father, but yours be done"*). How well he succeeded was shown by his glorious resurrection some three days later!

Likewise, to fulfil our sainthood and to enter into all its splendid privileges we too must put aside our normal inclinations, our natural desires, and set ourselves to do one thing alone – *discover the Father's will, and do it*! For us, nothing less can be called success; nothing less can be reckoned *saintly*.

The Barrier of Satanic Opposition

See the story in *Matthew 4:1-11* and *Luke 4:1-13*. None of us has ever been so ferociously attacked as Jesus was at the end of six weeks of fasting and prayer in the desert. The severest part of it was the challenge to resume the powers of deity – *"If you really are the Son of God, then turn these stones into bread!"* But Jesus would have none of it. He was not there as the Son of God, but as representative *man*. So his first word in response to Satan was, *"<u>Man</u> shall not live by bread alone . . .!"* He defeated Satan, not in the power of his eternal Godhead (which he had laid aside, Ph 2:6-8), but simply as a man filled with the word of God and with the Holy Spirit.

If Jesus had succumbed to the temptation, if he had even for a few moments resumed the powers of deity, then his mission would have been undone. Had he turned stones into bread, our salvation would never have been accomplished. Hell would have triumphed over heaven. Why? Because to be our true High Priest he had to live and die as we do, and to face temptation and overcome it, not as the Son of God, but as a son of man (He 4:14-15).

But because he triumphed he can now offer us help in our time of need (vs.16).

Likewise, to live in the fulness of his life, we too, following his example, must set ourselves to resist Satan, and to break through every devilish barrier that the powers of darkness may set in front of us (Ja 4:7; Ep 6:16-17). We will then truly know what it means to be called a *saint*!

Christ depended upon the same resources that are available to us, namely –

- the testimony of scripture concerning him
- prayer mixed with unshakeable faith
- submission to the will of God
- and the revelation and power of the Holy Spirit.

Like Christ, we too must receive and believe the message that comes to us from scripture. No matter how improbable it seems, no matter what opposition you face, determine never to fear but only believe! (Mk 5:36; Lu 8:50) Break through the barriers! Discover who you are in Christ, what you have in Christ, where you are seated in Christ, in the heavenlies, and how by faith in his name you are and can be all that he has ordained for your life! [6]

A Walk of Power

Not only are we *called* "saints", we are also called to *be* "saints" (1 Co 1:2); that is, actually to *live* as the supernatural people of God.

How can natural men and women do such an impossible thing? How can we gain access to miracles, heal the sick, cast out devils, do the works of God, live righteously, fulfil the Father's purpose?

Again we have the example of Jesus –

<u>First</u>, as we have seen, we must follow his example of boldly embracing the identity God has given us in Christ. We need to live with a *"throne-view"*! It is wonderful how a change of position can change a person's outlook – *"I was robbed! I was robbed!!" cries the buyer. But as he walks away he boasts about the bargain he got."* (Pr 20:14). How much better things look when you see yourself as being on top and

---

(6) Someone may ask here, "If Jesus worked all his miracles only as a man filled with the Holy Spirit, how is it that we cannot do the same – walk on water, multiply loaves of bread, hush storms, raise the dead, and the like?" The plain answer is that you can! But only if such things lie in the purpose of God for your life, as they did for Jesus (Lu 4:17-21). For most of us, of course, most of the time, they don't. But if the call of God does require one to work a miracle, then, as one of God's saints in Christ, by faith and in the power of the Holy Spirit, it should be done.

not on the bottom. One moment he's a victim, and moaning; the next he's a winner, and joyful! But that's just where scripture says you are! You may look down and out. But in reality, as a *saint*, you are strong in the strength of God. Able to do all things in Christ. Rich with divine possibilities. Believe it and make it yours indeed.

Second, follow the example of Christ by utilising all the resources of the kingdom through the power of the Holy Spirit, and the authority of the Word of God, which should be the anchor of our souls, the foundation beneath our feet.

There is a delightful story in the writings of the ancient Greek historian Herodotus that illustrates this –

> Among the Athenians the man who gained most glory is said to have been Sophanes ... who showed himself the best of all the Athenians in battle ... He carried an anchor of iron bound by chains of bronze to the belt of his corslet; and this he threw whensoever he came up with the enemy, in order, they say, that the enemy when they came forth out of their ranks might not be able to move him from his place; and when a flight of his opponents took place, his plan was to take up the anchor first and then pursue after them. [7]

Herodotus doubted the truth of the story – and it does seem fantastic – but it makes a great parable about the manner in which we should trust in both the defensive and offensive strength of scripture. [8] Paul uses a different analogy. He calls scripture the *"sword of the Spirit"* (Ep 6:17), but the basic idea is the same – by the Word of God we can overcome every foe and set ourselves to be totally victorious

---

(7) *The Histories* 9:73, tr. by G. Macauley.

(8) However, Sophanes himself is usually thought to have been a real person, a hoplite warrior, who was later killed in another battle.

in our spiritual warfare. Anchor yourself in the Word. Arm yourself with the Word. Determine only to advance and never retreat; only to win and never surrender. In Christ, and by his Word and by the Spirit, your ultimate triumph is assured.

Section Two:

In The Heavenlies

Two:

Over The Hills and Far Away

Tom, Tom, the Piper's son,
Learned to play when he was young,
But all the tune that he could play
Was, *"Over the hills and far away!"*

Tom with his pipe made such a noise
That he pleased right well both girls and boys,
And they all stopped when they heard him play,
"Over the hills and far away!"

"Tom" was an ancient nickname for a piper, and the nursery rhyme of his adventures goes on for many more verses. The poem is more than 500 years old, and its tag – *"Over the hills and far away"* – has been called the most beautiful and haunting expression in the English language. G. K. Chesterton described it as *"the finest line in English literature and the silent refrain of all English poems"*. Another great writer said that if he could be credited with inventing it, he would gladly toss all his other works onto a rubbish heap. Indeed, many have wished that the privilege of coining the poignantly lovely line had been theirs, but its origins are lost in the mists of antiquity.

"Over the hills and far away!"

How old is the yearning those words express! Yet it is as modern as tomorrow. People today, as in the past, still long for an escape into a new world. They still search for a greener valley, a happier city, a chance to begin again, a new life. They still sigh to be over the hills and far away in a land of brighter opportunity and sweeter dreams.

Why is this so? Simply because people have a deep feeling that something precious is missing from their lives, that somewhere over the horizon the fulfilment of their most earnest desires and deepest needs can be found. Yet the very words "far away" are an admission that they will never arrive at that distant Elysium.

But there is no need for anyone to despair nor to search in vain. The land "far away" is closer than you think! Paul tells us about it –

> *Blessed be the God and Father of our Lord Jesus Christ, who has blessed us in Christ with every spiritual blessing* **in the heavenlies** *... God raised Jesus from the dead and seated him at his right hand* **in the heavenlies** *... God has raised us up with Christ and has enthroned us with him* **in the heavenlies** *... The wisdom of God in all its infinite variety is now made known through the Church to rulers and princes* **in the heavenlies** *... We are not fighting against human enemies but against ... superhuman and evil forces* **in the heavenlies** *(Ep 1:3,20; 2:6; 3:10; 6:12).*

Especially notice in each of those verses the use of the term "heavenlies", or "heavenly places". Precisely what Paul meant by that phrase is uncertain; but it does suggest a spiritual realm, to which God has given us access by faith, in which all of our real spiritual warfare occurs, and in which every divine blessing is found.

This and the following five studies all explore aspects of who we are and what we have *"in the heavenlies"* in Christ.

Introduction

> *"Blessed be the God and Father of our Lord Jesus Christ, who has blessed us in Christ with every spiritual blessing in the heavenlies"* (Ep 1:3).

Here is another answer to the age-old question that opened my previous chapter, *"Who am I?"* It presents us with a choice –

To Accept a Human Definition

There are many in the church who refuse to see themselves as God sees them in Christ – that is, fully righteous and fit for the highest heaven. For example, the chaplain of a national youth organisation, just before Christmas one year, sent out a circular that described his young charges in degrading terms, as if they were trash. He denied them any merit of any sort, and told them to reckon themselves as the offal of the earth. They were vile creatures, said he, whose only value lay in being sinners redeemed by the grace of Christ. [9]

Now we certainly do need to be aware of our sinfulness and of our need for God's grace, but the basic image conveyed by the chaplain was offensive. What can be gained by causing any group of Christian people, young or old, to think about themselves in a debasing manner? Rather, we should think and talk about ourselves as God does. And what is that? The Father in Heaven, says Paul, never stops *"eulogising"* us! (Ep 1:3) The Greek word translated "blessed" is *eulogeo*, which means much the same in Greek as in English – "to speak well of ... to eulogise ... to praise and honour someone." So then, pause a moment, and ask yourself, "What is God saying about me right now? Is he cursing me, denouncing me, declaring how vile I am, how much he loathes the sight of me? Hardly! According to scripture, if you are in union with Christ by faith, he is *eulogising* you! Yesterday he was speaking well of you. Today he is speaking well of you. And tomorrow he will still be speaking well of you, calling the angels to hear his eulogy!

---

[9] I still have a copy of the document, but prefer not to identify the author or the denomination, except to say that it was not myself nor mine!

Now that *eulogy*, of course, is spoken *"in the heavenlies"* – which means, to benefit from the Father's good opinion, you must position yourself there too, by faith, with Christ. Which brings us to the second option –

To Accept the Divine Definition

As Christian people we should bravely affirm what scripture says about us –

I am Divinely Righteous in Christ

There is a sense, of course, in which that chaplain's document is true; but what God says about us in Christ is even more true, namely, that the righteousness of Christ is always greater than my sin (Ro 5:17). John Bunyan showed this in his story about the *Interpreter* [10] –

> Then Christian began to gird up his loins, and to address himself to his journey. So the other told him, That by that he was gone some distance from the gate, he would come at the house of the Interpreter, at whose door he should knock, and he would show him excellent things. Then Christian took his leave of his friend, and he again bid him God speed.
>
> Then he went on till he came to the house of the Interpreter, where he knocked over and over; at last one came to the door, and asked who was there.
>
> . . . Then said the Interpreter, "Come in; I will show that which will be profitable to thee." So he commanded his man to light the candle, and bid Christian follow him: so he had him into a private room, and bid his man open a door; the which when he had done, Christian saw . . . a

---

(10) *The Pilgrim's Progress* – "The Second Stage." The "Interpreter" is the Holy Spirit.

place where was a fire burning against a wall, and one standing by it, always casting much water upon it, to quench it; yet did the fire burn higher and hotter.

Then said Christian, "What means this?"

The Interpreter answered, "This fire is the work of grace that is wrought in the heart: he that casts water upon it, to extinguish and put it out, is the devil; but in that thou seest the fire notwithstanding burn higher and hotter, thou shalt also see the reason of that." So he had him about to the backside of the wall, where he saw a man with a vessel of oil in his hand, of the which he did also continually cast, (but secretly) into the fire.

Then said Christian, "What means this?"

The Interpreter answered, "This is Christ, who continually, with the oil of his grace, maintains the work already begun in the heart; by the means of which, notwithstanding what the devil can do, the souls of his people prove gracious still (2 Co 12:9). And in that thou sawest that the man stood behind the wall to maintain the fire, that is to teach thee that it is hard for the tempted to see how this work of grace is maintained in the soul."

Thus we have a duty to recognise that our union with Christ by faith has brought with it the gift of God's own righteousness (2 Co 5:17,21). Yet many are still like those foolish people whom Paul sternly denounces for rushing about trying to establish some righteousness of their own (Ro 10:3). But how absurd! Why would I cling to the rags of my own righteousness (even supposing I had any) when God offers to replace it with his infinitely more lovely righteousness? Even had I never committed any kind of sin, I would still be crazy if I preferred *my* righteousness to *God's*! So instead, I happily cast aside any claim of personal righteousness and present myself to God clothed only in robes woven out of the glorious and eternal righteousness of Christ.

This leads us on to a second affirmation –

I am Divinely Victorious in Christ

So long as you refuse to let go of Christ, you cannot be defeated! I have a daughter-in-law who turns rags into beautiful quilts; just so, God turns even our "defeats" into splendid victories. We are like an army that has lost a battle yet knows that it will still win the war. Our cry should be: *"I cannot be discouraged by discouragement, nor made poor by poverty, nor fail by failing, nor made sinful by sin, nor sick by illness!"*

That, of course, is all pre-conditioned upon the sinner clinging to Christ, with the corollary that anyone who does cleave to the Saviour cannot help but hate what he hates and love what he loves. In other words, one cannot love sin while at the same time claiming to possess victory over it. Therefore, even when succumbing to temptation a true Christian will loathe his or her weakness, and hasten as quickly as possible to repent and reclaim faith and holiness in Christ.

But through it all, in triumph or defeat, in success or failure, in holiness or impurity, still I will declare boldly, and will never deny, *"This is the victory that overcomes the world, even our faith!"* (1 Jn 5:4). Still I will insist that the Father is eulogising me in the heavenlies, and I will see myself there in Christ. Let me but believe in Jesus, and refuse to allow anything (not even my own failures) to pull me away from him, and I know that I will in the end prevail over every foe, even death itself!

I Am Divinely Identified in Christ

See *John 10:34-35*, in which the people of God are themselves called "gods". How startling that sounds! How can it be proper to call you or me a *god*?

The ascription *gods* was given to the people of God because –

The Word Came to Them

That is true of **_everyone_** who believes in Jesus, for how can we believe until we have heard, and how can we hear unless someone has preached the gospel to us? (Ro 10:13-15) Problems arise, though, when people stop there. To live in the **_authority_** of scripture we must keep that good word coming to us, by reading it and meditating in it continually (Ps 1:1-3).

Notice how full of the word of God Jesus was! He was surrounded (Jn 10:24,31) by angry, savage men who were eager to kill him; yet he remained calm, and was always able to give them an immediate answer, even if he had to call upon an obscure passage of scripture (Ps 82:1,6). The serenity, the authority, the victory that Christ displayed did not happen of themselves. Rather those qualities arose out of his absorption of the promises of the Father. He was, above all other men who have ever lived, a man of the Word.

Jesus read the scriptures, he absorbed them, he meditated on them day and night (Ps 1:1-3), he declaimed them, he trusted them, he knew they were the words of God and that they would endure for eternity. In this, as in all things, he set us an example.

They Stood in the Place of God

The judges were God's agents on earth (see Ex 7:1; 22:28), hence they were called *gods*. Likewise, when you and I act in Jesus' name and in harmony with the word of God, then we speak with the authority of God. That authority is such that should it lie in the divine will, we can command mountains to move! (Mk 11:22-24)

So in Christ we gain a divine identity, which Paul insists gives us a place in the heavenlies, gives us authority over all the powers of darkness, and provides a right of access to the very throne of God and all heaven's abundance. Therefore scripture calls us *"gods"*, and bids us to conduct ourselves accordingly.

Conclusion

If you are *"in Christ"*, then

- you are not a "filthy slime bucket", but the very righteousness of God!
- you are not a "muck-pit", but more than a conqueror!
- you are not a "low-life slob", but the true image of your God on earth, bearing his name, possessing his authority, reflecting his beauty, and destined for his everlasting glory!

Three:

Your Provision in The Heavenlies

"I never stop thanking God for you and remembering you in my prayers!" (Ep 1:15-19; 3:14-19)

There is an inexorable spiritual law that ***faith*** must precede ***practice***. Many Christians fail to live victoriously because they break that law. They try to reverse it into *practice* first, then faith. For example, they say, "When I see myself *doing* good, then I will believe that I *am* good." But spiritual law is as unremitting as natural law; the rule cannot be violated: ***faith must always come before practice***. That is, before you can truly **behave** like a saint you must first **believe** that you **are** a saint! So we are required to say, "Because I know that I <u>am</u> good, in Christ, therefore I will <u>do</u> good!"

Christ presented the same law in his saying, *"You will know the truth and the truth will set you free"* (Jn 8:32). Before freedom comes knowledge. Liberty arises from revelation. Power in action is a product of the promise believed.

So here is something we all want: ***freedom***! Freedom to serve God and to love him; freedom to rejoice in his goodness; freedom in worship and prayer; freedom to live righteously and to walk soberly and godly in this present world; freedom from sickness, and from every dark work; freedom to prosper every day in the favour of God! And how can we obtain that freedom? Jesus said simply, ***"Know the truth!"***

Therefore, before you start praying for some need to be met, or for some freedom to be enjoyed, you should take these two steps –

- find out what God says about his willingness and ability to meet your need (that is, discover the truth, find the right promise); and then
- believe God's promise with all your heart.

Your knowledge of, and faith in, the word of God, is the initial key to all his wonderful treasures.

A Constant Rule

This *law of the precedence of faith* is applied continually in the New Testament. Before demanding Christian **practice**, the apostles explained Christian **belief**. Doctrine came before doing; affirmation before action; trust before trying; faith before the fact.

Thus in **<u>Romans</u>**, Paul writes eleven chapters of powerful argument on the plan of salvation before he adds five chapters on practical living.

In **<u>Galatians</u>**, the closing two chapters of warning, instruction, and exhortation, are preceded by four chapters of reasoned faith, climaxed by the pungent challenge, *"Stand fast in the freedom for which Christ has made you free!"* Not until he has brought the Galatians onto the ground of full Christian liberty does Paul tell them how to display true godly characteristics. Always, it is **believe** before you try to **behave**!

In **<u>Ephesians</u>**, Paul begins with three breath-taking chapters that show the glories of Christ, the immensity of salvation, and the vast scope of God's plan for the Church. He explores the infinite wealth of the gospel, and reveals the riches of grace and glory God has given us in Christ. Only then, and not before, does he bring a practical application of the truth. He was careful to declare what God has **done** for us before stating what we should **do** for God.

<u>Colossians</u>, too, follows a similar pattern. Discover who you are in Christ, and your place in Christ in the heavenlies, and then you will be ready to live joyfully and victoriously in Christ.

And in many other places in the New Testament the same principle can be observed: before urging Christian **duties** the apostles were careful to teach the people Christian **doctrine**. They wanted them to find a place of security in faith **before** they tried to walk on the stormy waters of life.

A Remarkable Prayer

This rule is particularly obvious in Paul's written prayers. Here is an apostle praying for a church and its people. What will be the theme of his intercession? Will he pray that they might conquer sin? or be healed? or that the church will grow? or that their needs might be met? No! He prayed for none of the things that fill the prayers of most Christians! Instead, he pleaded with passion, not that they might be given *things*, but that **they might know the truth**! Again and again, he longed for them to know ... know ... **KNOW**!

So with fervent intercession he prayed that God would give them wisdom and revelation in the knowledge of Christ; that they might know the hope of their calling and the riches of God's glory; that they might understand the limitless power available to them in Christ; that they might comprehend the love of God, and perceive his will, and gain spiritual illumination – see *Ephesians 1:15-19; 3:14-19; Philippians 1:9-10; Colossians 1:9*; etc.

Paul knew this: if people familiarise themselves with the truth in Christ; if they steep themselves in knowledge of the gospel; if they grasp the significance of all that Christ wrought at Calvary for their full salvation – then they will need nothing else. All the other things they might desire will come to them as a natural consequence of discovering and believing the truth. Prayer will then no longer be a desperate cry in hope of some kind of answer, but, like the simplicity of the *Lord's Prayer* (Mt 6:9-13), an affirmation of trust in divine providence. We still pray, but with heartfelt confidence in the promise of God (1 Jn 5:14-15; and cp. Ja 1:6-8; 4:2-3; 5:14-18).

In The Heavenlies

Perhaps the most thrilling presentation of the wealth God has freely given us in Christ is found in Paul's letter to the *Ephesians*. In this letter the apostle fathoms the utmost depths, and scales the transcendent heights, of the glories of the gospel, and he reveals them to us in those five pungent sayings about our position **"IN THE HEAVENLIES"** in Christ. In particular, let us here consider the divine supply that awaits us in that supernal realm, beginning with a verse we have already looked at in a different connection –

> *Blessed be the God and Father of our Lord Jesus Christ, who has blessed us in Christ with every spiritual blessing in the heavenlies* (Ep 1:3).

Like every passage of scripture that contains a promise, or a statement of something God has done for us in Christ, those words demand *faith*. We are expected to *believe* them. But what does it mean, to "believe"?

A true "believer" heartily accepts the witness that God has given of himself and of his will in the scriptures. In particular, real faith requires acceptance of two things –

- you must believe what the Bible says about **_Christ_**; and
- you must believe what it says about **_yourself_**.

To believe either one of those testimonies without the other is largely futile. The purpose of scripture cannot be fulfilled unless you accept who **_Christ_** is in God, and who **_you_** are in Christ. That second article of faith is as important as the first; yet there are many people who fail at this very point –

they are willing to accept all that the Bible says about **Christ**, but they decline to accept what it says about **themselves**.

What happens to such people?

They are condemned to spiritual frustration and to defeat; the work of Christ on their behalf becomes largely vain; the earthly benefits of the work of Christ are negated or at least hindered in their lives. To refuse to accept the reality of the identity scripture gives to every believer in Christ is in fact to call God a liar, which can hardly please him! (1 Jn 5:10).

Indeed, it could be said that your faith in what the Bible says about **Christ** is finally only as great as your faith in what it says about **yourself**. It is, after all, much easier to believe that Christ is enthroned in the heavenlies than to believe that *you* are! The first can be held as a mere theory, it demands no special revelation; but the second can be maintained only by those who really have had *"the eyes of their hearts enlightened"* (Ep 1:17-18).

When you show that you truly know who **you** are in Christ, then you show also that you truly know who **Christ** is in God!

Which brings us to Paul's use of our text phrase, *"in the heavenlies"* –

What Are "The Heavenlies"?

I have already mentioned that no one is sure what this strange expression means. But we can assume at least this – it describes a spiritual dimension in which we have right of access to bountiful blessings through faith in Christ. In this dimension, God has deposited all the treasures of salvation; there, every spiritual blessing is located in abundance; whatever you need from God, whatever God wants to give, is placed there already in your name. There also, all our real spiritual warfare occurs. In fact, nothing can happen effectively on earth until it has first happened in the heavenlies; thus –

- you cannot gain victory over Satan on earth until you have first seized the victory that is yours in the heavenlies
- you cannot live in the abundant blessing of God on earth until you have first seized the treasures that are yours in the heavenlies;
- indeed, once you have positioned yourself in the heavenlies in Christ, and there grasped the promises of God, those promises will soon begin to be fulfilled on earth.

But many Christians try to wage all their spiritual warfare on earth, struggling against *"flesh and blood"*, using *"carnal"* weapons (Ep 6:12; 2 Co 10:3-4). They are doomed already to frustration and defeat. Rather, you should focus your faith on the heavenlies, where

Every Blessing is Already Yours

Notice, Paul says this great work has already been done. This is not a promise. It is a statement of **fact** – *"God HAS (already) blessed us with every spiritual blessing in the heavenlies."*

You say you have need of blessing? But God has already blessed you! And what has he given you? It is nothing less than *"every spiritual blessing"*!

Can you even begin to measure the profusion revealed by that statement, or can you ever exhaust that limitless treasure?

See it again: **_all_** spiritual blessings – all the good things you have ever longed for and prayed for; every blessing the human heart could desire, and every kindness divine hands can provide; all the riches of glory, and all the stores of earth, restricted only (and this is important) by *the larger purpose that the Lord may have for your life.* ⁽¹¹⁾

Nor should you suppose that "spiritual" means only ethereal blessings in heaven. No! These blessings are "spiritual" only in the sense that they originate from the Father and they repose in the "heavenlies", waiting to be accessed by faith. Otherwise, they comprehend every blessing for your **_body_**, in health, ability, and victory; for your **_mind_**, in all understanding, satisfaction, and belief; for your **_soul_**, in all cleansing, salvation, and life; and for your **_spirit_**, in all illumination, faith, and quickening!

With such superlative provision the Lord God has already blessed you!

But, you say, "I do not see that I have all these things!" Perhaps you have looked in the wrong place? Where are all these spiritual blessings to be found? In yourself? In your church? In your own good works? Emphatically, again, "No!" The scripture tells us quite plainly where to locate them – God has blessed us with every spiritual blessing **_"in the heavenlies"_**.

Here then is a particular realm, known as "the heavenlies" where you have unlimited credit. In this place, deposited in your name, is untold spiritual wealth. It is yours now! If you and I are not enjoying this divine provision it is only because

---

(11) For an example, albeit somewhat crass, I would love to be a concert pianist, or perhaps an astronomer. But there is little point me asking God to bring either dream into reality. First, I lack the requisite skills; second, they do not accord with what I know to be the Father's unchanging purpose for me – of which a part sits in your hand right now! Which is simply to say that everything must be measured against the Father's purpose for our lives. Within that purpose, ask what you will and you will have it! (Jn 14:12-14). But God will hardly grant a prayer that will take you out of his will or diminish your capacity to do what he wants, or undermine your true prosperity and success.

we are not looking in the right place or walking along the right path or have not appropriated it in the right manner.

Illustration. Suppose there was a commercial bank called *The Bank of the Heavenlies*. If a friend deposited a large sum of money in that bank, in your name, you would at once become wealthy. But your new wealth will do you no good until you go to the bank, present an authority that gives you the right to draw on the account, and then withdraw as much as you requir.

So it is with your riches in God's "heavenlies" – you must accept that they are there, that they belong to you, and then enter this spiritual dimension with authority and claim by faith what is yours in Christ.

"Spiritual Blessings"

What are these "spiritual blessings" Paul is talking about? We have seen that it is wrong to think of them as blessings that are "spiritual" in contrast with physical and material blessings. They are called "spiritual" blessings, not because they are unearthly, but because they have a spiritual basis – that is, they arise from the ministry of the Holy Spirit in the Christian's life; they stem from our union with Christ; they are located in the heavenlies. But the blessings themselves comprehend every promise God has ever given us of pardon, healing, victory, supply, success, and so on.

Paul gives a kind of analysis of these blessings in *Ephesians 1:3-20*. He lists them as

- a blameless and holy life (vs. 4)
- destiny as the children of God (vs. 5-6)
- redemption and forgiveness (vs. 7-8)
- knowledge of the plan of God (vs. 9-10)
- freedom to live for God's glory (vs. 11-12)
- the promise of the Holy Spirit (vs. 13)

- a guaranteed inheritance (vs. 14).

Then he sums it all up in three great statements (vs. 18-20) –

- the **hope** to which he has called us
- the **riches** of his glorious inheritance
- the immeasurable greatness of his **power**.

Hope, riches, great power – those three expressions embrace every spiritual blessing God has provided for you in the heavenlies –

- there is ***hope*** – for our future is secure in Christ; we have a destiny, a kingdom, a reward appointed for us, of which none can deprive us, save we ourselves, by unbelief, or by such wilful continuance in sin that the sinner loses all capacity to believe, and thus loses Christ;
- there are ***riches*** – of pardon, of grace, of healing, of life, of supply of every need; indeed, all the treasures offered in the good promises of God; and
- there is ***power***, immeasurably great power, over all the kingdom of darkness, over the principalities and powers of evil, over sin, over the opposition of the world, over death and the very gates of hell.

Two keys are needed to unlock these treasures –

Revelation

I never stop giving thanks for you (wrote Paul), *and in my prayers I keep on asking that the God of our Lord Jesus Christ, the Father of glory, will give you a spirit of wisdom and of revelation in your knowledge of him. I pray that the eyes of your hearts will be enlightened, so that you may know all about the hope your calling brings you, and how rich you are because of the glorious inheritance that is yours, and how immeasurably great is the power of God at work in all who believe.* (Ep 1:16-19)

Our ears and eyes need to be opened so that we might understand that all these promised blessings are ours right now; for these are not future **promises**; they are present **possessions!** But such knowledge is beyond the natural mind; it must be revealed by the Spirit. A merely mental understanding of the promise is not enough; these things must be spiritually perceived. People can read, say, the first chapter of *Ephesians*, and mentally agree with every word, yet remain as impoverished before God as ever they were. The truth has to get from the mind into the heart – *"With the heart a person believes"* and so obtains the blessing of God (Ro 10:8-10).

If it were enough merely to read the promise, and to accept it in your mind as true, then Paul, having just instructed the Ephesians (1:13-14), would not have said immediately, "Now I am going to pray that God will reveal these things to you!" But he knew that his written words, no matter how sincerely they might be received, were insufficient by themselves – the touch of God was needed to make those words come alive in the hearts of the readers. They needed an **inner revelation** of the truth of what was written.

So, having described all the spiritual blessings in the heavenlies that belong to the people of God, Paul at once began to pray that they might be illuminated on the inside, that they might see inwardly and know absolutely what belongs to them in Christ. He is talking about divinely imparted knowledge; it is *head* knowledge become *heart* knowledge; it is knowledge perceived by a spiritual quickening of the things the mind has received. What has been "heard" by the ear is now "seen" in the spirit. It is the Lord opening the eyes of your heart, giving you spiritual awareness, so that his word suddenly becomes to you the only reality.

All other knowledge is overwhelmed by this inner knowledge of the promise of God. By divine revelation we grasp his presence and power, and faith then laughs at every foe, and rejoices in the sure victory of God (cp. 2 Kg 6:15-17).

This spiritual insight comes to people in different ways – sometimes while reading scripture; sometimes while sitting under the preaching of the word; sometimes while praying; or in some other way. But pre-eminently it comes by taking up a promise of God and praying over that promise until the Lord does impart *"a spirit of wisdom and of revelation in the knowledge of Christ"*.

But whatever way it comes, there is simply no substitute for *"having the eyes of your heart enlightened"*; for without this, the promises of God will remain for you a dead letter.

How will you know when it has happened? You will know, because you *know*! That is, the promise of God will not be merely something you have memorised; it will now be as real as life itself. It will burn inside you. It will throb with vitality. It will seem as inevitable as tomorrow's sunrise. You will have an awareness, deep within, that the promise of God is irresistibly true; incredulity will change to total belief. The hiatus between you and the promise will be bridged; the credibility gap will no longer exist; you and the promise will be fused together. You will become identified with the promise and the promise with you. It will then be inconceivable to you that the promise could fail.

Illustration. The change is something like what you might experience if you were told by a stranger that he was about to give you a million dollars. At first you would be incredulous, perhaps even angry at his seeming attempt to mock you. But he insists that you take his cheque, and he is so earnest and sincere you begin to have second thoughts. You finally take the cheque and, hardly daring to hope, go off to the bank against which it is drawn. You enquire at the bank, and to your utter astonishment discover that the cheque is good, and the money is yours whenever you want it. Now all doubt is gone! Now you know! Suddenly the truth of it strikes you! What merriment fills your heart! You have not yet taken out a penny of it, but already you begin to think and talk differently, for now you know that you truly are a millionaire!

That same kind of assurance has to come to you concerning the riches God has laid up for you in the heavenlies; and it will bring the same kind of gladness. Those riches are yours now, if you can believe it.

Then the second key needed to unlock the treasures that are already yours in the heavenlies is

Release

If "revelation" is the first key needed to unlock your spiritual blessings in the heavenlies, then the second is the "release" of faith. Those things that are already your *potential* possessions will become your *actual* possessions when you make a faith commitment to receive them from God. You will be like old Israel, of whom the prophet said that one day they will *"possess their possessions!"* (Ob 1:17) That oracle can have its fulfilment in you, if you can believe.

But this faith must be specific. You cannot reasonably expect to reach out and grasp every spiritual blessing in one moment any more than you can eat a whole warehouse full of food in one meal. You must determine which is the proper spiritual blessing for you at the present time, and then decide to believe God for that one thing.

People frequently fail to obtain the thing they need, simply because they are too vague in their application of the promise. But real faith cannot function until a particular promise is applied to a particular need.

For example, people say, "I know that God can meet my financial needs." But that is more a statement of doctrinal belief than of specific faith. Real faith would say, *"I know God will help me to overcome this particular debt!"* In fact, real faith would be even more bold: *"I know God has already blessed me with the solution to this money problem, in the heavenlies in Christ!"*

Faith possesses its possessions; faith rejoices in the provision God has already made; faith shouts with gladness, *"Blessed be the God and Father of our Lord Jesus Christ, who <u>has</u> blessed me in Christ with <u>every spiritual blessing</u> in the heavenlies."*

Four:

Your Power In The Heavenlies

> *I pray that you might know how immeasurably great is the power of God that is at work in us who believe. It is the same limitless strength that he exerted when he raised Christ from the dead and enthroned him at his right hand in the heavenlies.* (Ep 1:19-20)

Paul does not ask God to give us power. He longs only that we might **know** the power that is already at work in us in Christ. This power, all of it, is the possession and prerogative of every believer. What is this power? How can we activate it in daily life and in Christian service?

The Measure of This Power

Paul describes the power that is ours in the heavenlies, and tells us two things about its greatness –

- *first*: it is *"**immeasurable**"*; no Christian need ever fear that this power will be insufficient to meet any difficulty that may arise; and
- *second*: it is *"**according to**"* a great demonstration of the might of God.

What was that demonstration? The power available to each Christian is *"the same as the limitless strength that God exerted when he raised Christ from the dead and enthroned him at his right hand in the heavenlies"*.

How astonishing then is strength that is ours in the heavenlies! It has the same character, force, and effect as that which broke the bonds of death from the crucified Christ, freed him from sin's darkness, and raised him in glory to heaven's radiant throne!

It is interesting to compare the standards of power of the old dispensation and the new –

- Before the resurrection of Christ, whenever people wanted to depict the power of God, they could cite no greater example than the Exodus of Israel from Egypt. Again and again the prophets used that striking event as the supreme demonstration of God's power. The Exodus showed what tremendous things the Lord could do for those who trusted him. So the measure of divine ability in the old dispensation was "according to" Israel's deliverance from Egyptian tyranny.
- But now there is a new standard. Now we are given an infinitely higher measure of revealed omnipotence. It is found in the resurrection, ascension, and enthronement of Christ. The manifestation of God's power in the former time was *great*; but now it is *immeasurably great*!

It took an act of astounding power to bring Israel out of Egypt; but that deed pales into insignificance against the limitless strength required to raise Christ from the dead and to set him at the right hand of the Majesty on High! (He 1:3, KJV)

There is also a contrast between the *effectiveness* of the old power and the new –

- if the first was a physical deliverance from temporal bondage, the second is spiritual freedom from eternal death; and
- if the first wrought national liberty, the second has created salvation for the entire race; and
- if the first offered Israel an earthly inheritance and natural wealth, the second has opened to all who believe the unlimited storehouse of God, and a kingdom eternal in the heavens!

The Purpose of This Power

The power of God is at once nullified if any attempt is made to use it in situations other than those approved by God. It is limitless power, irresistible in heaven and on earth; but it is not available to any person for any purpose. It is not like an electric power socket, open for anyone to plug into whenever they please! Indeed, even an electric socket will yield its energy only to a suitable device that is correctly connected to it.

So the power of God cannot be used to do the will of man; it is available only to accomplish the will of God. No one can appropriate this power to do merely his own pleasure; but believers can and should appropriate it to do all that they know is the pleasure of God.

Hence Paul writes –

> *May you be strengthened with all might, according to his incredible power ... to lead a life worthy of the Lord, one that always pleases him, abounding in every good work ... so that you will be able to endure with patience and joy whatever life brings* (Cl 1:9-11).

So this glorious might of God – the same force that raised Christ from the dead – is available to strengthen you to accomplish all that lies in the Father's purpose for your life. You need never feel inadequate for any situation into which you are brought by obedience to God. In the strength of his power within you (that power which you draw from "the heavenlies"), you can do whatever God has appointed – whether to *"conquer kingdoms, enforce justice, receive promises, stop the mouths of lions, quench raging fire, escape the edge of the sword, win strength out of weakness, become mighty in war, put armies to flight, raise the dead"*; or to *"endure torture, refusing to accept release, suffer mocking, scourging, chains, imprisonment, destitution, affliction, ill-treatment, and death"* (see He 11:32-38).

Once you have discovered the will of God in any situation then his power is yours to do his will – whether to change that situation by a miracle, or to endure it with steadfast patience! We become like Jesus, able either to hush a storm with a word, or in the midst of it create an epicentre of calm. Even as he was being pinned to the cross, still he was in command, knowing that no man could touch him if it were not the Father's will. As they buried him, he was in command. And by his own command he rose from the dead three days later! So long as he held to the Father's purpose he was actually invincible, and could not fail to triumph in the strength of God. In this, as in all things, he set us an example to follow.

The Location of This Power

Since the power of God exists only to do the will of God, this power is not carelessly left where anyone may improperly abuse it. It was drawn up with Christ (when God raised him from the dead), and it remains with him, secure in the heavenlies. It is not there, however, for his benefit, but for **ours**. It is not extended toward the angels; it belongs to ***"us who believe"***, and towards us it is proffered.

Moses had his rod: it was marked for him by God; he held it up, and it became for him the guarantee of God's power. By that rod, and by the signs and wonders it produced, he smashed imperial Egypt and created an example that for many centuries was the summit of God's power among men and women.

Do you stand in wonder before that staggering display of divine omnipotence, and do you envy Moses?

Moses certainly should be admired; yet that ancient example has been utterly eclipsed by God's stupendous new feat in Christ! And now, right now, offered to you who believe, as surely as the rod was tendered to Moses, is the right to grasp that enormous power! It wrenched Christ from death and exalted him to the highest glory. It can do the same for you!

In the heavenlies Christ reigns in splendid authority, *"far above all rule and authority and power and dominion, and above every name that is named, not only in this age but also in that which is to come"* (Ep 1:21). But here is the most marvellous thing: this victory was not accomplished for heaven's benefit, but for yours! So grasp it by faith!

God had no need to establish his power over the devil, for that was done in the very beginning, when Satan was thrown out of the Garden of Eden. Nor did Christ personally need to be exalted above the kingdom of darkness; for he had long before cast down Lucifer and the angels who rebelled with him, leaving them bound in chains of darkness (2 Pe 2:4; Jd 1:6).

So Christ was raised from the dead and lifted into the heavenlies, not to establish heaven's power (which was never at risk), **but to establish power for us who believe in Christ.** This *"immeasurably great"* power is not meant to be a weapon in God's hand, but a mighty resource in **your** hands, so that you and I, in the matchless name of Jesus, might be fully delivered from every satanic oppression.

All for You!

It is indeed true that *"God has put everything under Christ's feet"* (Ep 1:22). But why? Again, solely for your benefit, and mine! For he goes on to say – *"... and has made him head over everything <u>for the Church</u>."* On behalf of the **Church**, God raised Jesus from the dead; on behalf of the **Church**, the Saviour was exalted on high; on behalf of the **Church**, he now reigns in the heavenlies; on behalf of the **Church**, everything has been placed under his feet.

But if you are part of his Church, then you also are there, in the heavenlies, with Christ, and all the power that is his, is also yours, to do the will of God and to receive his promise.

Here, too, is victory over the prince of evil, deliverance from the grip of sin, liberty from the dominion of temptation, healing from the imprisonment of disease: it is all found by seizing what is already yours in the heavenlies in Christ.

Paul waxes even more bold. So sure is he of our complete identification with Christ, so certain that we are already seated with Christ in the heavenlies, he declares that this immeasurably great power is even now *"in us who believe"*. Yes, it is **in** you at this moment; you may not feel it, but you can believe it! And if you believe it, then that power will begin at once to fulfil God's marvellous work in your life.

Do you find it hard to believe that the resurrection power of Jesus is in you right now? Paul gives an illustration that clinches the matter. He says, *"God has put everything under Christ's feet and has made him Head over everything for the Church, which is his body, the fulness of him who fills all in all"* (vs. 22,23).

If Christ is the Head, and we are his body, then where he is we must be also; what he is we must be also; what he has must be ours also. How can it be otherwise? Christ is no monstrosity. He is not deformed. His body is perfectly matched to himself, the Head.

Consider your own body: where your head is, your body is. In natural life, every good thing your body is to receive first enters the body by the head – through the mouth, the eyes, the ears – and then is shared by the whole body.

So also, all the fulness of Christ, the Head, belongs to the Church, his body – *"the Church is the fulness of him who fills all in all"* (Ep 1:23). What is given to the Head, Christ, inevitably belongs also to his body, the Church, and hence to every "member" of that body.

A Spirit-Filled Church

If you have come into union with Christ through faith, then all his heavenly power is yours as much as it is his. Only unbelief can block its mighty flow. But if you can believe it, then his resurrection power is in your hands when you lay them on the sick in his name; it is in your voice when you speak a word of faith and authority; it is in your mind as you search out the wisdom of God in scripture; it is in your flesh as you stand against the kingdom of darkness and seize the triumph of God. It permeates your entire being; it is the law of life in Christ Jesus setting you free from the law of sin and death! (Ro 8:2)

But let me add this. The church Paul wrote to in this letter was a Spirit-filled church (Ac 19:1-6; Ep 1:13; 2:22; 3:16; 5:18; 6:17-18). Everything he writes is premised upon the fact that those people were **baptised in the Holy Spirit**. Even their activation of the resurrection power of Christ rested upon the inner working, not only of faith, but of the Spirit –

> *I pray that God will give you, according to his glorious riches, strength and power in your inner being* **through his Spirit** (3:16; and cp. Ac 1:8).

Whatever you, dear reader, may feel about speaking in tongues in our day, there is no denying that the church in Ephesus was a *glossolalic* church (Ac 19:6), and its members had enjoyed a glossolalic baptism in the Holy Spirit. Paul was well aware of this. After all, he was the one who had imparted the Holy Spirit to them, accompanied by speaking in tongues and prophesying. Indeed, in the letter itself, he urges them to maintain this gift in their worship, instructing them to *"keep on being filled with the Spirit, sharing with each other psalms, hymns, and spiritual songs. You should always sing and make music to the Lord with all your heart, giving thanks to God the Father for everything in the name of our Lord Jesus"* (5:18-20).

Note the three kinds of song he wants them to employ –

- **Psalms** – singing scripture, especially from the *Book of Psalms*.
- **Hymns** – formal songs, composed especially for worship, similar to the hymns we still sing in church.
- **Spiritual Songs** – almost certainly a reference to *"singing in the spirit"*, that is, in other tongues (cp. 1 Co 14:14-16; and see also Ep 6:18; Cl 3:16; Ju 1:20).

Indeed, in scripture, the working of God's power is always linked with the Holy Spirit, and, in the NT specifically with Holy Spirit baptism. And Holy Spirit baptism is commonly associated with glossolalia, or at least with some charismatic gift (cp. 1 Co 12:7-11). Despite the cavalier abandonment of the charismata in some Christian circles, I can see no valid reason why they should not be as much part of Christian life now as they were then.

This is not really the place to engage in a debate on the nature of Holy Spirit baptism, but clearly the church at Ephesus had experienced it as an event discrete from the new birth, and accompanied by glossolalia. It was to such people that Paul wrote his letter. It was they whom he described as being blessed in the heavenlies with every spiritual blessing. And it was they whom he urged to keep on being filled with the Spirit. And it was they to whom he said that God's glorious riches, strength, and power would be given through the Spirit.

So faith alone is insufficient. If we would enjoy all the fulness of God, then faith must first bring us to the fulness of the Spirit, and then, in the strength of the Spirit, faith can progress to seizing all that belongs to the believer in the heavenlies.

Five:

Your Position in The Heavenlies

"God has made us alive together with Christ, and through our union with Christ by faith, he has raised us up and enthroned us with Christ in the heavenlies" (Ep 2:5-6, free translation).

Two Kinds of Truth

There is a difference between what might be called "situational" truth and "positional" truth –

- **<u>Situational truth</u>** describes your condition at the present time, that is, your **situation** as observed by the natural eye. It is the state you are apparently in just now, whether spiritual, mental, emotional, or physical; it is the way you feel, the condition of your health, the measure of your finances, the extent of victory or defeat you may be experiencing. It tells the facts about your present circumstances, what is actually happening in your life day by day.
- **<u>Positional truth</u>** describes your condition as God sees it in Christ. It is your **position** in the heavenlies in contrast with your *situation* on earth. On earth, you may be incomplete in sin, and you may lack many things; but in the heavenlies you are complete in Christ and lack nothing (Cl 2:10).

The Bible in fact declares five things about your "position" in the heavenlies –

1. You are **<u>crucified</u>** with Christ.

That is, you are united with him in his atoning death, thus becoming the recipient of all the mercy, pardon, and grace made available to each repentant sinner at Calvary.

    2. You are **_buried_** with Christ.

That is, you are united with him in destroying deep in the tomb all that belonged to your old nature.

    3. You are **_risen_** with Christ.

That is, you are united with him in his victory, and with him you become more than a conqueror over the power of sin, the strength of death, the grip of the grave, and all the power of the enemy (Ro 8:37).

    4. You are **_ascended_** with Christ.

That is, you are united with him in his endless life and in his unlimited access to the throne of God.

    5. You are **_enthroned_** with Christ.

That is, you are united with him in his invincible reign, working with him from the throne to extend his empire, and helping to enforce his triumph over Satan, his crushing of the powers of darkness, and his overthrow of all that is antagonistic to the kingdom of God.

Now you should understand that those events are not set only in the *future*; rather, they are true of you NOW! They describe the position you already hold in Christ. This is how God sees you at this moment! Not in isolation, of course, but as you are in Christ.

In the reckoning of God, whatever Christ accomplished through his crucifixion, resurrection, ascension, and enthronement, belongs to you already. When Christ died, God saw you dying; when Christ rose from the dead, God saw you rising; when Christ ascended into heaven, God saw you ascending; when Christ sat down upon his glorious throne,

God saw you sitting there. In the matter of your salvation, all that Christ is, God reckons you to be.

Naturally, if the Father looked at you apart from Christ, he would not see you crucified, risen, enthroned, and victorious; on the contrary, he might see you defeated by sin, sick, and oppressed. But he has resolved never too look at any believer apart from Christ. Every time the Father sees you, he sees you in the virtue of Christ; you are identified in the mind of God with all the perfections and triumph of Christ.

The Basis for Victory

Now we are told these things, not to establish a pretty theory nor a cosy doctrine, nor to provide some kind of licence for sin. Rather, the gospel is given to create a basis upon which we should embrace the ability of God in our daily lives. By it we can overthrow sin and Satan, and complete all that the Father has given us to do in life.

God's desire is obviously that what is true of each Christian *positionally* may become true *practically*. We are told what we have become in the *heavenlies* only so that we might become the same on *earth*.

Here then is a great decision taken in the councils of heaven: ***God has resolved to position in the heavenlies and upon the throne every person who believes in Christ.*** This is a spiritual enthronement, wrought in conjunction with the ascension and glorification of Christ, and established irrevocably by God's own decree in scripture. He has also declared that knowledge of this "position" is both the **_legal_** and **_practical_** basis upon which each believer can gain victory and fulness in his or her daily life –

It is the Legal Basis

Because our union with Christ in the heavenlies, by faith, frees us from the reach of God's broken law, it enables God righteously to answer our prayers and to act on our behalf as Saviour (instead of acting against us as Judge). Knowledge of your true "position" in Christ is therefore the best way to prevent the law from barring your access to the throne of God.

But the reverse is also true. Unless you are secure in the free gift of righteousness that is yours in Christ the door will be closed against you. Every time you try to approach the throne of God the Accuser, or even your own conscience, will raise against you the barrier of your sins. You will then be crushed by a sense of unworthiness; the boldness you had as you approached the throne will be vitiated; you will no longer dare to expect a great answer from God; you may even reckon you deserve only scornful rejection.

But neither the law, conscience, nor the devil, has any influence over a believer who by faith is securely seated with Christ in the heavenlies. Irrefragably, that believer is freed of all condemnation and has access to every spiritual blessing (Ro 8:1).

It is the Practical Basis

God has promised to respond in power to every person who grasps the truth of the heavenly position he has given to us in Christ, and who affirms that position with bold faith.

When you know, regardless of your actual situation on earth, that you truly are spiritually enthroned in the heavenlies with Christ, and when you begin to assert that enthronement, then God will begin to make it actually happen for you.

Here then is a law: when your _confession_ matches your _position_, then your _situation_ will be made to match your _confession_.

Change your **confession**, and your **situation** will also change. But many people want to reverse that rule. Their attitude is that they will not profess to be enthroned with Christ in the heavenlies until they actually see themselves living like a king on earth. But in God's economy **profession always precedes possession.** So, if you say that you are defeated and enslaved, you will effectively abdicate your enthronement; but if you say that you are enthroned and triumphant in Christ, then you will effectively revoke your enslavement!

This is not mind over matter. You have no need to deny earthly reality. If you are sick you are sick. If you are defeated you are defeated. If you are poor you are poor. You cannot say that those things are not true, nor that they are an illusion, for that would be a lie, and God has no use for falsehoods. What you *can* do is replace that earthly reality with the greater *heavenly* reality, that is, replace a weak law with a stronger. It is like the law of aerodynamics keeping an aeroplane in the air despite the competing law of gravity, or the law of displacement that keeps an iron ship afloat. [12] So we are called to affirm the heavenly truth against the earthly one, to overcome the strength of our earthly *situation* with the greater strength of our *position* in the heavenlies in Christ.

What Do You Reckon?

So then, what God declares you to be now, in Christ, you should reckon yourself now to be. If you see yourself as seated on his throne in the heavenlies, then you will also be able to proclaim yourself a king and begin to act like one on earth.

You cannot stay experimentally on the throne if your reckoning and profession are wrong. You must think about

---

(12) This idea is taken up again in the next chapter.

yourself as God thinks about you; you must get a mental image of yourself that reflects what you are in the heavenlies, not what you are on earth. No matter what your earthly state might be, you must declare yourself by faith to be now **all** that God says you are in Christ.

However, it could also be said that there are two aspects of our heavenly position that are still future – the <u>visible</u> manifestation of that position; and the full <u>realisation</u> of it. In other words, prior to the resurrection, **(a)** we have to walk by faith rather than by sight; and **(b)** we cannot hope to experience here all that our heavenly position implies. But after the resurrection, the throne will be visibly ours, and all that it represents will be immediately possessed and held for ever.

In the meantime, God's desire is obviously that what is true of us "positionally" may also become increasingly true "situationally". We are told what we have become in *Christ* in the heavenlies, so that we may become the same in *fact* on earth. How that can happen is theme of the next chapter.

Six:

Your Profession in The Heavenlies

> *"We are not contending against flesh and blood, but against ... the spiritual hosts of wickedness in the heavenlies"* (Ep 6:12).

You should stir your imagination, in response to scripture, to see yourself where God has placed you, in the heavenlies, on the throne of Christ. As we have seen, only from that vantage point can you find the right kind of strength and authority to change your present situation.

If you want God to walk with you and to act powerfully in your behalf, then you had better keep on saying what he is saying (Am 3:3). What does God say when he talks about you? Good things! He has resolved to speak about you only as you are in Christ. He speaks well of you in Christ. He has *"blessed you with every spiritual blessing in Christ"* (Ep 1:3).

Remember that the Greek verb *"to bless"* is *"eulogeo"*, which simply means *"to speak well"* of, or eulogise, someone. You will hardly please God by constantly speaking ill of a person (yourself) about whom God is constantly speaking well! Indeed, if Christians persist in refusing to profess themselves to be what God says they are in Christ, if they refuse to fix their minds and mouths on their heavenly condition, and insist on professing only their earthly situation, they risk angering God and depriving themselves of his highest favour.

We are commanded to fix our attention upon the reality that is in heaven, not upon the reality that is on earth (Col 3:1-3).

What are the Real Facts?

Someone will protest that to say you are enthroned when in fact you are enslaved is to tell a lie. But that is not so; you are merely supplanting one set of facts for another set of greater facts; you are changing one truth by the application of another truth.

An example. For centuries, people were bound by the obvious fact that iron and steel cannot float. They have no natural buoyancy. So everybody scoffed at the idea of an iron ship. But then somebody was bold enough to apply the laws of displacement and, behold! the world was amazed to see an iron ship float! The fact that iron sinks in water was overcome by a greater fact: if the weight of the iron vessel is less than that of the water it displaces, it will float.

Likewise, humans dreamed for centuries of being able to soar through the sky like an eagle, but gravity bound them firmly to the earth. And gravity prevailed relentlessly until someone discovered a greater law, aerodynamics. Suddenly a heavier than air machine could fly, and now every year millions of people soar higher and faster than the mightiest eagle! There is no denial of reality. But there is one law replacing another, a higher fact overcoming a lower, a weaker force being mastered by a stronger.

Likewise, nobody can deny the truth of your ***situation***, which may be one of sin, fear, sickness, defeat, or poverty. But then, I am not suggesting that you should deny it. Rather, what you should do is replace ***situational*** truth with ***positional*** truth. Whichever one you choose to believe has power to nullify the other.

If you decide to cling to your situation, to talk only about your poverty and failure, to believe that your situation represents the dominant fact in your life, then you will never gain an experimental knowledge of your enthronement in the heavenlies

But if you decide to accept your rightful position in Christ, and by faith step up to the throne, confidently affirming and insisting upon your throne rights, then all that God has wrought for you in Christ will increasingly become your actual experience.

Another illustration. Let us suppose that a letter has come to you, saying that you have inherited a vast estate in a foreign country. The name of the estate is "The Heavenlies". It comprises a million acres of prime grazing and agricultural land, stocked with thousands of quality sheep and cattle. It also contains many beautiful buildings and a vast quantity of machinery; it has huge investments in many industries, and enormous capital reserves. The wealth of the estate is almost incalculable.

Now, assuming you are a person of modest income, that letter represents a truth that has power to transform your present situation utterly. All you have to do is claim what is yours.

But suppose you think the letter is a hoax, or perhaps are fearful of so much wealth and power, so that you refuse to claim what is yours, and in fact you throw the letter away? Or, suppose you allow a false claimant to usurp your title, or an unscrupulous lawyer to contest your claim and to impoverish you? Then all that was promised by the estate, The Heavenlies, will be lost to you.

Enforce Your Rights

Many people fail to obtain *"every spiritual blessing"* for just those reasons. They simply cannot believe that this inheritance, this kingly right, is already theirs. Or else they have such an image of personal defeat, they cannot bring themselves to think, speak, and act like an enthroned monarch. Or else they allow the usurper, Satan, by force or guile to deprive them of their inheritance.

So Paul, having said that *"every spiritual blessing"* is found in the heavenlies, also says that we will have to contend for those blessings against the thievery and usurpation of *"principalities ... powers ... world rulers of this present darkness ... spiritual hosts of wickedness"* (Ep 6:12).

But how should you contend against that deceiver, Satan, and his dark hordes? From the weakness of your earthly situation, or from the strength of your heavenly position? If you are wise, you will possess the throne first, in the name of the invincible Christ, and then war against Satan with a crown on your head and a sceptre in your hand!

Our weapons are not carnal, not *"flesh and blood"*, but they are mighty through God to pull down every stronghold of Satan (2 Co 10:3). Even when Paul speaks about us donning our armour and sallying forth to battle, he is careful to show that we fight, not with natural energy or weaponry, but with spiritual resources: *"take up the shield of faith and the sword of the Spirit, which is the word of God"* (Ep 6:16-17).

Claim Your Inheritance

Go back for a moment to my illustration about inheriting a magnificent estate. Suppose you refused to be intimidated either by the splendour of the inheritance, or by the threats and accusations of a usurper. You are determined to possess your possessions (Ob 17). What would you do? Sit down dejectedly, wringing your hands, and decrying your wretched situation? I hope not! Rather you would establish your identity as the rightful owner, then you would boldly claim your estate, march onto it, and possess the land, driving off any false claimants who stood in your way. If necessary you would call on the authorities to come to your assistance, and to evict all trespassers.

You should do the same for your heavenly estate.

Get your identity right to begin with. Are you truly a Christian? Are you the actual person Paul was speaking about when he said *"you were made alive together with Christ, and raised up with him, and enthroned with him in the heavenlies"* (Ep 2:5-6)? If you are, then you have an unassailable right to the throne. Press your identity against the enemy. Put up a shield of faith against his accusations and fall upon him with the word of God. Call for the legions of heavens, those *"ministering spirits"* (He 1:14), to hasten to your assistance. Give your enemy no quarter, nor allay your demands, until he leaves you in undisputed possession of your rightful inheritance.

Those who sit upon a throne have throne rights. God says that by virtue of your union with Christ you are at this moment enthroned in the heavenlies. So exercise your rights, and be oppressed by Satan no more!

Maintaining a Balance

Someone may protest: "Too much emphasis upon the believer's position will make people careless about their situation. They will feel so secure in the 'heavenlies' that they will stop caring about the 'earthlies'."

That statement is both true and false. It is *true* in the sense that an emphasis on "position" alone, without a balancing demand to use that position to change our "situation", may certainly lead to spiritual arrogance and carelessness.

But the statement is *false* in the sense that a proper and forceful presentation of our position (when it is understood and believed) can have only one result: a life steadily brought into conformity with that position.

How closely is it possible for our "situation" to equal our "position"? Can they ever be the same?

The hiatus between our heavenly *position* and our earthly *situation* should be steadily closing as we walk with Christ.

Nonetheless, on this side of the resurrection that hiatus cannot be altogether removed. Yet we should never stop trying to close the gap – not by sweaty effort, but by vigorous faith and lively application of the tools of grace God has put into our hands – scripture, prayer, fellowship, and the indwelling strength of the Holy Spirit.

Seven:

Your Protection in The Heavenlies

We have learnt that all the blessings of the gospel are already ours in Christ. You say, *"Why then don't I have them?"* Answer – because they are all located *"in the heavenlies"*, and you have to position yourself in the heavenlies before you can seize them. Therein lies our difficulty – how do we get from where we are (our situation) to the throne of Christ (our position) so that we can grasp those limitless "spiritual blessings"?

Although I have suggested that *"the heavenlies"* describes a special kind of spiritual location, I do not want to infer that you have to go looking for this place. You do not have to <u>go</u> anywhere to be in the heavenlies, you only need to be in Christ. Neither do you have to <u>be</u> anything, or <u>become</u> anything different from what you are now. The immense privileges and power God has provided in the heavenlies are reserved for none except the sinner who believes in Christ.

Paul identifies those who are the proper beneficiaries of the heavenly inheritance, and he describes them as those who were *"dead through trespasses and sins"*, who were *"disobedient children"*, who *"lived in the passions of the flesh, following the desires of the body and mind"*, and who were *"by nature the children of wrath"* (Ep 2:1-3). But they have now resolved to find life in Christ.

In other words, if you are a sinner, who is trusting Jesus for salvation, then you qualify for every spiritual blessing in the heavenlies!

God did not *"make us alive"* when we were worthy, but when we were *"dead in sins"*; he did not raise us up because we deserved such goodness, or had merited it in any way at all, but because *"he is rich in mercy"*. We have not been exalted into the heavenlies because we have a claim upon God's reward, but solely because of *"the great love with which he loved us."*

Throne Rights

But now that we ***are*** alive, and raised up, and enthroned with Christ, we are expected to exercise our throne rights and to live victoriously over all the works of Satan: *"For we are his workmanship, created in Christ Jesus for good works, which God prepared beforehand, so that we might do them"* (2:10).

So God did not perform his mighty work of redemption and renewal in us because we were living godly and righteously. The reverse is true. Just because we were dead in sins and totally incapable of doing good, God has quickened us, and raised us, and seated us together with Christ in the heavenlies. We could never have climbed there by ourselves! His grace alone could so exalt us; and faith alone can give us access to these God-created rights. But now, because we know we are enthroned, and because we understand our rights, therefore we can overthrow the deadly grip of sin. We can tread underfoot every spiritual enemy, and live victoriously, fruitfully, and happily before the Lord. [13]

Speak What You Believe

Note that true faith always expresses itself in confident speech. Many verses in the Bible, in both Testaments, stress the importance of what we say; our lives are shaped by the

---

(13) This idea of our *Throne Rights* is taken up in more detail in a later section. It is also the theme of an eponymous Vision College text book

words we speak – see Pr 13:3; 16:24; 18:20-21; Mt 21:18-22; Ro 10:8-10; 2 Co 4:13-14; etc.

All those verses express a spiritual law – what you truly believe is what you will speak; and what you speak is what you will get. [14]

So then, away with that false humility, that spurious servility, that hidden carnal pride, that lustful desire to create one's own goodness, that wicked unbelief that godlessly clings to a position of defeat and of separation from God's blessing.

How dare we say we are not alive when God says we are! How dare we deny the resurrection that God says has happened to us in Christ! How dare we shun our throne rights when God says we are seated with Christ in the heavenlies! How dare we detract from his glorious demonstration throughout *"the coming ages of the immeasurable riches of his grace and of his love for us in Christ"* (2:7). How dare we try to secure his favour on the grounds of our own good works!

The order is plain. Not good works first, then the throne; but the throne first, then good works. Not overcome sin first, then every spiritual blessing; but first every spiritual blessing, then overcome sin. This is a fact – unless you first grasp *"every spiritual blessing in the heavenlies in Christ"* you will never properly overcome anything! But when you understand your throne rights, and possess them, and begin to use them, then you will find yourself more than a conqueror through Christ!

Illustration. Have you ever used a camera that is brought into focus by bringing two images together in its view-finder?

---

(14) So long, of course, as what you speak is in harmony both with the word and the will of God. No one can speak into existence anything that has neither divine promise nor divine purpose to support it.

You begin with separate, blurred images; you end with one distinct image in sharp focus.

Just so, you begin with yourself and Christ separated and out of focus; but as you learn to identify yourself with Christ, bringing yourself together with him by faith, your whole perspective will change. You will see the world from the throne, looking down from the heavenlies; you will no longer be controlled by **situational** fact, but by **positional** truth.

By the exercise of your throne rights you will change your situation to conform to your true identity and position.

Fight for Your Rights

Through your union with Christ by faith, you are a king. So think like a king. Speak like a king. Act like a king. Let nothing deny you your throne rights – not even being arrested, flogged, and crucified! Christ never for a moment surrendered to his enemies. Even when they believed themselves his conquerors, he was still Master, for he knew that they could not truly harm him. He knew that he would rise victorious over every foe. He knew that he would reign for ever in unassailable majesty. And so will you, if you bind yourself to him by faith.

But you must be ready to contend vigorously for your rights, to refuse to be denied what is yours in Christ. Unhappily, *"every spiritual blessing"* is not the only thing to be found in *"the heavenlies"*; there are also *"spiritual hosts of wickedness"* (Ep 6:10-12), and one of their main weapons is to implant doubt in your mind as to the reality or security of your position in Christ.

But notice also that victory is closely allied with faith; thus all the parts of *"the whole armour of God"* (Ep 6:13-17) are linked with righteousness, peace, and salvation, which come out of the word of truth and out of our faith in that word. So the "armour" is another vivid way of describing what God has wrought for us in Christ, and of bidding us to stand unwaveringly in that heavenly provision.

The inference is this – whoever will take his/her position in the heavenlies, clothed in that "armour", will be inviolable against Satan. So resist the devil, steadfast in faith, holding fast to the profession of your God-given identity in Christ.

The Problem of Sin

"What if I sin; will I not lose my heavenly position?"

Normally, sin does not affect the believer's position in Christ. However, if someone persists in sin, or refuses to allow God's gift of righteousness to be translated into practical holiness, then a condition can be reached where *"Christ is crucified afresh"* and that person may become cut off from the grace of God (He 6:4-8; 12:15-17). [15]

But I do not think such a condition can be reached easily or lightly; it is the result of a long process of careless neglect of the means of grace and of deliberately stifling the gentle voice of the Holy Spirit (He 2:1-3; Ep 4:30).

Conclusion

Put yourself where God puts you, on the throne with Christ. From that throne you have access to all the treasures of the Father's kingdom. You have power and authority over all the works of Satan. **No earthly "situation" can long resist the strength of that heavenly "position"!**

---

(15) That sentence touches on a long-lasting quarrel in the church about whether or not a Christian can lose his or her salvation. Obviously, I think it is possible to do so, although not easily, and not by an occasional sin. I think scripture shows that one has to renounce Christ and deliberately revert to a sinful life (in a sense, committing spiritual suicide) before all claim upon the life of Christ can be lost. But this is not the place to pursue that debate. It is discussed further in my book Great Words of the Gospel.

Section Three:

Inheritance and Strength

Eight:

A Guaranteed Inheritance

> *"I pray that the eyes of your hearts will be enlightened, so that you may know what is the **hope** to which God has called you, and how abundant are the riches of his glorious **inheritance** in the saints . . . The Holy Spirit will remain God's **guarantee** until we finally take possession of this **inheritance** . . . There is one body and one Spirit, just as there is one **hope** that belongs to your calling in Christ"* (Ep 1:18; 1:14; 4:4).

Hope! Treasure! Inheritance! Guarantee! What a delightful collection of happy ideas. Yet we sometimes find it hard to grasp their reality. Who has not discovered that hope can turn sour under the battering that life hands us? Who has not felt the bitterness expressed in the proverb – *"When hope is delayed, the heart is made sick with longing"* (Pr 13:12)? And the promises of riches seem inadequate when financial woes are assaulting us, and as for an inheritance – perhaps it is only a dream?

Out of such situations a deep cry arises from the human spirit. We may describe it thus –

There is the Cry for Innocence

The thing we most admire in little children is their innocence – the thing we most regret is the first sign of the loss of that innocence. Our sadness at the loss of innocence results from an ineradicable memory of the idyllic Garden of Eden. Hidden within the human spirit fragmented images remain of how things were before Adam and Eve ate the forbidden fruit.

Those first fallen humans tried to regain their lost virtue by covering themselves with leaves. But as it was then, so is it now – unless the Lord God clothes us, we cannot escape a sense of nakedness, and a deep longing to regain lost beauty.

But behold the riches of his grace and the wonder of his love! For in Christ we do indeed regain all that Adam lost and more, and we find ourselves arrayed in gorgeous robes of righteousness, sparkling with purity and beauty. Then the remainder of the proverb becomes real. After knowing the anguish of hope deferred, in Christ we find that *"hope fulfilled is like an open door to the tree of life!"*

There is the Cry for Independence

An article in the *Sydney Morning Herald* mocked people who willingly make themselves "slaves of God". The author insisted on his right to freedom from any kind of divine restraint. His words echoed sentiments expressed by William Henley more than a century earlier, in the poem *Invictus*. Henley contracted tuberculosis of the bone when he was still a boy, which led to his left leg being amputated below the knee when he was 20. Five years later he found himself once again confined to a hospital bed, threatened with the loss of his other leg. He resolutely declined the surgery, and instead penned the famous lines –

> Out of the night that covers me,
> Black as the Pit from pole to pole,
> I thank whatever gods may be
> For my unconquerable soul. . . .
>
> It matters not how strait the gate,
> How charged with punishments the scroll
> I am the master of my fate:

> I am the captain of my soul. [16]

Stirring words indeed! And they have stiffened the courage of many people over the years. Yet in the end they are a delusion. Death is the great leveller that mocks all human hubris, and scorns all claims to ultimate freedom.

Thus in the same year that Henley flung his defiance at heaven, other writers were declaring a different theme –

> Thou orderest all things well; . . .
> Hark!! from the opening skies
> The anthem's echoing swell,—
> "O mourning Land, lift up thine eyes!
> God reigneth. All is well!" [17]

Here then is a remarkable paradox. The way to hold independence is to lose it! For the only people who are truly free are those who have surrendered to the Lord. As the *Book of Common Prayer* has it, in the service of Christ alone "there is perfect freedom". [18] Or, as Phillips Brooks said, "No man in this world attains to freedom from any slavery except by entrance into some higher servitude. There is no such thing as an entirely free man conceivable." [19]

So indeed, we will either be slaves to

> Sin
> Fear
> Death

---

(16) *Invictus*, first and last stanzas. Henley put himself in the hands of the renowned physician and pioneer of antiseptic surgery, Lord Joseph Lister, whose treatment saved his leg and enabled him to enjoy another 30 years of active life. (Wikipedia)

(17) Oliver Wendell Holmes, in "A Hymn", from *Songs of Many Seasons*.

(18) A Collect for Peace.

(19) *Perennials*. I have no other information about this quote.

– or we will joyfully serve Christ, in whose service alone can we find true liberty!

There is the Cry for Transcendence

All of life is far more boring than words could ever say. Our eyes and our ears are never satisfied with what we see and hear (Ec 1:8, CEV).

Or, in the words of the KJV –

The eye is not satisfied with seeing, nor the ear filled with hearing.

Or we could call on this vivid picture of the poor in ancient Israel –

They carry the sheaves, yet stay hungry; they crush olives to make oil and tread grapes to make wine – yet cannot slake their thirst. (Job 24:11)

But is that not a metaphor of us all? Is our thirst ever satisfied? Is our hunger ever removed? Are our deepest yearnings ever fulfilled? Does our toil ever bring its promised reward? Certainly not without Christ!

Furthermore, we have all experienced the phenomenon of desiring something, only to find, when we get it, that it fails to satisfy us. Yet we *know* that somewhere true fulfilment exists, and we cannot desist from restlessly seeking it!

Yet in the end, only Christ brings deep joy with never any risk of either satiation or disillusion. Christ is never either too much or too little – he is always just right! As the psalmist cried –

Thou wilt show me the path of life: in thy presence is fulness of joy; at thy right hand there are pleasures for evermore (Ps 16:11, KJV).

There is the Cry for Inheritance

One of the most universal things in human society, from the distant past until now, is a belief in the right to an inheritance. It feels right when parents leave a substantial inheritance, and wrong when they cannot do so (Pr 13:22), or, as Paul puts it –

> *Children should not have to provide for their parents, but parents for their children.* (2 Co 12:14)

And Sirach, too, two centuries before Christ was born, insisted upon this rule –

> *It is better for your children to expect an inheritance from you than for you to be dependent upon them (33:21).*

It cannot be surprising then that the Lord God follows the same rule – that is, he has undertaken to provide a munificent inheritance to his own children –

> *God raises up the poor from the dust; he lifts the needy from the ash heap to make them sit with princes and inherit a seat of honour.* (1Sa 2:8)

Which promise, Jesus himself repeated –

> *Then the King will say to those on his right hand, "Come, you whom my Father has blessed, inherit the kingdom prepared for you from the day the world was first created"* (Mt 25:34).

So we who believe in Christ are promised a kingdom, an inheritance, a crown, a throne! Can we be sure of this? Is there any doubt? No! For this stupendous prize is sealed by the Holy Spirit, *"who is the* **guarantee of our inheritance** *until we acquire possession of it, to the praise of his glory"* (Ep 1:14). Are you full of the Holy Spirit? Have you been baptised in the Spirit? Then you have a strong witness, even a vision, within your own spirit that the inheritance is real, and extravagant, and will certainly be yours in the day you enter heaven.

But there is also a part for us to play in gaining the prize –

> *Do not be sluggish, but be imitators of those who through faith and patience inherit the promises.* (He 6:12)

> *Therefore, dear friends, work hard to make your calling and election sure . . . for then God will provide you with a rich entrance into the eternal kingdom of our Lord and Saviour Jesus Christ* (2 Pe 1:10-11).

I love that expression, *"a rich entrance"*! One person can enter a city unheralded, unknown, unobserved, and unrecognised. But another will enter with acclamation – bands playing, flags waving, trumpets blaring, people cheering, honours and wealth bestowed! That is the difference between an *entrance* and a *rich* entrance! Peter tells us to make sure that our entrance into the eternal kingdom will be glorious. Won't that be true of all Christians? No, for although every believer will certainly be *saved*, not all will be *honoured*. A rich entrance into heaven will belong only to those whose works, when they are tried by fire, emerge as gold, silver, and precious jewels (1 Co 3:12-15). Those whose works burn up because they are akin to wood, hay, and stubble, will be saved surely enough, but their entrance into heaven will be poor and unheralded.

Some people think that it is impious to serve God with an eye upon the promised reward. They insist that we should serve the Lord for his own sake, not for the sake of any possible recompense. No doubt that is true, to a point. It is true in the sense that anyone who loves God will indeed be willing to offer their lives to him whether or not there is a prize to gain. But it is wrong in the sense that the promised rewards – the crown, the trophies, the dominion, the honours, the treasures – are all described in scripture itself, and it is *scripture* that encourages us to labour for them – so it can hardly be ungodly to do so!

I began this chapter with Paul's prayer that the eyes of your heart will be enlightened, so that you may know what is the glorious hope and the rich inheritance to which God has called you in Christ. Here is the most urgent quest in Christian life – to **know**. To know the promise of God so deeply, so passionately, so fully, so believingly that you cannot possibly doubt it. To know it so mightily that it becomes a transforming force in your life. It is as Jesus said, if you would only but **know** the truth, that truth would set you free!

So read your Bible! Meditate constantly in the word of God (Ps 1:1-3). Search out the promises of God. Pray over them. Emulate Paul and give yourself no rest until the eyes of your understanding are opened, until revelation bursts into life inside you, until you know beyond all question, past all doubt, with thrilling conviction, that what God has spoken is true and that you are indeed the possessor of a guaranteed hope and an eternal inheritance in Christ!

Nine:

Beyond Measure

> *"I pray that you will know how far beyond measure is the great power of God that is at work in us who believe"* (Ep 1:19a).

In the year 107 a Christian bishop was thrown to the lions in the great arena in Rome. The vast crowd howled with delight as the ravenous and ill-treated beasts fell upon the martyr and tore him to pieces. The bishop's name was **Ignatius.** Church tradition holds that he was the child whom Jesus placed before his disciples as an example of humility and vulnerability (Mt 18:2). After the boy grew up, so the story goes, he became a friend and disciple of the apostle John, and later bishop of Antioch.

When Ignatius was about 45 years of age the Roman emperor Trajan ordered a persecution against the Church. The bishop was arrested, but steadfastly refused to worship the gods of the empire. So he was condemned to death in the arena in Rome. Placed in chains, he was given into the hands of a guard of 10 brutal soldiers, and began the long march to Rome. Every mile was made a dreary misery for the manacled bishop, as the guards endlessly taunted him and forced him to move faster, denying him rest and water.

But Ignatius remained serene in faith and gentle in love, and along the way he wrote seven letters to various churches that they passed, including one to the church in Rome itself –

> All the way from Syria to Rome I have been chained to a detachment of soldiers who have behaved like animals toward me. I tried giving them money, but the more I gave them, the more roughly they treated me. Quite

> honestly, they are like a pack of leopards . . . (but) that has some advantages, for I may as well get used to "leopards" now, since it will be lions, and real ones at that, when I get to Rome. . . . Forgive me for writing like this, but I do know what is best for me. . . . Whether the way be fire, or crucifixion, or wild beasts in the arena, or the mangling of my whole body, I can bear it. . . . So far as I am concerned, to die for Jesus Christ is better than to be king of the whole world! (20)

So the brave bishop, resigned to martyrdom, told his friends in Rome not to make any effort to secure his release.

He finally arrived in the city, was condemned again to die, thrown into the arena, and in a few moments was torn to pieces by the lions.

However, in this study I am more interested in another letter written by the saintly and courageous bishop. I mean his letter to the *Ephesians*, in which he deliberately used a word that Paul had also used in *his* letter to the same church. That word is part of the text that stands at the head of this chapter (Ep 1:19). In Greek it is *hyperballo*, which is a piece of hyperbole made up of two other words, *ballo* = to throw; and *hyper* = beyond/above. The two together create a superlative expression, which is literally *"to throw out of sight"*, but means *beyond measure,* or *past comparison,* or *immeasurable*.

Here is how Ignatius twice used *hyperballo* in his *Letter to the Ephesians* (9:2) –

> How then was Christ manifested to the world? A star shone brightly in heaven, **_far above_** all the other stars, with indescribable brightness . . . All the stars, with the

---

(20) Taken from Ignatius' letter to the Romans ch. 5 & 6, translator unknown to me.

sun and the moon, formed a chorus to this star, and its light was ***immeasurably great*** above them all!

So *hyperballo* conveys a picture of the limitless glory and power of Christ, which Ignatius knew well enough had been applied by Paul, not to Christ, *but to each believer!* [21] What measureless honour then is ours! What incomparable splendour! What boundless strength and glory! As Christ is, so are we! (1 Jn 4:17) And not tomorrow, but, as John says, *now*, in this present world!

So Ignatius quite rightly applies *hyperballo* to Christ. But Paul, with breathtaking boldness applies it to us! He uses this word, which seems as though it really should belong only to Jesus, to give an extravagant description of the invincible strength at work in the Church. But not content with this, Paul heightens its force by linking it with two other extravagant words: *megethos* = vast power; and *dunamis* = miraculous force, supernatural acts.

That phrase (*hyperballon megethos*) occurs only here in the NT, and with *dunamis* added it presents the strongest possible description of what every true Christian possesses in Christ –

> *How far beyond all measure is the illimitable and supernatural power of Christ that is at work in us who believe!*

Our problem, of course, is that such extravagant words seem far removed from reality. On the face of it, they could hardly be more out of touch with the facts of everyday life! How often can you look into a mirror and declare of yourself,

---

(21) Paul uses *hyperballo* five times, always in connection with some gift of God to those who believe – 2 Co 3:10, the gospel; 9:14, the excellence of his grace; Ep 1:19, his power at work in us; 2:7, the riches of his grace; 3:19, his measureless love.

"There is an image of power, strength, glory, miracles, and splendour beyond all measure!" You don't look like such a creature, nor do you feel like it!

How then should we understand Paul's words? Are they really too profligate? Should we tone them down to a more practical level? Can I truly believe that the power of Christ in me is immeasurably great, far above any human appraisal, surpassing all telling, working all miracles?

In fact, they become very believable once you realise that the apostle is affirming two divinely sure things –

The Sure Victory of the Church

The first modern state to try to banish religion was not (as most people think) Communist Russia, but France, at the end of the 18th century, when its blood-drenched Revolution was raging. The revolutionaries seized all the churches, banned the priesthood, and tried to replace Christ by a white statue of the Goddess of Reason. They placed their statue on the high altar of the cathedral of Notre Dame in Paris. But their sacrilege met with little success, and eventually was overturned by Napoleon.

In the middle of this crass attempt to abolish Christ, a rationalist philosopher complained to Prince Talleyrand about the difficulty of converting the French peasants to the new religion: "What can I do to impress these people?" he asked.

Talleyrand replied: "You could try getting crucified, and rising again after three days." [22]

The turmoil in France finally settled into a democratic republic, but there is still a fierce war going on between –

The World

- with its philosophy of might makes right; its admiration of riches; its adulation of power, strength, achievement, material success; and

The Church

- with its philosophy of humility, love, gentleness, self-denial, and sacrifice on behalf of others.

On the face of it, the contest is absurdly unequal! How can the Church, with its softly loving weapons, hope to defeat the world, with its ruthless force? But there are two things we should never lose sight of –

- We serve the King of kings, whose ultimate and absolute victory is assured in heaven and on earth (cp. Da 7:9,10,13,14; etc).
- We belong to a kingdom whose ruling principle is love.

The Church may lack guns, planes, tanks, worldly power; but still we will win, because we *love*! And this love is the <u>highest</u> expression of the *"immeasurably great"* power of Christ in us. For it has now become true that whereas –

---

(22) The story is well known, although I have not been able to trace its source. Talleyrand's response is sometimes wrongly attributed to Voltaire. Talleyrand was a renowned statesman in France at the time. He survived the Revolution and went on to serve Napoleon until he fell into disfavour with the emperor and had to retire from high office.

- once we lived by the rule of *hate*, now we are governed by *love*
- once we were controlled by the principle of *greed*, but now we are more eager to *give* than to receive
- once we were driven by the need for *revenge*, but now we are quick to *forgive*
- once we *laughed* but had no real *joy*, which is now a bubbling spring in our souls
- once only *death* worked in us, now we possess an indestructible force of *life*
- once we lived only for *ourselves*, now our focus is upon the welfare of *others!*

This change from what we were to what we are in Christ is one that nothing but the power of God himself could have accomplished. It is beyond the skill of psychology, self-effort, personal makeover, or any other human tool, which can do little more than hang plastic fruit on a thorn bush. It might look pretty, but it's still not the real thing. To get good fruit you need a healthy tree producing fruit from its own inner dynamic, which God alone can make.

Unhappily, Christians have often forgotten these things, and have resorted instead to worldly weapons; they have tried to turn the *"immeasurable power of Christ"* into a thing of muscle and money. But as Jesus said, *"Those who live by the sword will die by the sword"* (Mt 26:52). A church that depends upon secular weaponry, or resorts to brute force, has *Ichabod* written all over it. I do not mean that churches should not use whatever resources are properly available to them, but only that in the end, if we cannot win the world to Christ by love, then we will not win it at all.

We are challenged to remain true to our calling in Christ, to believe in the invincibility of divine love, to find there our *greatest realisation* of the limitless power of Christ at work in us. For indeed the Church is made strong not by gaining some physical or material strength above that of its enemies – for instead it remains poor, weak, defenceless in the eyes of the world – but by the possession of an infrangible love, against which its foes are ultimately helpless.

The church that loves cannot be destroyed; the church that resorts to carnal weaponry will fall.

The Sure Victory of the Believer

Two Weaknesses

We believers confront two seemingly fatal weaknesses –

We are Mortal

I heard somewhere that for the first 20 years of his life a man hears his *mother* asking him where he is going; then he spends 50 years hearing his *wife* asking him where he is going; then at his death the *mourners* stand around wondering where he has gone!

We must all die. But what then?

In Christ alone is immortality found, and in him all who believe are guaranteed victory over death and the grave. This was undoubtedly a major part of Paul's concept of the *"immeasurably great"* power of Christ that is at work in us, for he calls it the very same power that raised Christ himself from the dead.

We are Fallen

Have you ever been teased with this conundrum: what happens when an irresistible force meets an immovable object? There is of course no answer, because the question itself is absurd. If there is such a thing as an immovable object, then an irresistible force cannot exist; and vice versa. Logically, only one of those items can exist at the same time. Whichever you choose, the other is at once negated.

But in the *spiritual* realm there is a sense in which the puzzle becomes real – what once had seemed to be the immovable object of our sin must now yield before the irresistible force of the blood of Christ. What else but a power beyond all measure or limit could suffice to redeem our fallen lives?

Hence in any warfare against sin, the believer should triumph, not by focussing upon either the temptation or the sin itself, but rather upon the weapons of our warfare: the **Blood**, the **Name**, the **Spirit**, the **Word.**

No one can truly overcome sin by warring against it personally. Some kind of outward victory, or even behaviour change may be won, but inwardly the sin principle will still be deeply pervasive and poisonous. So don't concentrate your eye or your prayer upon what is defeating you, but rather upon the sources of victory. Let the irresistible force of the gospel make temptation otiose and break the seemingly immovable grip of iniquity.

Victory Assured

If by the power of the indwelling Christ we are able to overcome sin and death, our mortality, and our fallenness, what is left to fear?

If our two most dread enemies have been destroyed, how can we be terrified by any lesser foe?

Should we tremble before the world, or sickness, or poverty, or anything that may come upon us from the devil? Nay, in all these things we are *"more than conquerors"* in Christ. We are destined to rule the universe as co-heirs with Christ of all the Father's domain. We cannot lose for winning. We cannot fall for rising. We cannot weep for laughing. For this is the victory that overcomes the world and all that is in it, *"even our faith"*! (1 Jn 5:4)

Summary

Paul prays that the saints will learn the *"immeasurable greatness"* of the power that is at work in them, and he defines that power in four ways (Ep 1:20-22). He says nothing about any secular sort of power – money, bombs, buildings, government, brute strength, and the like – rather he finds Christian strength in something quite different – *love that works by faith* (Ga 5:6). And how strong that weapon is! We see it demonstrated in Christ. It –

- raised him from the dead
- enthroned him in the heavenlies
- put all things under his feet
- made him Head over all things.

And all this, says Paul, was done *"FOR THE CHURCH"* – that is, for the benefit, enrichment, and triumph of the Church, so that no enemy might ever finally prevail over us. They may rob us of goods, spouse, children, wealth, position, and indeed, of anything that is of this world, including life itself – but while Christ is ours, and we are Christ's, we remain indestructible (cp. He 10:32-35, and note especially the word *"cheerfully"*!).

Conclusion

The last of the pagan Roman emperors was Julian the Apostate (reigned 360-363). He was the nephew of Constantine the Great, and was raised a Christian. Sadly, he reverted to paganism, and when he became emperor tried to revive the old Roman religion. He refused to call Jesus the "Christ", but always referred to him scornfully as the "Galilean".

War broke out between Rome and Persia, and in an attempt to secure the support of Rome's ancient gods, Julian resolved to rid his army of officers who were Christians. He made a special example of a high-ranking man named Mercurius, whom he put to death cruelly.

Soon after the war began, when Julian was leading his troops in battle near the site of modern Baghdad, he was mortally wounded by a Persian spear. Some soldiers carried him to his tent and laid him, bleeding copiously, upon a bed. Julian saw his approaching death as God's vengeance upon him for killing Mercurius, so he thrust his hand into the wound and bathed it in his own blood. Then, holding the dripping hand up to heaven he gave one last despairing cry in his Latin tongue: "Vicisti Galilaee!" – "Thou hast conquered, O Galilean!" [23]

The pagan emperor's lament of *defeat* is our shout of *triumph*.

Christ has won the victory. In him we cannot ever be finally defeated, for his *"exceeding great power is at work in every one who believes"*, guaranteeing our ultimate triumph over sin, death, and the devil, and ensuring our glorious entrance into God's supernal paradise (Ep 1:19; Ro 8:18).

---

[23] Theodoret, *Church History* 3:20 (circa 429 A.D).

Ten:

An Extraordinary Strength

I pray that your inner eyes will be enlightened until you have fully grasped, not only the hope to which God has called you, but also all the riches and glory that lie in your share of the inheritance that belongs to his people. And I pray that you will truly know how far beyond all measure is the strength he has planted in us who believe! (Ep 1:18-19)

I want to ask again, How shall we understand this *"strength that is far beyond all measure"*?

It is certainly not "power" as the world understands it. Nor is it "power to rule over others", nor even "power to escape all harm" – rather, it is

Power to Love – and Not Hate

This does not mean that we are required to have *affection* for every person, nor to be fond of them. Wisely, scripture does not say, "You must *like* your enemy," but, "you must *love* him!" There are many people I cannot like; indeed, there are some whom I loathe –child rapers; torturers; wife-beaters; people who advocate genocide; and the like.

I'm in good company – Jesus didn't like such people, either; and he was harshly vituperative against religious hypocrites! (Mt 23:13-33)

Yet still Christ *loved* each man and woman (even the vilest, even those who murdered him) and gave his life as a ransom for us all, albeit requiring from the sinner genuine repentance and faith.

Thus we too must *love*, even if we cannot *like*, and that love will behave toward all people as Christ himself did.

One mark of true love is that it will offer pardon to those who have offered offence. Where there is no forgiveness there is no true love. Which does not mean that a person who has done wrong should be allowed to escape all penalty. But it does mean that whatever punishment may be required by law or social custom must be imposed with restraint, with justice, with equality, and with a forgiving heart.

If we do not allow love to prevail, even over the worst offences against us, then we will stay bitter, resentful, and looking for revenge. What a foul way to begin each new day! What an ugly burden to carry into each new tomorrow! Why would you want to fall asleep with such darkness in your soul, festering, poisoning, marring the image of Christ in you?

No wonder Paul says, *"If you get angry about something, do not let your fury become sinful, and make sure that you are rid of anger before the day ends"* (Ep 4:26). [24]

When does anger become sin? When it is based on the hurt someone has done to yourself rather than to someone else! Jesus was often furious with people who were cruel and unjust to others, but he never allowed anger to rise up against a personal injury. Indeed, he pleaded the Father's pardon even for those who were brutally hammering great spikes through his wrists and feet, savagely nailing him to the cross (Lu 23:34).

Francis McNutt suggests this exercise: first read *1 Corinthians 13:4-8*, replacing the word "love" with "Jesus"; then read it a second time, replacing "love" with "I". You

---

(24) I will take up this theme again in Section Four (below) – *Forgiveness*.

should find that all wrongful anger will be driven out of you, or at least that it will begin to dissipate.

Power to Give – and Not Grasp

Christian giving will show cheerful generosity – *"Give and it will be given to you, in rich measure, pressed down, shaken together, and running over. For by the measure you give so will it be given back to you"* (Lu 6:38).

So then, by what measure should we give? Based upon OT practices, the tithe, or a tenth, is usually thought to be a good rule of thumb,– *"'Bring one-tenth of your income into the storehouse so that there may be food in my house. Test me in this way,' says the Lord of Armies. 'See if I won't open the windows of heaven for you and flood you with blessings'"* (Ma 3:10). However, the laws placed upon Israel are not necessarily mandated for the Church, and no Christian should feel under any binding duty to tithe his or her income. Nonetheless, many people agree that the tithe is a practical basis for Christian giving, so long as it remains voluntary, cheerful, and an act of faith, not of obedience to some law.

One principle enunciated by Paul is that we should give regularly according to how much God has prospered us (1 Co 16:2). But we can be sure of this, the Holy Spirit is not likely to bid anyone to give parsimoniously, coldly, or indifferently! Rather, in accord with Jesus' teaching, and with the tenor of scripture, we may expect to be directed to give freely, generously, sacrificially, and to apportion our giving to the church, the poor, and world missions.

Notice how Jesus spoke about a "law of proportionate return" (measure for measure). Paul stresses the same rule in 2 Corinthians 9:6-11 –

> *The point is this – if you sow sparingly you will also reap sparingly, but if you sow bountifully you will also*

*reap bountifully. You should each give on the basis of a firm inner conviction – not reluctantly, nor because you have been forced, but with cheerful willingness, which God loves. And God is able to make **every** grace **abound** to you, so that you will be **all**-sufficient in **all** things at **all** times, **abounding** in **every** good work. For God will both supply you with seed for sowing and **multiply** it, so that you will be enriched in **every** way and also able to be generous in **every** situation!"* (abridged)

That passage has been called the most extravagant in the entire Bible. It contains ten superlatives (seven of them in verse 8 alone), which I have tried to show by the underlined words in bold print. There God promises to the generous, cheerful, sacrificial giver –

- every grace
- abounding grace
- all sufficiency
- in all things
- at all times
- abounding success
- in every good work
- enriched in every way
- generous in every situation!

Or, to look at it in another way –

- God wants you to have a surplus
- he is able to provide for you abundantly (vs 8,9)
- he does this by using "the law of sowing (vs 6) and reaping" (vs 10), that is, sow sparingly, reap poorly; sow generously, reap richly.

Those promises we are called to believe with all our heart! They are not just empty words, nor hollow theory. They are packed with life! They oblige us, if we sow in harmony with

God's laws, to expect confidently that his generous harvest will follow.

But there is an aspect of this law of sowing that is often overlooked. Every gardener or farmer knows that there is an optimum amount of seed to put into the ground. Too much seed, and the plants will strangle each other. Too little seed, and weeds will strangle the harvest. Each kind of seed must be planted in the right quantity at the right time in the right soil to ensure a bountiful crop.

So with Christian giving. For each person there is a proper amount to give, about which you should ask God. Sow too little, and God will be offended by your parsimony or unbelief – probably both. It is a sin. Sow too much, and God will be offended by your arrogance, going beyond what he requires. It is a sin. The Lord wants only that we should each give just what he has told us to give, no more, nor any less. To give less is disobedient; to give more is presumptuous.

It is sometimes said that one can't out-give God. But in the case of money, at least, that saying is folly. Whether too much or too little of anything, to give other than what the Lord requires is rebellion, and will scarcely attract his blessing.

But, again, how can I know what God wants? What should one's motivation be? Apart from what I have already said about cheerful, generous, and sacrificial giving, and using the tithe as a useful guide, note the following –

- One should never give with the hope of buying some favour from heaven, nor of bullying the Lord into releasing some blessing. God cannot be cajoled; he cannot be bargained with; you can't trap him in a corner.

Some people give away too much, or spend beyond their means, expecting the Lord to bail them out when the bills fall due. But he is under no obligation to do so, and usually won't. If one plays the fool, one can expect a fool's reward – that is, either nothing, or even worse, more loss.

- Emulate Paul, and base your giving upon the laws of harvest, the principle of sowing and reaping.

A sensible farmer does not try to bargain with God – "Look, I've made this great sacrifice and sown all this seed, more than I can afford, now it's up to you to do the right thing and make it grow well!" Rather, he knows that God has ordained certain natural laws – sow well and you will reap well – and he co-operates with those laws. He does not require God to respond to his initiative; instead, he is responding to God's initiative. He knows that if he works his farm well, in harmony with natural law, then he may expect to prosper. He is not demanding that God should obey him; on the contrary, he is obeying God.

In response to this harvest law, says Paul, we must *"make up our minds"* – that is

- Do not allow your giving to be controlled by sentiment, nor by an emotional response to some appeal, nor by some kind of manipulative tactic, nor even by the fear of giving too little.
- Let all your giving be a planned, disciplined, and obedient response to what you perceive to be the will of God for you – *"Each of you should give what you have decided in your heart to give, not reluctantly out of a sense of duty, nor under any kind of duress, nor out of mere emotion or whim, but with firm intention and cheerful goodwill, which God loves"* (2 Co 9:7, paraphrased).

In that way, working with God in accordance with the law of harvest, he will *"make you rich enough so that you can always be generous, and your generosity will produce thanksgiving to God"* (vs. 11, GW).

Eleven:

An Extraordinary Strength – 2

We are still trying to grasp the meaning of the *"extraordinary strength"* that Paul says is at work in us believers. That power is certainly unlike what the world considers powerful, consisting as it does of deeply inward spiritual forces – the qualities of *love, generosity, forgiveness*, and the like. But now we turn to a quality that church history, in the stories of its martyrs, has shown to be immeasurably strong – the power to *suffer* and yet never yield. This has been a constant mystery to the secular world. How can ordinary people endure such torments without wavering, the world cries, and all for the sake of a religious belief? We confront here –

Power to Suffer – and Not Fail

Christian suffering takes two forms, the trial of *temptation* and the trial of *pain*. Both of them are normal parts of Christian life, and belong to our call to be *witnesses*, that is, *martyrs* for Christ. You will find more about being a martyr below, but here let us look at –

The Trial of Temptation

The person who is truly victorious is not the one for whom sin has no appeal, but the one who craves, yet firmly resists the devil. The bravest people are not those who are fearless, but those who are terrified, yet persevere in doing what is right. The strongest are not those who crush the weak, but those who face overwhelming odds yet press on, knowing that no matter how many battles they might lose they will still win the war. Thus the power of Christ at work in us does not rid us of temptation, but enables us to meet every sort of enticement while never succumbing to its allure. Or if we sometimes *do* yield, to shake off the chains of sin and to rise up again in righteousness, purity, and the beauty of holiness.

We should have the same heart as the prophet –

> *You can stop rejoicing over me, O my enemy. I may have fallen, but I shall stand up again. I may be sitting in darkness, but the Lord is still my Light. Yes, I have sinned against him, and he is angry with me; but I know that he will nonetheless plead my case and argue in my defence. Then he will bring me out into the light again and make everything right for me!* (Mi 7:8-9).

Now, on this matter of temptation, there is a passage that is at once the most encouraging, and the most discouraging in the entire Bible! –

> *There are no unique temptations. Whatever trial comes upon you is part of human experience and has been faced by other people. But God is faithful. Either he will keep you from being tempted beyond your strength, or he will provide a way of escape from it, so that it does not defeat you* (1 Co 10:13).

Why is that the most *encouraging* text in the Bible? Because it provides firm assurance that no Christian will ever be confronted by a temptation that cannot be resisted and overcome.

Why is it the most *discouraging* text in the Bible? Because it robs us of every excuse we have ever made for yielding to sin!

Now that is a bit hard to take, for we are all prone to think that the fiercest temptations in our lives are somehow unique to ourselves. We like to persuade ourselves either that no one else has ever faced quite such a temptation, or that, like ourselves, they crumpled beneath it.

But Paul is adamant – there are no *uncommon* temptations. He insists instead that every temptation is *common* to human experience. How can he say that? Simply because, in the end, all temptations (and hence all sin) can be reduced to just three categories –

- the hunger of the eye
- the hunger of the flesh
- the pride of life
  – see *1 John 2:15-16; Matthew 4:1-11; Luke 4:1-13*.

In that list there is again good news and bad news. The good news is that those three tools comprise the entire satanic armoury. The bad news is that with such a small array of weapons he has been able to wreak awful havoc upon humanity.

But now, because of the gospel, we have the advantage of knowing just what fiery darts the devil will be throwing at us, and can arm ourselves against them (Ep 6:11-18). So don the armour of God, take up the weapons of your spiritual warfare and send Satan to rout!

Think too, about the martyrs who defied all secular expectations when they endured with unflinching courage the most horrific barbarities. Thousands of men, women, young people, even children, were burned, racked, torn apart, mutilated, raped, subjected to every conceivable torture, and endured every sort of pitiless agony – yet in the grace of Christ they held firm, and often died with a song on their lips!

In like manner we should expect to find in Christ whatever strength and tenacity we need to master every foe and enforce the triumph of Christ. And when temptation presents itself, act on Paul's advice –

- affirm the promise of the limit – no trial will go beyond what God allows, nor surpass the strength God himself will give you;
- search for the way of escape – whether that be a way to avoid the trial altogether, or to find in Christ an inner place of refuge; and in all cases
- rise up in the power of the Holy Spirit, and win the victory!

That victory may sometimes mean the demolition of your foe, or it may mean an ability to resist being overthrown, or it may mean remaining serene even while battle rages around you. But it always means that in every situation we are *"more than conquerors in Christ"*! (Ro 8:37)

The Trial of Pain

> *It has been granted to you, for the sake of Christ, that you should not only believe in him <u>but also suffer for his sake</u>* (Ph 1:29).

How disturbing that sounds. We are more accustomed to thinking about faith in Christ attracting blessing, not pain. Yet the theme is strong in the teaching of the apostle –

> *I rejoice in my sufferings for your sake, because in my body I am filling up whatever might be lacking in Christ's afflictions for the sake of his Body, the Church ... I want to share in the sufferings of Christ, becoming like him in his death, so that by any means possible I may attain the resurrection from the dead ... I want to share in suffering for the gospel by the power of God* (Cl 1:24; Ph 3:10; 2 Ti 1:8).

In one way or another we are all called to live out those verses. And what extraordinary riches Paul attaches to Christian suffering –

Completing the Suffering of Christ

In some mysterious sense we *"fill up what is deficient in the sufferings of Christ"*. Commentators struggle with this, because it seems to imply that Calvary was inadequate and that we have to add something of our own to the Cross. Yet we know that we are saved by grace alone, apart from any work, whether good or bad, and solely through faith in the finished work of Christ (Ga 2:16). We can add nothing to that redemption; we can take nothing from it.

So why does Paul say that what Christ has done is somehow "deficient"? I think he has in mind the whole world, and that its redemption requires a suffering church. I think he is saying that while the death and resurrection of Christ have provided full and effectual salvation for each believer, the actual rescue of the *world* demands the presence of a church that suffers – not a proud, complacent, self-satisfied church (Re 3:14-18), not a church that craves domination, not one that wants to rule the world, but a church that is willing, like its Saviour, to die so that others might live.

We are to be *witnesses* of Christ; but we can do that only as we are also *martyrs*. Thus, when Christ told his disciples to go and bear witness to the ends of the earth (Ac 1:8), he used a Greek word (*martus*) that can mean either a *witness* (2 Co 13:1) or a *martyr* (Re 17:6). And indeed, Christ himself was both witness and martyr (Re 1:5), and so must we be who are part of his suffering Church, his Body on earth. No one can truly follow Christ without in some way sharing his reproach. Discipleship is costly. But if we share in his *grief*, we shall also share in his *glory* (Ro 8:17).

Establishing a Resurrection Claim

Paul wanted to be like Christ in suffering and death, so that by any means possible he might *"attain the resurrection from the dead"*. He is not expressing uncertainty about his hope of resurrection, for he knew full well that all who believe in Christ are assured of being raised to everlasting life in Paradise with Christ. But he means that if it were necessary to suffer as Jesus suffered, to die as Jesus died in order to gain that resurrection (as Christ did), then he would joyfully embrace whatever anguish life and ministry might bring.

Paul was also determined that he would never, under any circumstances, or despite any persecution, allow anything to turn him aside or put at risk his gaining of the resurrection. To him, the resurrection was a prize so staggering, a joy so immense, a treasure so alluring that he could not imagine anything of greater worth or more to be desired. Even a cross would not be too high a price to pay to ensure rising from the grave to meet Christ when he comes again.

Suffering by the Power of God

Nothing so marks the difference between worldly power and the power of the gospel than Paul's assertion that he would suffer *"by the power of God"*. I have preached many sermons and heard many more that have urged people to call upon the power of God for victory, health, prosperity, and other blessings, but not many that have suggested the listeners should depend upon the power of God for suffering!

Yet where else would we have more need of the power of God than to give us courage, patience, and faith to endure and defeat fierce persecution and terrifying violence?

Whatever befalls us, we have no cause to complain if God imparts his power to sustain us and bring us safely home to heaven.

So this *"immeasurably great power"* that is in us in Christ enables us, not to play petty tyrants, nor to stomp proudly through the world like despots, but to overcome hatred by love, to stifle greed by giving, and to defeat suffering by his empowering grace.

But finally, and perhaps most important, it is –

Power to Live – and Not Die

This was probably the dominant thought in Paul's mind when he cried, *"How extraordinary is his strength planted in us who believe!"* For he straightway went on to exclaim that this power is akin to *"the working of his great might, which God worked in Christ when he raised him from the dead and enthroned him at his right hand in the heavenlies"* (Ep 1:20).

There the power of God in each believer is unbreakably linked with turning mortality into immortality, and with our destiny to live and reign with Christ for ever. It's an idea that Paul states even more forcibly in another place – *"We are waiting for our Saviour, the Lord Jesus Christ, who will transform our lowly bodies to be like his glorious body, by the power that enables him even to subject all things to himself"* (Ph 3:20-21).

Behold, nothing less than divine omnipotence – the power that enables God to bend everything to his will – is required to call the dead out of their graves and transform them into the glorious likeness of Christ! Our "low" bodies, corrupted by sin, decayed in the grave, blown dustily around the planet, will nonetheless be brought back together, transformed, and fashioned into bodies of radiant and supernal beauty. Incandescent as the sun. Shining with the loveliness of Christ. More splendid even than those towering infernos of golden flame, the sublime seraphim, who stand before the throne of God crying day and night, *"Holy, holy, holy is the Lord of Hosts!"* (Is 6:1-3)

Indeed, Christ will *"transform our bodies to be like his glorious body"* – of which we can gain some feeble sight in the vision of the beloved disciple –

> *I saw someone who looked like the Son of Man. He was wearing a robe that reached down to his feet, and a gold cloth was wrapped around his chest. His head and his hair were white as wool, like dazzling snow, and his eyes burned like flames of fire. His feet were glowing like red hot bronze, and his voice thundered like the roar of a mighty waterfall. He held seven stars in his right hand, and out of his mouth came a sharp double-edged sword. His face was shining as brightly as the noonday sun.* (Re 1:13-15)

No wonder we are told that John *"fell at his feet like a dead man!"* (vs. 17) But not for long. He was soon back on his feet, marvelling at the splendour of heaven, the majestic throne of God, and the illustrious destiny of the Church.

Death, we are told, is the *"last enemy"* (1 Co 15:26), and if in the end we conquer death, then we have indeed conquered all!

Section Four:

Christian Life

Twelve:

Forgiveness

If you become angry don't turn it into sin. Don't let the sun set on your anger ... Cast off all bitterness, passion, and fury. Stop squabbling and insulting each other. Let there be no more nasty feelings of any sort. Rather, you should be kind-hearted to one another, compassionate, and eager to forgive one another, as God has forgiven you through Christ (Ep 4:26, 31-32).

Introduction

There is a peculiar formula in the early chapters of Amos. It occurs eight times in connection with the judgment of God upon various nations. The Lord said: *"For three transgressions and for four, I will not revoke their punishment"* (1:3,6,9,11,13; 2:1,4,6).

Because of that Amos formula, the Jewish rabbis in the time of Jesus argued that it was enough to forgive your neighbour three times. They said that even God forgave only thrice and then punished a fourth offence. Why should we be more generous than God?

Hence Peter, when he offered to forgive an offender no less than *seven* times, was probably proud of his piety (Mt 18:21). Was he not willing to go twice as far as popular practice required? But Christ scorned Peter's offer of seven-fold forgiveness. He knew, of course, that the rabbis were wrong. The formula *"for three transgressions and for four"* was just a vivid way of saying, "it is not possible to count the number of sins the nation has committed." Someone has explained it thus –

> When the perfect number (three) is followed by four ... God not only declares that the measure of iniquity is full, but that it is filled to overflowing and beyond all measure.

So Amos was not saying that God's patience is exhausted after only three or four transgressions. Rather, he meant that despite countless warnings the people had not repented (compare 4:6-11, and the refrain *"yet you did not return to me"*). For that reason judgment became inevitable (vs. 12). Even so, had the people wept for their sins and turned to the Lord with all their heart, he would have pardoned them with joy (5:4,6,14).

So Christ told Peter (and us) – *"You must forgive those who offend you, not seven times, but seventy times seven!"*

Yet we should not be too quick to judge Peter. I have met many Christians who refuse to forgive even *one* offence, let alone multiple misdeeds.

When Jesus declared that we should be willing to forgive our neighbour at least 490 times, did he mean that we could count to 490 and then, on the 491st offence take savage revenge? Of course not! He was actually teaching that our willingness to forgive must be *limitless*. If you are counting off the number of offences ("488 ... 489... 490 ... 491 – wham! *now* I can strike back!") you simply show that you have actually not forgiven the offender even once – you have merely postponed your retaliation.

But how can such limitless forgiveness be demanded? It would seem to impose upon our frail humanity an intolerable burden. Is Christ a tyrant, requiring of us a greater forbearance than even God shows? Hardly! For *our* benefit Christ insists that we forgive *"seventy times seven"* (that is, without limit). *Refusing* pardon, not *giving* it, is the thing that turns life into a crushing burden. Hence we learn –

The High Cost of Limiting Forgiveness

Failure to forgive freely and heartily those who have hurt you exacts a heavy toll – [25]

To Limit Forgiveness Places You Under the Tyranny Of Hate

We Christians are obliged to live by the royal law of love. But those who refuse to forgive, no matter how they try to disguise it or to justify it, are actually living by a law of hatred. It is pointless to pretend otherwise. We cannot love and yet not truly forgive – see *1 John 2:9-11; 3:14-18; 4:19-21*

If you refuse to forgive your neighbour, then you are saying that he does not deserve God's forgiveness, which means that you think he deserves to suffer the torments of hell forever. The most virulent hatred could not wish any greater pain upon an enemy.

If you have not truly forgiven, then you will be seeking an opportunity to retaliate – but God says, *"Vengeance is mine, I will repay"* (Ro 12:19-21; 13:9-10). To take vengeance into your own hand, or even to wish that you were free to do so, will make you just as guilty in the sight of God as the person who offended you – even more guilty if God knows that your opponent's offence was unintentional or done innocently.

Note however, that God prohibits only *personal* revenge. In other circumstances the Lord himself acts to cast down wrongdoers – sometimes through the law (Ro 13:1-7); sometimes through the church as an agent of discipline (Mt

---

[25] Some parts of the following outline are based on an article, or perhaps even a book, that I read many years ago. I have long since lost any record of the original.

18:15-17); sometimes through natural disasters, or through adverse circumstances; or else divine vengeance may be delayed until after death (Lu 16:19-31). There are times, too, when the Lord inflicts punishment by seemingly chance occurrences, as when King Ahab was killed in battle by an arrow shot *"at a venture"* – that is, randomly, without aiming, or without the archer even knowing that he had struck the king between the joints of his armour (1 Kg 22:34; 2 Ch 18:33).

In any case, God reserves to himself the right of ultimate revenge because he alone knows all the factors that cause people to behave in certain ways; he alone knows the real extent of their guilt or innocence.

Therefore, any Christian who lives under the tyranny of hatred will pay a heavy price. At the very least, he or she will be unable to enjoy fulness of life in Christ, will suffer some measure of separation from his Body, the Church (1 Co 11:28-30), and will be robbed of some part of a clear vision of heaven's bliss.

To Limit Forgiveness Places You Under The Tyranny of Selfishness

Those who limit forgiveness condemn themselves to a double blindness – they no longer see any *virtue* in the offender; they no longer see any *fault* in themselves. That blindness may not fully darken their lives immediately; but if they remain implacable, it will eventually cause both a distorted concentration upon the faults of the offender and a corresponding distorted emphasis upon their own virtues.

If the offender is a *believer*, ongoing rancour will prevent the victim from seeing Christ *in* that Christian; if the offender is an *unbeliever*, ongoing rancour will prevent the victim from bringing Christ *to* that person. Both faults are serious offences against the love of Christ; they expose a self-centredness that is antagonistic to joyous Christian life.

To Limit Forgiveness Places You Under The Tyranny of The Past

Do you really want to enter each tomorrow under the shadow of yesterday? Do you really want to darken the beautiful prospect of each new day in Christ by bringing into it the bitterness of the past? Paul's advice is wiser: *"Do not let the sun go down on your anger"* (Ep 4:26).

Can any Christian afford to jeopardise the wonderful future God has planned for us by stubbornly clinging to the faults of yesterday? Indeed, those who withhold forgiveness are actually turning their backs on God's tomorrow and foolishly facing only the shadows of their past. It is a sin that ruins Christian life.

So that is why Christ insisted upon forgiveness without limit – for any sensible Christian, the cost of limiting forgiveness is absurdly too high.

Yet having said that, let me also warn against some common faults –

(1) Do not pretend that forgiveness is easy

It can be very glib for someone who is happy, say, in his or her marriage, serene, comfortable, prosperous, to lay a burden of pardon upon someone who is tortured by a sense of injustice suffered, of heartless cruelty, or of irretrievable loss. The wronged person may be struggling simply to come to terms with what has happened, to find a way to restructure life, to see some light in the darkness. Adding the further burden of demanding forgiveness may provoke final rebellion.

There are times when a deeply hurt person may be able to offer sincere, heartfelt pardon only after hard striving in prayer. Even arriving at a place of *willingness* to forgive may require a miracle of grace! Here is a time indeed when the strong should help the weak, not with harsh demands, but with sympathy, love, and gentle counsel (Ro 15:1). Yet still we cannot condone an implacable heart. No matter how hard it may be, we must all learn to forgive or we may find ourselves forfeiting the Father's pardon of our own wrongdoing –

> *If you forgive others for the harm they have done to you, then your Father in heaven will forgive you. But if you do not forgive others, then <u>your Father will not forgive your sin against him</u>.* (Mt 6:14-15)

(2) Be careful not to trivialise vile behaviour

Someone who has been badly hurt may feel that any demand for free and full forgiveness may seem horribly unjust, as if the offence were trivial and should be easily overlooked. But some offences cannot just be ignored. Hurt people may need time to rid themselves of anger or bitterness, they may need space in which to align their lives with God's purpose, they may need counsel to help them put everything back into a proper perspective, or to come back to the love and grace of Christ.

Offering pardon too easily may also seem to encourage wrongdoers to repeat their offences, since their faults cause them little or no loss. So balance is required. We neither want to show a disposition that is too ready to forgive, no matter what hurt has been done to us or others, nor to pressure offended people to offer pardon before they can truly do so. Our task always is to show our own readiness in Christ to pardon every wrongdoing, and then to guide others with all compassion and sensitivity toward the same place of Christian kindness.

(3) Be careful about shifting the blame

Sometimes the demand that a victim should forgive the person who inflicted pain turns into a subtle shifting of blame. The counsellor may end up making the suffering person a victim all over again, this time by being bullied into offering pardon. But without the enabling grace of Christ, people cannot truly forgive those who ravage their lives. Our task is not so much to impose a duty of pardon upon them as to bring them into such fellowship with Christ that holding unforgiveness becomes impossible. We should forgive every offence, not as a matter of duty, but because in the love of Christ we can do no less.

(4) *Make sure that pardon is the real issue*

I mean here that it is easy to confuse forgiveness with such attitudes as –

- *A patient resignation to the inevitable*. Truly, if something cannot be avoided then it must be endured, and even, if possible, enjoyed. But accepting what one cannot escape, while remaining angry or bitter about it, is scarcely following the example of Christ.
- *Learning to tolerate behaviour that should be intolerable*. There is a real distinction between forgiving someone and condoning his or her behaviour. Wrongdoing, if possible, should be rebuked and corrected, and may even need to be punished. Do not confuse an easygoing tolerance with genuine Christian forgiveness.
- *Excusing blameworthy conduct on the ground of some defect of character*. If there is a failing in the behaviour of a person, or if he or she has come under some unhappy influence, and the like, then these matters need to be addressed. They should not be overlooked, nor excused on a spurious understanding of what forgiveness means. Certainly, faults can be pardoned, but they should still be corrected.

How then can we help a victim to break out of the prison of resentment, without imposing upon him or her more burdens of fear, guilt, or shame?

The key is not to press people further than they are able to go. Rather, we should encourage a forgiving heart to arise out of a process of healing and restoration, teaching the victim first how to *receive* pardon from God, then how *offer* that same quality of forgiveness to others. The ideal is to bring people to a place where forgiveness no longer has to be demanded, but will be freely offered, whether with joy or with tears. Only an adamant refusal to allow the softening influence of the Spirit can finally close the door and lock a person into bitterness.

By the grace of Christ, and through the work of the Holy Spirit, forgiveness is possible *for* anyone *to* anyone for *any* offence. In doing so we simply show ourselves to be true followers of the Saviour who, while the spikes were being driven through his flesh, cried, *"Father, forgive them!"* (Lu 23:34)

What is the Nature of This Forgiveness?

True forgiveness demands a threefold renunciation –

Renounce the Right of Revenge

We have already seen that God reserves to himself the right of vengeance against those who have wronged you, and we are forbidden to usurp that divine right. But two quailfications need to be added to this –

(1) True forgiveness brings a loss of all desire to hurt the person who has hurt you. So let us not pretend to have forgiven an offender just because we are not actively seeking to extract some penalty from him. Many people suppose they have forgiven their enemies because they refrain from trying to hurt them, when in fact they are deterred from vengeance only by circumstances, cowardice, or the fear of God. The question is this – would you in fact take revenge if circumstances permitted it, or if you knew that you could escape

the eye of God? If you can honestly say "No!" then divine grace is indeed possessing your soul.

(2) If the offence involves some crime, you may be entitled (or even obliged) to initiate legal action against the offender. The same might apply if the offender has caused loss to others as well as to yourself. Some examples –

- You might forgive a thief from robbing you, and might not seek restitution from him, but if he is a habitual criminal you might need to report the matter to the police, and so protect other people from his depredations.
- Sometimes the law may require you to report certain forms of wrongdoing (for example, child abuse). But as a Christian you should do so without any personal malice.
- A drunk driver may damage your car, or even injure you bodily, and you should be ready to pardon him. But if you know that he is likely to drive again when he is drunk then you should probably take action to prevent him, but do so without vindictiveness.
- A woman whose husband has beaten her should forgive him, but may need to take out a court order to keep him away from her and from their children. She might also be entitled to separate from him completely, until he displays genuine reform in his behaviour. Nothing about the grace of forgiveness obliges anyone to accept foul or violent behaviour if it can be avoided.

In other words, Christian forgiveness does not require you to put yourself or others into the hands of cruel, irresponsible, or criminal people. If the only way to gain protection from such people is to take legal action, then that would be the proper thing to do, always making sure (as I have said) that your personal motives remain pure. All our actions must be motivated by the love of Christ, even if we must take steps to protect ourselves, or to save the offender from himself, or to protect other people.

Renounce the Right of Resentment

What is your reaction when you look at, or think about, the offender – is it love or loathing?

Resentment is a luxury you cannot afford; it is a crippling poison; it will dwarf your soul; it will stunt your spirit; it will bring disease to your flesh; it will eat at your very bones (see Ep 4:31,32; He 12:15, quoting De 29:18-20; and compare Pr 15:13,15; 17:22; 1 Co 11:29-31; etc.).

Renounce the Right of Estrangement

A true Christian cannot say, "I forgive you, but I never want to see you again!" If you have really forgiven, you will make every effort to restore sincere friendship. Reconciliation is an integral part of forgiveness. God was not content merely to pardon our sin; he also acted in Christ to reconcile us to himself, to make us his friends, although we had once been his enemies and the murderers of his Son (Ro 5:8-11).

But there are two qualifications to this –

(1) You cannot compel another person to befriend you. If a person is determined to remain your enemy, you must still forgive him but you cannot be reconciled with him. In such a case, you are absolved from blame (Ro 12:18; see also verses 14-17).

(2) There is a difference between forgiveness and trust. I owe forgiveness to everyone who asks, as often as they ask, and even if they don't ask; but no man can demand that I trust him.

Because of what Christ has done for me, pardon is a debt I owe every person; but trust is a privilege that must be earned. So, if a man steals from me, I will forgive the theft, but I am not obliged to put him in charge of my financial affairs!

Likewise, if a drunken husband beats his wife, she should forgive him; but she may rightly refuse to live in the same house with him until he proves that he will properly cherish her, or will pose no risk to their children.

Thus people cannot rightly demand that you trust them unless they have shown themselves trustworthy (see 1 Th 5:12-15; 2 Th 3:6,10-15; and compare 1 Ti 3:1-10, *"Let them be tested first, and only if they prove to be blameless should they be allowed to serve."*)

Christians often confuse forgiveness with trust, supposing that forgiveness is proved by offering to trust the offender. That is not so. Mark this again: we cannot deny *pardon* to any person; but *trust* must be earned.

Failure to understand that rule has foolishly allowed people to be exploited over and over again in the name of Christ. A common case is that of Christian wives who allow their husbands to abuse them maliciously, each time forgiving them, even though scripture specifically allows them to abandon the brute (cp. 1 Co 7:15-16).

An abused wife is certainly not *obliged* to leave her husband; but neither is there anything in the gospel that obliges her to remain in a violent and humiliating situation.

Jesus gave a similar principle to the disciples: if the means of escape were available to them, they were forbidden to stay wilfully in an antagonistic community (Lu 10:10-12). Sometimes we are more pious than Christ and demand of ourselves and others things that the Master does not require.

God's Right to Make This Demand

The quality of forgiveness demanded by Christ is quite extraordinary. Consider, for example, this passage –

> *If a fellow Christian sins, offer correction, and forgive the ones who say they are sorry. Even if someone mistreats you seven times in one day and says, "I am sorry," you must forgive that person every time* (Lu 17:3-4).

Consider this. A man deliberately knocks you down, then comes back a little later and with tears begs your pardon. You will (I hope) forgive him. Then, an hour or so later, he knocks you down again, and again pleads for pardon. You will, I suppose, be rather more tardy this time with your clemency. An hour later, he approaches you a third time. How will you react? Probably the least you will do is defend yourself, and may even seek to flatten him before he can swing his fist at you again. But if he does prevail, what then? Jesus said that you must forgive him, and an hour later for a fourth blow, and an hour later for a fifth, a sixth, and even a seventh blow! Though mistreated seven times in one day, each time followed by a plea for pardon, the battered believer, said Jesus, should grant unhesitating and cheerful forgiveness!

How can God make such a demand? Who is equal to it? Am I? Are you? Why should one even try to be so magnanimous?

Please read the parable told by Jesus in *Matthew 18:23-35*, which begins with the arresting phrase – *"This what the Kingdom of heaven is like."*

The story demonstrates how willing God is to forgive us, and therefore why we should forgive our neighbour. There was an official who owed his king ten thousand talents. That is equivalent to the wages of 150,000 soldiers for one year. It was an astronomical debt, but the king cancelled it. By contrast, a second man owed the official a mere one hundred denarii (equal to the wages of one labourer for about three months), and the official ruthlessly demanded payment on threat of imprisonment. The king, when he heard about it, was furious. He imposed a massive penalty upon the mean and unscrupulous official.

The first debt, absurdly vast, utterly beyond the official's ability to pay, represents our indebtedness to God – which he has fully and freely forgiven us for Christ's sake. Remember that scripture treats us as though each one of us were there with the hostile mob, screaming, *"Crucify him! Crucify him!"*

The second debt represents the worst that any other person can do to us. Think of any hurt that has ever been done to you, any loss you have suffered, any injustice or cruelty, any defamation or unkindness – it is 100 denarii. But the injury we have done God, each of us, is akin to 10,000 talents.

The point is, nothing that any person can do to me can be compared with the enormous injury I have done God. If, then, I am willing to *accept* pardon from God, I should be even more willing to *offer* pardon to my neighbour. Whenever my neighbour offends me, and I become resentful, or want to retaliate, the parable reminds me that at worst my neighbour's fault, when compared with my fault against God, is like comparing a handful of dollars to a debt that is beyond computation.

In the parable, the other servants were *"greatly distressed"* when they saw the injustice that was being done. Just so the Father looks with horror upon those whom he has forgiven yet who refuse to forgive their neighbour.

Jesus said that the implacable official was delivered up to be tortured until he had paid all his debt (which he could never do). Then Christ added the stark warning: *"So also my heavenly Father will do to every one of you, if you do not forgive your brother from your heart."*

Conclusion

Christian forgiveness is not a learned art; it is not merely a coping skill, nor a way of handling a difficult situation.

Forgiveness is not an act of patient resignation, nor of passive tolerance. Even less is it simply a reflection of a quiescent as distinct from an aggressive personality, a gentle temperament in contrast with one that is stern. It does not depend in any sense upon any sort of natural emotion or disposition. Rather, Christian forgiveness is a direct product of the grace of God, it is a miracle of divine love, it cannot be given without the enabling work of the Holy Spirit; it is active, inspired, divine.

Christian forgiveness is a re-enactment of the Passion; every time we truly forgive an offender in Christ's name, we follow in the Master's steps. When we forgive we walk with Jesus to Golgotha and to death to self. We pass with him through the grave and into a resurrection into a new dimension of life.

Each person who from his or her heart truly forgives someone who has done them harm gains a foretaste of heaven and has taken another step towards Paradise.

Thirteen:

Transformation

Nearly 300 years ago the first English translation of *Tales from the Arabian Nights* was published. Included in the collection was the charming *History of Aladdin*, which soon gained immense popularity. No one who has read the story can help wishing for their own magic lamp. And how astonished we are by the folly of the princess who heeded the wicked sorcerer's cry, "Who will change old lamps for new ones? . . . New lamps for old?" [26]

The idea of something new for something old is memorable because it is improbable! Yet that is what God offers us in Christ – give him your old self, and he will give you a new self! –

> "*Put off your old self . . . and put on the new self, created according to the likeness of God in true righteousness and holiness.*" (Ep 4:22-24).

Paul uses that metaphor of transformation to present an amazing picture of Christian life, which can be summarised in two main aspects –

- the **_character_** of Christ revealed in the believer's *life* (Ep 4:13); and
- the **_power_** of Christ displayed in the believer's *walk* (Zc 12:8).

---

(26) The original story was set in China, not Arabia, and dates back at least a thousand years.

The joining of those two things creates God's *"new person"* in Christ, in contrast with the *"old person"* of sin. But we must respond to God's action in Christ by our own action of *"putting off"* the old nature and *"putting on"* the new nature. How can we do this? Simply, by two observing two vital rules –

A Word of Faith.

Notice a surprising contrast –

- on the one hand Paul says that because of our union with Christ we have *already* put off the old and put on the new (Cl 3:9-10); but
- on the other hand, he says that we must *now* do so, as if it were not yet done! (Cl 3:12; and our text).

Underlying that seeming paradox is the biblical principle that what God has wrought in Christ we must *implement by faith*. This is the proper way to victory over all the iniquities Paul lists in the context of his command (see Cl 3:5-9; Ep 4:17-32; 5:3-5) – fornication, theft, violence, excessive anger, deceit, drunkenness, sloth, foul language, malice, blasphemy, bitterness – and indeed, every kind of sin. Yet there are many people who ignore God's prescription, and prefer instead the way of drenching tears and begging prayers. They hope that by abasing themselves before the Lord, and by passionate entreaty, they can persuade him to do something special for them; that somehow he will carry them to victory by an extraordinary act of power.

How foolish and ignorant that is!

Rather, we must open our eyes to see what God has wrought for us in Christ, then by boldly spoken faith, bring his triumph into reality in daily life. There is hardly anything more futile than begging the Lord to do what he has already done! [27] Rather, just *believe* it and *act* on it!

I remember once hearing the weeping confession of another pastor. He had been caught in repeated adultery, and he complained bitterly that despite pleading many times for God to help him overcome his sin, his prayers had remained unheard. The hidden inference? Since heaven had chosen to ignore his cries, the real person to blame for his repeated iniquity was not the pastor, but God!

My reaction was to name him a blasphemer.

What should the pastor have done? Instead of foully blaming God for his sin, he should have understood how the Father has already acted in Christ to provide a powerful way of overcoming sin and Satan. All we need to do is to appropriate god's gift by faith. But if we fail to grasp the Lord's method of victory, then we must grapple with sin alone, bereft of divine aid. It is no wonder that people in that condition keep on failing!

So resolve to speak, not what your natural eye sees (a fallen and sinful person), but what God says. And what does he say? Simply that you are a person who is dead to sin and alive only to righteousness in Christ. (Ro 6:11) So determine to see things as God sees them! Settle it in your mind that you are who he says you are, that you can do all he says you can do, that you will be all he says you can be – not because you have any strength in yourself, but because you fervently believe in all that God has wrought for you in Christ! Thus –

---

(27) Only think how irritated most people are when someone demands they do something they have already done! It annoys the Lord, too!

- ***if you are "dead in Christ"***, who can truly hurt you, cause you to sin, offend you, rob you? No one, unless you allow them to do so.
- ***if you are "alive in Christ"***, how can you fail to live in righteousness, showing all the gracious fruit of the Spirit? (Ga 5:22-25) You will fail only if you refuse to believe in and act upon the promise.

I do not mean that such a faith-reckoning will immediately solve every problem or give you instant victory over every sin. It takes time to put off old garments and put on a new set! But truly, the more firmly you declare yourself *"dead indeed to sin"* in Christ and *"alive to God"*, the more fully that promise will be actualised in your life each day!

That is what Paul means by *"putting off the old self"* and *"putting on the new self in Christ"*.

A Walk of Power

The leading characteristics of the *"new self"* are frequently linked with the Holy Spirit –

"Where the Spirit of the Lord is there is liberty, and by the Spirit we are changed into the image of Christ from glory to glory (2 Co 3:17-18) . . . We rejoice in afflictions and opposition, because the love of God has been poured into us by the Holy Spirit (Ro 5:3-5) . . . There is no condemnation for those who walk in the Spirit, for the law of the Spirit of life has made us free from the law of sin and death . . . So if you, through the Holy Spirit put to death the works of the flesh, you shall truly live . . . You have received adoption by the Holy Spirit, who enables us to cry, 'Abba! Father!' . . . The Spirit himself bears witness with our spirits that we are the children of God . . . The Holy Spirit helps us in our weakness, and through us intercedes for the saints (Ro 8:1-26) . . . We abound in hope through the power of the Holy Spirit,

and mighty signs and wonders are done (Ro 15:13,19) . . . *The fruit of the Spirit is love, joy, peace* (Ga 5:22) . . . *We are mightily strengthened within ourselves by the Holy Spirit, so that we are rooted and grounded in love and filled with all the fulness of God* (Ep 3:16-19) . . . *The word of God is the sword of the Spirit . . . so in the Spirit always keep on praying with all prayer and supplication* (Ep 6:17-18) . . . **You will be filled with power after the Holy Spirit has fallen upon you"** (Ac 1:8) – *plus many other references.*

To live in the fulness of Christ, then, requires an initial Holy Spirit baptism; plus daily walking in and yielding to the Spirit. Are you filled with the Spirit? Are you living in the fulness of divine power? Are you holding fast to your confession of faith in Christ – by faith putting off the old self and putting on the new? Then I can hardly believe other than you are a person living joyously in the victory and abundance of Christ!

And if you are not, don't blame God! Rather get filled with the Spirit, then set yourself to search out the promises of God and to saturate them with prayer until they come alive inside you – then believe with all your heart and be made whole!

Conclusion

What will you be if by faith and by the power of the Spirit you discard the old and replace it with the new? Perhaps not the richest or greatest person in the world, but you will be –

- gentle where once you were harsh
- forgiving where you were vengeful
- tolerant where you were critical
- gracious where you were offended
- peaceable where you were angry
- loving where you were hateful!

And where you were weak against sin and the works of Satan you will now be **prosperous** in holiness and **powerful** against the kingdom of darkness, set to win the overcomer's prize in heaven! (Re 2:7-3:21). Indeed, says the Lord, *"Those who win the victory will inherit all things, and I will be their God and they will be my children!"* (21:7)

Fourteen:

Meekness

As a prisoner of the Lord, I urge you to walk in a way that proves you have truly been called by God. Be humble and gentle, patiently bearing with each other in love, eager to maintain the unity of the Spirit in the bond of peace (Ep 4:1-3).

Paul there uses a colourful Greek word, *praotēs*, which has no real English equivalent, although it is often rendered as *gentle* or *meek*. [28] I have come across a claim in several books, no doubt correct, that Aristotle defined *praotēs* as the mean between the extremes of too much aggression and too much passivity. A "gentle" person is one who knows when to be angry and when to restrain wrath. He is humble and kind, but also knows how to be furious and exacting. But in every case he adheres always to the proper degree, always keeping within the appropriate bounds

A person who has *praotēs* is ruled neither by timidity nor arrogance. He is gracious but not insipid, restrained but not supine. He understands what action is right for each occasion, does not go beyond what the occasion demands, nor holds back when more is required. Neither too much nor too little, is his motto, as he chooses just what is right for every situation. Both his actions and his emotions are tempered, so that he *does* neither more nor less than each situation demands, nor *feels* either less or more than he should.

---

(28) Also *prautēs*; and adjectives *praos* and *praus*.

Meekness may be the nearest English equivalent to *praotēs*, so long as this is understood, not as *weakness*, but rather as controlled strength. Hence Jesus describes himself as *"meek" (praotēs;* Mt 11:29), yet he was able to make a multi-thong whip with his own hands and then, in blazing anger, drive money-changers out of God's temple (Jn 2:15). Meek he was, but he was certainly not weak!

"Gentle Jesus, meek and mild," goes the child's prayer; yet the seeker then depends upon a strong Christ to *"look upon a little child"* and bring that trusting child safely through the night and one day into heaven's home –

> Fain I would to Thee be brought,
> Dearest God, forbid it not;
> Give me, dearest God, a place
> In the kingdom of Thy grace. [29]

So this meekness is an inward quality, not shown by some outward aspect of servility, but by the depth of love we have for both neighbour and God. Nor is it dependent upon a naturally gracious character, but goes further than any innate human attribute. It is not just an inborn disposition toward humility nor even kindness. It is a Christian grace, resting entirely upon the work of the Holy Spirit, who continually strives to mould each believer into the likeness of Christ.

What must we do or become to make this divine meekness ours in daily life?

---

[29] Charles Wesley, *Hymns and Sacred Poems* (1742), stanzas one & two of "Gentle Jesus". There are a further six stanzas which are actually a separate hymn ("Lamb of God") that is now joined to this one.

Basic Sources

The first mention of meekness in the NT is found in Jesus' *Sermon on the Mount* – *"Blessed are the meek (praus), for they shall inherit the earth! (Mt 5:5)* [30]

Here is a great promise indeed! It surely encompasses every favour God has bestowed upon us in Christ, both in this world and the next. It includes answered prayer, victorious life, fruitful service, good health, prosperity, and many other bountiful blessings, climaxing in our ultimate inheritance in the eternal Kingdom of God. But the inescapable condition for the fulfilment of the promise is *meekness*, without which there is no hope of pleasing God.

Now here is just where many Christians are deprived of their rightful possessions –they try to practice a kind of meekness that is unscriptural, unpleasant, unspiritual, and unnatural, which must fail of the promise! Let us then attempt a true understanding of this important biblical concept – *praotēs*, meekness – beginning with a list of scriptures that show how vital this matter is–

In The Gospels

- see *Matthew 5:5; 11:29; 21:5*.

In The Letters

- to an erring and haughty charismatic church, Paul twice presented the meek character of the truly Spirit-filled Christian (1 Co 4:21; 2 Co 10:1).
- meekness is a major fruit of the Spirit (Ga 5:23), and in that spirit of meekness Christians should seek out, support, and restore each other in love (6:1).

---

(30) Jesus was quoting *Psalm 37:9-11*.

- only through meekness can the church maintain the unity of the Spirit (Ep 4:2), and every true Christian will endeavour to clothe himself or herself with that meekness (Cl 3:12).
- in place of greed and violence the true person in Christ will find all real wealth and invincible strength in meekness (1 Ti 6:11); nor will such people forsake meekness when seeking to correct those who oppose them (2 Ti 2:24).
- all Christians should show meekness toward all their neighbours (Tit 3:2), and with meekness they should continue to receive an implanting of the word of God (Ja 1:21); thus they show themselves to be truly wise and full of understanding (3:13).
- meekness clothes Christian women with pure beauty, and ornaments them with loveliness (1 Pe 3:4).
- meekness infuses the preaching of the church with winsome appeal for those who are not yet saved. (vs. 15).

We are left in no doubt about the importance of *praotēs* to the apostles! It is a major concept in gospel teaching and Christian living. That is because this meekness is –

A Uniquely Christian Virtue

Not Admired

Meekness has never been admired by secular man. The secular world cries that *"Might is right,"* and reaps a bloody harvest. But the Church says that *"Meekness is mighty!"* and steadily moves toward inheriting the earth! Yet still the world stubbornly clings to the kind of arrogant self-sufficiency Nietzsche taught. He dreamed of *"Man as Superman"*, which inspired Hitler to create his race of so-called *Aryan Supermen*, with all its attendant horrors.

Yet even if they wished to be meek, they could not. For until the world knows Christ it will never know meekness, which only he can teach them (Mt 11:29). So the world is condemned to trust in the delusion of its own might, which is so easily fractured, while God's mighty meek, resilient, tough, invincible, will go on to be kings with Christ for ever!

Paul was able to speak of the *"meekness and moderation"* of Christ (2 Co 10:1), thus setting before us two of the cardinal virtues, and showing us the true character each Christian should display to the world. They are virtues, however, that can be born in the human heart only as –

A Result of Knowing God

Knowledge of Self is Insufficient

A proper sense of human frailty should keep all of us humble, but strangely fails to do so. Small and great alike delude themselves into thinking they are strong. Yet even the most despotic tyrant is prisoner to the need for sleep, and is as vulnerable and helpless in his sleep as the meanest peasant; the mightiest of men can be bruised and broken as easily as the weakest; and a tiny virus can lay low the haughtiest of emperors. Yet despite this manifest fragility, human instinct, because of the Fall, remains opposed to meekness. Instead of our vulnerability making us humble toward ourselves and others, we are more prone to disguise that frangibility beneath a facade of self-aggrandisement. Hence irrational hubris, not meekness, is the common characteristic of fallen man.

Since knowledge of ourselves is ineffectual, meekness must then come from knowledge of God. At once we discover two things –

- God called us into being out of nothing, and only his grace keeps us from falling back into non-being (He 11:3; 1:3).

- Meekness should be sustained and increased in us by the knowledge that we are sinners saved by grace.

That is we are both created and re-created by God through Christ, hence we are doubly dependent for our continuance upon him and the upholding power of his Word. This discovery begins the infusion of divine meekness into human character.

The Meekness of Jesus

How can Jesus be said to be meek? Through the incarnation

- he adopted a subordinate form.
- he accepted a sinful identity.
- he submitted to a shameful death.

Thus he humbled himself, abandoning all use of the attributes of his deity, and taking upon himself both the form and fashion of a man, vulnerable to hunger, weariness, wounds, and death (Ph 2:6-8).

"Ah!" cries the despising world, "see how weak he was in all his meekness!" But they fail to see what strength he also displayed – withstanding every temptation, overcoming every trial, fully completing his earthly mission, preventing anyone from hurting or killing him until his time had come, raising himself from the dead (Jn 10:17-18), and then displaying his utter triumph over all his foes in his ascension back to heaven! From that gentle yet tough example of the meek Christ we learn –

The Nature of Christian Meekness

Sir Christopher Wren took 35 years to build the sublimely majestic St Paul's Cathedral in London. When it was completed he invited Queen Anne to inspect the building. She gave her judgment: *"It find it awful, amusing, and artificial!* What do you suppose was Sir Christopher's reaction? Actually, far from dismay or fury, he was delighted!

For in the early 18th century, *awful* meant *awesome*, *amusing* meant *amazing*, and *artificial* meant full of *skill* and *artistry*. Thus words have so much changed in meaning over three centuries! (31)

Something similar is true of the word *meekness*. It once had a positive feel, conveying a sense of courtesy, of someone who was kind and ready to forgive an injury. Now it has a more derogatory sense of weakness, of someone who is too easily imposed upon, who has no courage to resist oppression, nor any zeal to fight for what is right. So, before a Christian can practise true meekness, he or she needs to know just what the biblical concept really means.

But let us do that by first learning what –

Meekness Does Not Mean -

Weakness

There is no support in scripture for the idea that we are meek only because we cannot help ourselves. On the contrary, for Christ meekness was an expression of strength; he had no need to assert himself, because he was inviolable, having access to the limitless resources of heaven. Only the insecure, the uncertain, the carnally vulnerable, have to protect themselves from peril by erecting a barrier of arrogance.

Those who know that they are ultimately invincible in Christ have no need of insolent pomp or pride, but can easily afford to conduct themselves graciously and kindly. Thus the meek are never impotent. Even if they must yield before violence, and appear helpless in the hands of the strong, they still retain spiritual mastery. There is always some action of faith

---

(31) This is a thought that Bible students need to keep in mind. The Bible spans at least 20 centuries, and the meaning that a word has at the beginning of the story is not always the same as the one it has at the end!

they can take, whether physical or spiritual. Despite appearances, was Jesus ever truly helpless in the hands of the Romans and the Jews? No! Then neither are we!

At the very least, the meek can seize *Romans 8:28*, so that the ultimate outcome of each event is determined, not by the will of their persecutors, but by their own faith. At other times, God will allow faith to perform mighty exploits and to make the meek outwardly invincible, quenching fire, taming wild animals, turning foes aside, breaking open prison doors, doing the impossible (cp. He 11:32-38).

Timidity

The modern idea that the meek are timid, flaccid, spineless, without opinion or will, tamely submitting to whatever life imposes upon them, has no place in scripture. On the contrary, Christian meekness, while it may be gracious and humble, and mostly gentle and kind, is still dynamic with courage and purpose. The saying of Jesus (quoting the psalmist) that the meek will inherit the earth pre-supposes that they are vigorous, and capable of marvellous things. After all, if the meek are always docile, supine, timorous, how could they ever hope to "inherit the earth", or do anything useful with it if they did inherit it?

Servility

Abject submissiveness, enervating softness, may characterise worldly notions of meekness, but they are not the Christian virtue. Here is a better description – *"The meek, the terrible meek, the fierce agonising meek, are about to enter into their inheritance"* (Charles Kennedy).

Jesus is the perfect exemplar of Christian meekness. Was he ever abject before any man, no matter how exalted his rank? Hardly! Did he ever allow anyone, even the highest in the land, to exact slavish docility from him? Never! Courteous, yes. Merciful, yes. Kindly, yes. But cringing abasement, fawning docility? Never! The meekness of Christ consisted of an unquenchable love for all people, even his tormenters, and a life devoted with irresistible strength to fulfilling the Father's will.

Temperament

Christian meekness is not primarily a thing of outward behaviour, for this might reflect only a *naturally* gentle and self-effacing temperament. Rather, it is an inwrought grace of God in the soul, displayed, *first*, in a disposition of loving obedience toward God; *second*, in a disposition of humble recognition toward ourselves; and *third*, in a disposition of amiable goodwill toward our neighbour.

This Christian grace may dwell equally well in those of shy character as of bold, in women as well as men, in the young as well as the old, in the physically strong as well as the weak, in the learned as well as the unlearned – that is, in every Spirit-filled believer. This meekness does not turn an extrovert into an introvert, nor the reverse. A shy Christian may remain naturally reticent, yet be able to act with great boldness when required; and the bold may find grace in Christ to draw back into the shadows. The naturally aggressive person will find it easy, when necessary, to behave gently, and the gentle to behave sternly.

So we discover that there is a supernatural quality in godly meekness that enables it, no matter the natural temperament or preferences of the meek person, to behave in whatever manner is most appropriate to the occasion. By contrast, people whose meekness is wholly natural are locked into one kind of gentle, unassuming, and patient pattern of behaviour, prevented by their disposition from acting out of character.

Meekness *Does* Mean

Submission to God

The philosophers of the ancient world, akin to those of today, greatly praised self-confidence and self-assertion. But true wisdom recognises this: *"Many are in high places, and possess great renown; but mysteries are revealed to the meek ... The Lord overthrows the thrones of princes and establishes the meek in their place"* (Sir 3:19; 10:14).

How extraordinary to realise that more than 2000 years ago the ancient rabbi had learned such wisdom, which the world has yet to learn! In the purpose of God the meek, sooner or later, do indeed rule the earth! Princes and potentates give way before them! Empires fall and the meek rise up out of the ashes. Crowns are removed from the arrogant and placed instead upon the heads of the meek! Which drives us again to ask – just what *does* this "meekness" mean? How can we take a sure stand among the meek whom the Lord God honours?

The ancient Greeks used the word that we are exploring (*praotēs/praos/praus*) to describe a wild animal that had been tamed, or a horse that was broken in and had become responsive to bridle and bit. The animals were now "meek" but hardly "weak"! Or, in everyday life, the Greeks saw agriculture, as opposed to war, as a *"meek"* pursuit – it was vigour and strength devoted to creation, not destruction, to fruitfulness not ruin. Hence, the apostles understood meekness as the strength of God in the believer under the control of the will of God, enabling us to fulfil the fruitful purpose of God. They saw it as a temper of spirit that yields to the hand of God, co-operates with his laws, accepts his providence as good, and surrenders to his purpose without argument or rebellion. Like a tamed elephant, it is strength under control, power under restraint. Yet it is more than mere *self-control*, for that might be only a natural attribute, and it might lead to failure to act when swift response is called for. Rather, it is *God-control*, based upon divinely imparted grace, grasped by faith in surrender to the Father's will.

Such an attitude of humble submission to the will of God results in new qualities of Christian character. In particular, the divinely meek person will have a disposition of gentleness and forbearance toward everyone, even those who are harsh and provocative. Indeed, the things people do to us, and the events of life, must be seen as the agents of God. The things we suffer must be accepted as just, even if unjust men are using unjust means to afflict us (cp. 2 Sa 16:5-12).

Divinely meek people will also know when and how to be either withdrawn or assertive, to act boldly or to remain passive, to press forward or to hold back, to accept the events of each day or to overthrow them in the name of Christ. Such people are always strong, both in action and inaction, because their meekness is supernaturally imparted and empowered.

Honesty With Yourself

There is no place in Christian meekness for false self-deprecation or wrongful self-effacement. The truly meek are able to accept both prominence or obscurity, power or weakness, wealth or poverty – whatever the purpose of God entails. They are aware of their true worth, of their actual gifts and abilities, of their strengths and their weaknesses.

The truly meek have no illusions about themselves. They know who they really are and are not. They are not reluctant to seize the limelight, but neither do they resist stepping back into the shadows. They gladly yield the floor to a more qualified person, but will also be willing to take preference over a less qualified one. If they think it is right in God to have prominence, they will claim it. If it is better that they should yield to another, they will do so gladly. Neither high office nor low is important to them, but only doing the will of God.

The truly meek follow the rule of Paul in *Romans 12:3* – that is, knowing their true worth, they reach for that position in society and in the church that best accords with that worth. They do not aspire to a rôle that is too high, nor are they content with one that is too low – except that they are always willing to yield to the sovereign providence and purpose of God.

Being truly aware, of their special gifts and abilities they are able both to seize leadership or to relinquish it; they know when to exercise authority and when to submit to authority; they are able both to grasp everything and to cast it all aside. Nothing is finally important to them except what the Lord decrees.

Hunger then, neither to be known nor to be unknown, to have all or to have nothing, to be at the top or at the bottom, but simply to be obedient to the will of God.

Service for Others

A grovelling self-abasement, a masochistic enjoyment of humiliation, an inability to stand up for either yourself or for others, a cringing subservience – all these often masquerade as meekness. Rather, beginning from a position of strength in Christ, we are to have a servant's heart, as Jesus did (Ph 2:1-11). If you meet someone who is truly meek in Christ you will find a person who is tough yet pliable, resolute in serving God, forceful in pursuing his or her goals, yet willing to surrender all rights in love, tolerant of the most foolish, patient with the most troublesome, having a true servant's heart, yet a warrior, sure of winning the battle in Christ.[32]

Forgiving

Meekness is never resentful, refuses to hold a grudge, does not seek revenge nor hunger for retribution. This is the spirit of one who is not easily provoked, but keeps in chains the natural urge to retaliate. This meek person knows there is a time to give vent to anger (Jn 2:13-17; Mt 23:13-33), and a time to control it. And even when furious anger is a proper response, the meek person still knows how to maintain emotional discipline and to fetter anger so that it becomes a tool of righteousness. As Paul said, you may indeed be angry when the occasion calls for it, but make sure that in your anger you do not sin and give a foothold to the devil (Ep 4:26-27).

Bold in Action

Meekness does not mean an incapacity for action; rather, the meek should be *mighty in the works of God* (cp. Nu 12:3; Jn 21:25). It is sometimes thought that the task of the meek is to keep the peace. But we are not bound to be peacemakers at any price, for there are times when we *must* act strongly, to defend the weak, to uphold the church, to advance the kingdom of God. Yet such actions gain special strength when they are done by someone who is normally gracious and gentle, who usually endures personal affront with calm restraint. An echo of this idea lies in the arresting phrase, *"the wrath of the Lamb"* (Re 6:16). What a paradox! Here is the gentle Lamb, who in his own body bore away the sins of the world. But tremble before him all ye nations! Do not

---

(32) Are you wondering if I had someone in mind when I wrote that sentence? Yes, I did. The meekest person I know – my wife, Alison!

arouse his fury! A Lamb he may be, but his wrath will be terrible past telling!

The thought of trembling before a lamb or fearing what wounds it may inflict, seems absurd. I have several times stood among a throng of hundreds of surging sheep, and the only peril I faced was the unlikely possibility of being knocked down and trampled. Even less would any harm be likely if the flock had been all small *lambs*. One does not stand afraid of a lamb, or even of a multitude of them. But this Lamb is of another sort! For he is also the Lion of Judah, and his avenging roar will one day resound across the heavens. So the ideas of "wrath" and "lamb" are curiously incongruous, but they beautifully reveal the nature of godly meekness. The ordinary character of Christ can be displayed under the figure of a lamb – gentle and lovely. But that same Lamb will know when the time has come to rise up in leonine majesty and to inflict the judgment of the Almighty upon the trembling earth.

Likewise, when it becomes clear that tolerance and patience are merely confirming a wrongdoer in his evil, and that he is not disposed to change his ways, then Christian love may demand that action be taken, to uphold the law, to preserve society, and to prevent the wrongdoer from increasing his guilt. As lambs of the Lamb of God, there are times when we too must display the wrath of the Lamb!

The Rewards of Meekness

"You shall possess the land, and delight yourself in abundant prosperity" (Ps 37:11; Mt 5:5).

Historically, that promise has always been fulfilled; for all tyrants eventually fall, and new and gentler regimes begin. The gunslinger may prevail for a time, but in the end the West is won, not by bullets, but by grocers, clerks, school teachers, pastors, farmers and shepherds. It is simply true – the meek always do inherit the earth!

Individually, we too we may anticipate a personal fulfilment of that promise in our daily lives, homes, and businesses. That is, we may normally expect to overcome the Evil One and all his minions and to receive good things from the bountiful hand of the Lord. But if life's changing tides deprive us of our inheritance, what then? The Hebrew word for prosperity is *shalom*. It means that whatever happens, nothing can rob you of the inner peace, happiness, wellbeing, health, salvation, satisfaction, that are abundantly yours in Christ. That is, if not the "land" itself, then still all that you might hope to get from material possessions, even if you are denied those actual goods. The "proud" may grasp the "land", but that is all they will ever have, and even that will finally be taken away from them.

Thus there are two aspects to the promise of inheriting the earth –

- There are the physical, material, and temporal blessings that may not always be fulfilled for us individually in this life; and
- There are the spiritual and eternal blessings, which belong unfailingly to all the meek, both now and forever.

Eventually, when the Lord has made the world truly worth having, then he will give it to those who most deserve it – ***"The meek shall inherit the earth!"***

Section Five:

Throne Rights

Fifteen:

Enthroned in the Heavenlies

"God has made you alive with Christ, and raised you up together with him, and <u>enthroned</u> you with him in the heavenlies" (Ep 2:6).

Paul uses the graphic idea of "enthronement" to display each believer's spiritual authority.

All Christians need to understand this authority, for the lack of it is a source of much frustration and failure. But note – I am talking here about true *spiritual* authority, not the kind of carnal religious tyranny condemned in *1 Peter 5:3*; nor about the secular power structures that are often substituted in our churches for true authority. The one can be and usually is easily overthrown; the other is invincible. Pastors who depend upon a power structure usually feel threatened, but pastors who are secure in spiritual authority, know there is never anything to fear. Power structures have to be constantly asserted, strengthened, reinforced; they are always subject to undermining. Spiritual authority is serene, secure, irresistible, assured of obedience, confident always of divine backing. I have seen several pastors fall because they depended upon some kind of secular power structure; I have yet to see any pastor truly fail who understood and depended upon spiritual authority. [33]

A local church will instinctively yield leadership to a man or woman who holds a God-given spiritual right to exercise it. But people acting only in the authority of a worldly power structure will have to impose command and will always be looking over their shoulders, wondering if a coup is being planned.

How then shall we define genuine spiritual authority? Paul says that it is the outcome of our enthronement with Christ in the heavenlies, which conveys to us –

A Royal Privilege

To say that we are *enthroned* is a vivid way of declaring that we have access, this very hour, to all that belongs to the throne of God. In Christ, we are as though we were already there, sitting at the Father's right hand, far above all other powers and authorities. And mark this – no future event can give us any more right to that lofty position than we *now* possess. The coming resurrection will only make the throne more visible, it cannot make it more real nor give us stronger possession.

Understand this – *every* Christian already has full legal right in Christ to that throne and to all that it represents.

But someone says, "Hold on! No one can convince me that I'm sitting on a royal throne, possessing kingly authority.

---

(33) Power structures that follow a secular model may be (but not always) revealed by a large salary difference between the senior pastor and those working under him, a demand for isolation from other staff members, a luxury office much larger than any others in the building, and similar distinctions. They emulate the organisational hierarchies, rewards, and perks of office that can be seen everywhere in the secular world. They are far removed from the pattern set by Jesus and the apostles.

Look at me! No crown, no robe, no sceptre, no palace – just an ordinary person with too many problems and not enough resources to cope with them."

But think about Queen Elizabeth II of Great Britain. She has often been far away from home, and has frequently walked the streets in foreign countries, greeting people while dressed in ordinary street-wear, looking just the same as the thousands of women lining the pavements. If she were to mingle with them, then someone who had never before seen her would not pick her as a queen. Yet she remains a monarch, as much when she is far away from London in some foreign city as when she is on the throne in her royal palace. She is just as rich, whether at home or abroad. Whatever authority she rightfully possesses remains hers, whether she is in the UK or fulfilling her duties in a distant nation.

Or consider a warrior monarch, like Marcus Aurelius, the 2nd century Roman ruler and philosopher. He spent only a handful of his 19 years as emperor actually in Rome. For the remainder, he was at war on the frontiers of the empire, defending it from invaders, living in harsh conditions in military camps, suffering illness and wounds, and enduring all the rigours of incessant campaigns. Yet, despite personally leading his army, despite being far distant from the pomp and splendour of his imperial palace, despite wearing battered armour instead of silk robes, and a helmet instead of a coronet, he remained firmly in control of his imperium, and his royal authority was never diminished. Today he is still renowned as one of the greatest of the Roman rulers and his greatest book, *The Meditations*, has never been out of circulation.

We should view ourselves in the same way. Our palace may be in heaven, our true glory hidden, and we are far removed from our throne, but kings we remain. We may be deeply involved in spiritual warfare, and obliged to live and fight on the frontier, but our sovereignty is fixed, and we are called to *"reign in life"* (Ro 5:17) through Christ.

Another analogy is to say that we are like *ambassadors*, having behind us the resources of the most powerful of all kingdoms (2 Co 5:20). Whatever we speak in God's name, expressing his will, in harmony with the laws of his kingdom, and with a firmness that brooks no denial, must be done!

How should the ambassadors of a powerful country behave? No better illustration can be found than in the conduct in 168 BC of Gaius Popilius Laenas, an ageing and irascible former consul of Rome. He is famous for drawing history's first "circle in the sand", which he did around the Syrian despot Antiochus IV Epiphanes. [34] Antiochus was determined to increase the size and power of his empire, by adding Egypt to his dominions. Only Alexandria, at the mouth of the Nile, had withstood the Syrian onslaught, so Antiochus set up a siege, surrounding the city with his army on land, and a large navy offshore. In despair, Pharaoh Ptolemy appealed to Rome for help, knowing that the Romans would never tolerate so much wealth and splendour being added to the Syrian throne. Ptolemy fully expected that Rome would send an army to rescue him. The senate debated the matter, but declined to mobilise their legions. Instead, they called Popilius out of retirement, and designated him a temporary envoy. He was given three ships, a small legation, a handful of soldiers, and told to set sail at once. His commission? To find Antiochus and order him to pack up his army and navy and go home! Daniel, in a remarkable prophecy (11:30), describes the event –

---

(34) Antiochus was so impressed by his own achievements that he began to reckon himself superhuman, and to have divine origins. So he awarded himself the title Epiphanes, by which he is still known. The Greek word means "God Manifest".

> *The Romans will come in ships from Cyprus and oppose him (Antiochus). In fear and anger he will march back to Israel and try to destroy the religion of God's people.* (35)

Daniel called the ships that carried the Roman legation to Egypt *"ships of Cyprus"* because they sailed from Rome to Cyprus, and then from Cyprus to Alexandria, where Popilius and his companions disembarked outside the walls of the city. Being, a little creaky from old age, and with a temper more cranky than usual, Popilius broke off a branch to help him walk across the sand toward Antiochus. Several ancient Roman historians tell the story, but here is the account given by Livy –

> (Popilius) set sail for Egypt to carry out the mission with which he was charged. He was anxious to meet Antiochus, if possible, before he approached the walls of Alexandria. ...
>
> Antiochus was now master of the rest of Egypt, (and was getting ready to attack Alexandria, but) about four miles from the city he was met by the Roman commissioners, to whom he gave a friendly greeting and held out his hand to Popilius. Popilius, however, placed in his hand the tablets on which was written the decree of the senate and told him first of all to read that. After reading it through he said he would call his friends into council and consider what he ought to do. Popilius, stern and imperious as ever, drew a circle round the king with the stick he was carrying and said, "Before you step out of that circle give me a reply to lay before the senate." For a few moments he hesitated, astounded at such a peremptory order, and at last replied, "I will do what the

---

(35) Paraphrased.

senate thinks right." Not till then did Popilius extend his hand to the king as to a friend and ally. Antiochus evacuated Egypt at the appointed date, and the commissioners . . . then sailed to Cyprus and sent home the fleet of Antiochus which had defeated the Egyptian ships in a naval engagement. The work of the commissioners won great renown amongst the nations, for it was undoubtedly owing to this that Egypt had been rescued out of the hands of Antiochus and the crown restored to the Ptolemaic dynasty. [36]

How stunning! On one side, the glittering emperor with his immense army and a powerful fleet spread along the coast; on the other, an elderly arthritic ambassador with a handful of attendants and three ships. The contest seems absurdly unequal. Yet the legate draws his circle and the man who thought he was a god gives way, pulls out of Egypt, marches home, and – just as Daniel had foreseen – on the way wreaks havoc on the Holy Land. Why did Antiochus leave? First, because Popilius was backed by the irresistible might of Rome, which Antiochus knew would destroy him if he ignored the senate's decree. But second, and just as important, because Popilius *himself* knew his right and his authority. With magnificent arrogance he ignored the king's outstretched hand, thrust his tablets upon the outraged Syrian, and forbade the king to take so much as one step before he had agreed to obey fully every line of the senate's demands. Antiochus knew that he had no choice. He did as he was told.

But if Popilius had been timorous and hesitant, if he been supinely apologetic, if he had trembled in craven fear of a Syrian sword, if he had approached his task with

---

[36] Livy (B.C 59-A.D 17), *The History of Rome* 45:10-11. Tr, by Rev Canon Roberts, 1905.

pusillanimous uncertainty, or had doubted the senate's support, do you suppose that Antiochus would have yielded so readily? Hardly! He would have measured Rome's strength by the weakness of its ambassador, cast the tablets aside, and sent Popilius home in shame. He would then have resumed his siege of Alexandria, and completed his conquest of Egypt. And who can say how much that would have altered history!

One ambassador, speaking with bold authority, changed the course of world events for centuries to come!

Likewise, we too are called to understand our throne rights, and to use our spiritual authority against our enemy and all his works. Those who do so will not fail to complete the will of God for their lives, treading down serpents and scorpions and all the power of the enemy, crushing Satan underfoot, fulfilling the purpose of their King, and bringing honour to his name (Lu 10:Je 1:9-10,18-19; Ro 16:20).

A Righteous Provision

A Common Complaint

Someone may protest: "What you are saying cannot be true of me. I am too sinful, weak, and doubting"

Perhaps what you really need is to get a clearer picture of who you are in Christ!

But still someone says: "A pretty doctrine; but how can I make it happen in my daily life?"

God brings our throne position into being in the same way he does everything – he simply **declares it to be true**.

The Example of Jesus

The power of the spoken word of God is revealed by the state of sin that was pronounced upon Jesus (2 Co 5:21). Though he was without sin, he was made sin for us, and this by nothing more than the decree of God.

If God can justly reckon his sinless Son to be a sinner, then he can also justly reckon this sinner to be a sinless son!

In neither case does the change depend upon human action, but only upon the divine decree. (37)

Jesus did no sin, yet he was proclaimed a sinner; neither do you have to do any righteousness before God can pronounce you righteous!

And see how powerful God's reckoning is! It is no mere abstract proposition. It is irresistible! Less than 24 hours after the word of sin was spoken (in Gethsemane, Mt 26:39-44), Christ was dead upon the cross. The penalty of sin was inescapably imposed upon him, which otherwise would have been impossible, since he was actually not guilty of any sin. Death is the penalty of sin; a sinless man cannot die (Ro 6:23). How then did this sinless man die? Because he was *made sin* by God's decree!.

Surely it is more difficult to call an innocent man guilty than to call a guilty man innocent? So if the decree of God can bring guilt and death upon Jesus, it can more easily bring innocence and life upon you and me.

But you might still protest: "How is it, then, that I am not living victoriously? If the reckoning of God actually took

---

(37) I do not mean that God may make any decree he pleases, contrary to his own law, but that whatever he can decree within a framework of justice and of truth, he may speak. In the case we are considering, the just decrees are built, first, upon the willingness of Christ to die for us, which enabled the Father to load him with our sin; and second, upon the work Christ accomplished on the Cross, which enables the Father to pronounce us innocent and righteous..

Jesus to the cross, why has that same reckoning not brought me just as surely to the throne?"

The example of Jesus again provides the answer – Jesus had to *hear*, *believe*, and *embrace* the Father's reckoning, otherwise it would have remained ineffective. This was the real cause of his struggle and anguish in Gethsemane – not cringing fear of physical suffering, [38] but revulsion against embracing a sinful identity. His holy flesh shrunk back from being declared <u>unholy</u>, just as our unholy flesh cringes away from being declared <u>holy</u>.

Hence, just as Jesus had to break through his awareness of righteousness, by prayer, before he could accept the Father's sentence of unrighteousness, so we have to break through our awareness of unrighteousness before we can accept the Father's sentence of righteousness.

This is important. Without Christ's willing acceptance of the Father's decree it would have remained ineffective – indeed, it could not have been justly made. God is no tyrant. In the Garden, God offered Jesus the cup of unrighteousness, and he could have declined it. Had he done so, he could not have been given a sinful identity, Calvary would have been avoided, and we would all have perished without hope. Instead, he cried, *"Your will be done!"* thus opening the way for the Father to declare him *sin* and to make his death inevitable.

---

(38) It is foolish to suppose that Christ's agony in the Garden was caused by fear of crucifixion. Countless martyrs bravely, even cheerfully, faced much worse and more prolonged torture than Jesus had to suffer. His pain went far deeper than any whip or spike could inflict upon him. Furthermore, long before his Gethsemane anguish, Jesus had been aware of his approaching death, and of its manner, and showed that he had no fear of it (Jn 3:14; 8:28; 12:32).

In the same way, if you and I are willing to yield to the Father's will and embrace the Father's decree, then, just as Christ's acceptance of the divine word led him irresistibly to the cross, so our acceptance of the divine decree will place us in actual possession of the privileges of the throne.

This, then, is God's righteous provision – Christ, who had done no sin, was declared guilty, and suffered, and died, so that we who had done only sin might be declared innocent, and saved, and might live. But remember that the decree of God remains ineffective for each of us personally until we vigorously believe and act upon it. So then, abandon at once all attempts to "work" your way up to the throne. Rather, take your stand there now, by faith, and boldly seize all that is rightly yours as God's gift to you in Christ.

A Rigorous Penalty

Any person who claims authority over another will have that authority tested: at home by children; at work by employees; in the church by members; in life by Satan; and so on. In the end, no one has any more authority than he or she has the courage, the strength, the will, the confidence to exert in each new circumstance.

So too, each Christian has only as much spiritual authority as he or she can hold under pressure, without panic, and without resorting to carnal strength. Your authority *will* be tested. Resolve now to know that authority, and stand firm in it, exercising all the throne rights that belong to you in Christ.

And never forget that a bitter penalty is exacted from those who, having authority, fail to understand it or use it.

A young trainee female school teacher was once put in charge of a class of nearly fifty 12-year old boys and girls. As children do, they at once tried to find out how much they could get away with before the teacher was provoked to action. They soon discovered that she had no idea how to control them, and the class descended into rowdy chaos. The young teacher, humiliated and helpless, took herself off to a corner and stood there, facing the wall, her head bowed into her arms, sobbing bitterly.

An older male teacher walked past the room, heard the racket, and for a few moments watched the mêlée through a window. Then he stormed into the room, hauled several of the worst offenders to the front of the class, both boys and girls, seized a cane, and, as they say in the classics, applied some vigorous knowledge to the seats of learning (this was in the days when corporal punishment was still permitted). He sent those children sobbing back to their seats, then angrily lectured the entire class, warning them that he would look through the window from time to time each day, and woe! woe! to any boy or girl who was in the least inattentive or rude to the young lady teacher.

For the remainder of the two weeks that she looked after the class, they were the best behaved children in the school!

But, you say, of course they were – after all, she was but a young untried girl, while he was a big experienced man. But it was more than that. There were 50 of those children, some of them well-developed. If they had decided to fall on the man and beat him savagely, they would fairly quickly have prevailed over him and done him serious injury. No, his triumph was more a matter of authority than brute strength. He knew his authority, and was not afraid to exercise it. The children, too, recognised the voice of authority, and at once submitted to it.

In reality, the girl had the same authority, and immense resources were ready to back her in the use of it. If she had found herself unable to control the children, she could have called upon other teachers to support her; if they had failed, there were all the resources of the state education department; if they had failed, the police, the army, the navy, the air force could have been called in – sooner or later, those children would have been obliged to yield!

But instead of using her authority she succumbed to despair and the children became her masters.

There is no escaping this rule – if you have been given an authority that has adequate resources behind it, and fail to use that authority, then you will face a rigorous penalty. That rule is as true in spiritual life as it is in the secular world.

Conclusion

Success in the service of God is dependent upon knowing who you are in Christ, what authority God has given you, and then acting accordingly. Notice how Paul uses the past tense when he describes the great work of grace wrought for us by Christ. He says that all these things were done for us by Christ while we were still *"dead in sin"* (Ep 2:5), and that we have now only to believe the promise of God and act upon it. And if God did all these things for us in Christ while were still *"his enemies"*, how much more will God do for us now that we are his friends!

Yet there are three cautions –

- *Suppose you abdicate the throne?* – Then you will be on your own, and whatever royal authority you might have had in Christ will be rendered ineffectual.
- *Suppose an enemy contests your claim?* – Then you must assert your legal rights as a person in union with Christ by faith, for whom the throne is a birth right of which you refuse to be denied.
- *Suppose you abuse your privileges?* – Eventually, any monarch who misuses his or her office will be dethroned – as in 1688, William of Orange invaded

England and, with the consent of Parliament, forced the abdication of James II [39] Likewise, spiritual authority is given to us only to implement the will of the Great King we represent, not to fulfil our own whims and ambitions.

So then, let us bravely grasp our God-given freedoms, align ourselves with God's opinion of us in Christ, accept our identity as royal priests (1 Pe 2:9), already enthroned with Christ in the heavenlies, and go on to serve God in true liberty and holiness.

---

(39) James opposed Protestant and Parliamentary supremacy in Great Britain. He tried to re-assert Catholicism and the divine right of the king to wield absolute power.

Sixteen:

Bravely Into The Holiest!

Everything God did in Christ was in agreement with his eternal purpose, which he has achieved through Christ Jesus our Lord, so that, because of our union with Christ and through our faith in him, we may now go boldly and with all confidence into the very presence of God! (Ep 3:11-12)

You will never read anything more amazing than those few lines! Why so? Because there Paul declares emphatically that the way into the holy of holies is wide open, and that anyone, any time, and in any condition, may simply walk in and converse with the Almighty! The only condition is that one must first embrace Christ as Lord and Saviour. But nothing else is required, except boldness and confidence!

Nothing like this had ever been written or even imagined in all previous human history. For ages it had been unthinkable that any mere mortal could boldly walk up to the throne of any god, let alone the Lord God, without ceremony, without sacrifice, without pain or price, and, standing tall, enter into fellowship with the Ruler of all heaven and earth. Those ideas are so astounding that no man of that time could have written them apart from divine revelation. [40]

Some critics have insisted that the claims made in *Ephesians* are literally incredible – that is, no one can sensibly believe

---

(40) I know that this and the following paragraph echo some of the ideas in the preface; but it does no harm, as both Peter and John once said, to remind you of them! (2 Pe 1:12; 1 Jn 2:21)

them. Yet it is indeed easier to accept the truth of Paul's assertions than to believe that he could have invented them. As a piece of fiction, their writing would nearly equal the miracle of what God has done for us in Christ! Remember that Paul was a Jew, deeply imbued with twenty centuries of Yahwistic monotheism, culture, and religion. He had nothing to gain and everything to lose by writing *Ephesians*. There is no rational explanation for the letter, unless what Paul wrote was so true that he could do no other, even if it meant fierce persecution and violent death.

So we turn again to his words, and we see why Paul defied Jew, Roman, and Greek alike. What a dazzling vision! No godly man, privileged to see what he saw and to hear what he heard, could have kept silent. So he gave us this letter. In it, Paul declares that the idea of free access to the throne of God is not new after all, but very old. Why? Because from the very beginning this had always been God's purpose, which at last he has accomplished in Christ. Nothing remains but for us to respond, to believe, and to come boldly to the throne of grace. There, scripture says, we will always find grace and mercy to help us in every time of need (He 4:16; and see also 10:19-23).

The Torn Veil

Open access to the throne of God was first revealed when Jesus cried aloud on the cross and the great veil of the

Temple was torn in two from *"top to bottom"*! (Mt 27:51; Mk 15:38; Lu 23:45) [41]

That rent curtain signified many things, among them –

- The old legal code, with all its burdensome rules, was now cast aside like an old and worn-out garment (and cp. Je 30:21).
- When Jesus died, the old sacrifices all came to fruition, which is why the place where they were offered was stripped of its sanctity. The holy places in the temple were no longer holy. They could be exposed for all to see.
- The atoning blood, which once every year was sprinkled within the veil, has now been presented at Calvary by the great High Priest for all time for all who believe. No longer was access to the glory of God restricted only to a Jewish high priest. When Christ entered the holy of holies in heaven with his own blood he flung the way open for all who so chose to follow him.
- Hence, no blood of bullock or lamb is needed now, for Jesus has gone through the veil and into the Holiest with his own blood.
- The torn curtain revealed all the hidden things of the old dispensation, thus confirming that now every

---

(41) Many events in Jesus' life are recorded in one or two of the synoptic gospels, but not many are in all three. This is one them. Two of the gospels (Matthew and Mark) add the remarkable detail that the veil was torn from top to bottom, thus precluding human agency. Robertson says, "This veil was a most elaborately woven fabric of seventy-two twisted plaits of twenty-four threads each and the veil was sixty feet long and thirty wide. The rending of the veil signified the removal of the separation between God and the people." (*Word Pictures*, in loc.) Some have said that this curtain was as thick as the width of a human hand, and if so, then no human hand could have torn it.

believer is a royal priest, with full rights to approach the footstool of the Almighty.
- In particular, the mercy-seat could now be seen, where the glory of God once blazed, showing that now, through Christ, we have a clear revelation of God.
- And the fact that the curtain was torn from top to bottom shows that this was a supernatural act, done by the hand of God, just at the moment Jesus died, to show that a new era had begun.

Paul, in the words of our text, expresses the wonder of this extraordinary event in five great affirmations –

Access to His Glorious Throne

We may now go boldly and with all confidence into the very presence of God.

The torn veil on the day of Christ's death showed most of all that *through the blood of the everlasting covenant the way into the holiest is now made wide open to everyone who believes*! Those words in italics comprise what is perhaps the single greatest statement that can be drawn out of the NT. May I suggest that you read it again, commit it to memory, and come back to it constantly! Why? Because its truth will be constantly attacked by the enemy. Satan will never stop suggesting that for you the way is *not* open, and that you will have to do something difficult, costly, or painful to achieve genuine access to God.

As often as not, those attacks will originate, not in the world, but in church! Many Christians are cheated of their throne rights by wrong teaching. They hear from the pulpit or read in a book that nearness to God is a high privilege attained by only a few remarkable people. Often, some special method (aside from simple faith) of getting close to God is presented, such as –

- One must get perfectly still before God, gaining an absolute quietness of mind and emotions, so that nothing can hinder the soul's approach to God. Such "stillness" may be achievable for a few people, but for most it means that they will never be able to enjoy close fellowship with God.
- One must reach a certain quality or intensity of worship to reach God. Hence people are urged to arouse themselves, to sing louder and longer, to "break through" into the presence of God. [42] Yet scripture names the one who "breaks through" – it is the Lord himself! His name is Baal-perazim, *The Lord of the Breakthrough*. (2 Sa 5:20; 1 Ch 14:11; Is 28:21). If any "break-throughs" are needed, they do not consist of us trying to force ourselves upon God, but rather of the Lord breaking down our hardened hearts and wilful barriers, and opening us to *his* invasion!
- One must arrive at a level of passion in prayer, as if prayer is ineffective unless it is wracked by groans, tears, and anguished pleading. Sometimes, I know, such heats are needed (He 5:7; Lu 22:44), and we may be, any of us, called upon occasionally so to agonise before God. But if the aim is to enter the presence of the Lord, then all those tears are in vain. We enter simply by faith, in response to his invitation, or we do not enter at all!
- One must attain a level of piety or holiness in order to qualify for admission to the Throne Room. But if the

---

(42) To me this idea of "breaking through" to God is almost blasphemous. Can you even "break through" to see the Queen of Great Britain? Try it, and you will quickly find yourself under arrest! How then can anyone force a way into the presence of the Almighty? What you need is an invitation – and with that, you just walk in!

Blood of the Lamb alone does not sufficiently qualify us, then nothing else on earth nor in heaven will avail.

Those common, but false, ways of trying to get near to God are all deeply tragic. Why? Because sincere believers do yearn to dwell close to the Lord, and their very eagerness makes them susceptible to delusion! They are told there is something they have to do, or be, or become, some price they must pay, before they will be worthy to access the throne. Yet our text opens to every believer an un-closable door!

Never allow anyone for any reason to shut it!

So long as you truly believe in Jesus, and have a humble heart of repentance and of faith, then the door will never be shut! If you ever hear anyone suggesting, for any reason, that for you the way into the holiest is not open, reject it. If you are truly Christian, it is a lie!

Through Union With Christ

Because of our union with Christ we may now go boldly and with all confidence into the very presence of God.

Access to the throne of God rests solely upon the fact of our union with Christ through the new birth. So long as we are in relationship with Christ, and trusting in the blood of the everlasting covenant, then the way into the holiest remains wide open.

Notice three things about our right of access to the nearest presence of God –

(1) There is no place closer to God than standing in the Holy of Holies

What would have happened in ancient times if anyone, having got into the holy of holies, tried to cut open the far wall of the tabernacle and advance further? Would they have come still closer to God? Hardly! Beyond the holy of holies there lay only one thing – *the desert!* Likewise today.

Someone who supposes that by laborious effort it is possible to get closer to God than anyone can by simple faith, will discover, not a sweeter nearness to the Lord, but a barren wasteland.

If by faith alone we can boldly enter the holiest, which is where the Lord himself dwells, how can it be imagined that there is any nearer place to God? If you go past where someone is standing, you don't get closer to him, but further away with each step! So with God. If he is in the holy of holies, and we can find him there in a moment simply by murmuring the name of "Jesus", why try to go any further or look in any other place?

Not even the resurrection will get us closer to God than we already are in Christ. The throne will then be visible, whereas it is presently invisible, and we will then see the Lord, whereas we do not now see him, but we will not be any *closer!* Right now, this moment, as the apostle says, simply because we believe, *"we have complete freedom to go into the Most Holy Place by means of the death of Jesus."* (He 10:19 Therefore, he adds, *"Let us draw near with a true heart, and with full assurance of faith . . .And let us hold fast the confession of our hope without wavering, for he who promised is faithful"* (vs. 20-21).

One either trusts that admonition and acts on it confidently, or one is condemned to struggle in vain to find some way to purchase access by human effort. There are no other choices. It is either the work of Christ, or your work. I know which one I prefer!

(2) <u>The high priest entered by right of birth, without any reference to character</u>

In ancient Israel, any man who could claim the high priesthood by right of birth could not be denied his right to take office. Character was not an issue, nor conduct. The priest *could* be removed from office for certain grave faults or crimes, but until he *was* so removed, he could not be denied the rights of his office. In general, it was very difficult to remove any priest, and even more a high priest. The presumption was always that a man who was born to serve Israel as high priest would, once he had taken office, do so until his death. And as high priest, he, and he alone, on the great annual Day of Atonement, had an undeniable right to enter the holy of holies and sprinkle the blood of the sacrifice upon the gold lid of the ark of the covenant. He was there solely by virtue of his birth as the eldest son of a descendant of Aaron. The office could not be purchased, earned, merited, nor gained in any way except by right of birth. He did not have to demonstrate any special virtue nor show any extraordinary spiritual qualities. There was no price to pay, no holiness to attain, no merit to achieve, nor any perfection of life to accomplish. Was he the eldest surviving male of the current Aaronic family? Then that was enough. He was automatically the high priest of Israel, and no one could lawfully deny him the right to walk into the holy of holies.

In a similar manner, we too are priests who have been given right of access to the holy of holies simply by the new birth. Are you in union with Christ by faith? Then no one can deny you the right to draw near to God; nor can any work, price, or sacrifice of yours gain you any better right than you already fully possess in Christ.

(3) We not only have access by right of birth, but by right of personal invitation

Does a child need to "break into" its own home? Should an invited guest ignore the open door and "break through" your front window?

When you have an invitation to enter, and an unassailable right to be there, you simply *walk in* !

Don't insult the Almighty by offering him broken glass! Just accept the invitation you have in Christ, go boldly into the holiest, and stand in the very presence of God. And there, at the throne of grace, you will find all grace and mercy to help you in every time of need (He 4:16).

Now let me summarise what we have so far discovered in this chapter –

- There is no place closer to God than where he dwells in the holy of holies. Any attempt to find him somewhere else will take the seeker only into some kind of bleak spiritual desert.
- We enter that sacred place and stand before his throne solely by right of the new birth. No human effort of any sort can gain us better access than we are freely given in Christ.
- And to give us double assurance, we also gain entrance into the holy of holies and access to the throne of grace, by right of a personal invitation.

Which brings us to the third great idea in our text –

Faith

Through our faith in Christ we may now go boldly and with all confidence into the very presence of God

If entrance to the holiest is by faith, then – I have to say this again – no work of ours, whether good or bad, can either add to or detract from this right. Notice, I am talking here only about *rights*, which cannot under any circumstances be removed from the church; but two things can prevent any *individual* from gaining the benefit of those rights –

(1) The rights every Christian possesses in Christ must be appropriated by faith, and faith can exist only in an environment of wholehearted surrender to the word of God. Christian people who deny the promise of God, or ignore it, or are ignorant of it, or refuse to yield to it, cannot properly believe, and thus cannot enter the holiest. This is because

faith is not a self-existent entity. It cannot dwell alone. Faith is not something one possesses by itself, like holding a loaf of bread. Faith has no substance. No one can say, "I have faith!" – because faith cannot exist independently. Something else must always be attached. Thus , "I believe in God!"– "I would always trust that woman's word!" – "Whatever he says, you can believe!" – "God said it; I believe it; that settles it!"

Faith is rather like love. I cannot just "love". The idea of love is meaningless unless it is linked with a beloved object, person, or some other lovely entity. Likewise, I cannot just believe. I must believe *in* or *for* something or someone, and in the case before us, that means the divine promise, which says that any *believer* has free and full rights to step into the holiest.

So Christian faith is a trusting response to something God has said, done, or promised. Hence, anyone who sweeps a divine promise away cannot believe and therefore will be unable to grasp its riches.

(2) Wilful continuance in sin must eventually paralyse the sinner's ability to approach the throne with any kind of confidence. How can a person who is in a state of rebellion against God, who is disobeying his command, who lacks repentance, who has no desire for holiness, or who is crushing underfoot the blood of the everlasting covenant, *believe* that covenant and grasp its promised blessings? (He 10:29)

However, do note that faith is not a virtue; even less is it a "good work". Rather, mark it again, faith is simply an attitude of unwavering trust in the irrevocable promise of God. Faith does not bring us any merit in the sight of God; rather, it links us with the merits of Christ! And if that is so, if the merits of Christ are enough to carry me right up to the very footstool of God, then what a fool I would be to turn away from them and proffer some sin-darkened worth of my own! Leave that folly to those misguided ignoramuses who run about trying to establish their own righteousness. I prefer the righteousness of Christ (Ro 10:3).

No one has better displayed (unwittingly) the utter futility of trying to earn the right to get close to God by human effort than the ancient monks and hermits. What privations they endured! What agonies they suffered! What sacrifices they made! What pains they inflicted upon themselves! And in the end, were they one whit nearer the Lord than any *believer* can arrive at in a moment? To ask the question is to give the answer. Scripture speaks so plainly. We enter the holiest only by faith, and through the efficacy of the blood of the covenant, not by any effort of our own, whether great or small.

Let one man stand for all the hermits – St Simeon Stylites (early 5th century), who lived for 39 years on a small wooden platform on top of a stone pillar near Aleppo in Syria. You can find his story in any good encyclopaedia or church history. [43] But no one has ever entered so well into Simeon's passions and agonies as Tennyson does in his eponymous poem. [44] Somehow, despite the passage of many centuries, Tennyson's astonishing portrait of Simeon captures the essence of his fierce spiritual struggles and his final despair. The saint knows that his tortured hunger for God will not be realised in this life, and he remains unsure even of the next.

Like so many before and since his time, Simeon failed to understand the gospel and the grace of God. He thought that the best pathway to heaven was through frightful privations. How wrong he and all his ilk were! How wrong such ideas still are! Jesus is the Way, the only Way, the all-sufficient

---

(43) For a description of the life and significance of St Simeon Stylites, see http://en.wikipedia.org/wiki/Simeon_Stylites

(44) You can find a copy of Tennyson's poem, *St Simeon Stylites*, at http://www.online-literature.com/tennyson/728/

Way, the perfect Way. Just take his hand, and he will carry you at once into the throne room, and the very presence of the Father. [45]

Boldness

Because of our union with Christ, we may now go boldly into the very presence of God!

On one occasion, with startling daring, Paul reversed scripture. The writer of *Exodus* tells us that the people could not endure looking at the shining face of Moses, so that most of the time he wore a veil. (Ex 34:29-35) But Paul turns it around. He says, the *real* reason for the veil was to hide the fact that the face of Moses had *stopped* shining! (2 Co 3:13-16) Moses feared that he might lose authority if this loss of glory were discovered. So he kept the people "blind" to what had happened. And, says Paul, that is just what still happens. People do not see that all glory has gone from the law as a way of pleasing God, and that instead it has been transferred to the gospel.

---

(45) Someone may have been quietly thinking during the last few pages, "What about all those books I've read, and saints I've heard about, where people claim to have had some numinous encounter with God – perhaps after countless hours of prayer, or many fastings. Or perhaps, in a hope of getting closer to God, they imposed upon themselves endless pain, awful sacrifices, and the like. And what about all the experiences of God they talk about – flooded by light, supernatural visions, dreams of heaven, streams of overpowering love, and so on?"

Well, it is not my place to doubt anyone's spiritual experience. If those encounters were a source of true blessing to them, then praise God! But I strongly insist that none of that is necessary to bring a person to the throne of grace. And I also ask – whom should I believe – the testimony of some person, or the clear affirmations of scripture? My choice will always be the Word of God. Let God be true, even if it makes every man a liar! (Ro 3:4) I refuse to believe that I have to do anything to come into intimate fellowship with the Father at the throne of grace except trust his promise and walk in.

Therefore, says Paul, wake up! Tear off the veil! Be blind no longer! See where the glory of God truly exists – in the face of Christ. And looking away from the dead, cold face of Moses, and looking upon the lovely, ever-living face of Christ alone, let his Spirit carry you from glory to glory! (vs. 17-18) Which is to say, be done with all self-effort as a means of gaining righteous credit in heaven, unveil your eyes, believe the gospel, and heartily accept God's splendid gift of the righteousness of Christ. Why would you ever prefer your own good works to his great work? Why would you choose your dirty rags over his beautiful sparkling robe? Why would you approach God in your own name, when you can come boldly in the name of Jesus?

We saw earlier that the curtain of the temple was completely rent from top to bottom – no small tear, but one that laid the Most Holy Place wide open. It was God saying that the way into the holiest is now open for ever to all who believe, and that we may come instantly in Jesus to the very throne of grace. And in particular, when we reach that throne, we may *speak boldly*. The Greek word is *parrhesia*, which is made up of two other words: a prefix – *"all things"*; and a verb – *"say"* or *"speak"*. It had a strong sense of being unreserved, open, free, and brave in speech, especially in the democratic assemblies in ancient Athens. From there, it came to mean also fearless confidence, cheerful courage, boldness, assurance, and the like.

But *parrhesia* never entirely lost its connection with freedom of speech, of boldness expressed through the spoken word. And that is the word the apostle applies to the way we should speak in the holiest, in the presence of God, at the throne of grace! There is nothing mean or cringing about it. We do not crawl in on our knees, wailing about our sins, hardly daring to lift our heads. There is a time and a place to repent deeply of sin, and to express our sorrow before God. There is a way to seek his pardon for our wrongdoing. But that way and that place is not begging like poverty broken worms in the holy place! Repent if you need to. Seek divine forgiveness if you have sinned. Trust in the grace of Christ and the efficacy of his blood. But then arise! Stand tall! Walk bravely and speak boldly, as you approach the throne. Indeed, take your very seat as a person enthroned with Christ himself in the heavenlies, and talk like a king! In our text, Paul is emphatic. God has fulfilled his eternal purpose in Christ just so that we might have access to his throne with *boldness*.

Confidence

Because of our union with Christ we may now go with all confidence into the very presence of God!

It does indeed take a measure of spiritual boldness to agree with the promise of God and to march bravely up to the throne. Yet by itself it is not enough. Once there, we are told to express our requests with joyful *confidence*. Do you wonder why? Simply because to pray without keen anticipation of a sure answer is to insult God. Why pray if you are unsure whether or not God is listening? Why ask if you don't expect an answer? Why approach heaven's throne if you doubt its authority or strength? You had better get all those things sorted out first, and then, when you are ready to *believe*, come boldly and with confidence to the throne of grace. There you will receive all mercy and every grace you need to help you in your time of need (Ep 3:12; He 4:16).

But there is a still higher dimension to the ripped veil. It shows that the way to Paradise is open to the children of God, and how eagerly we are waiting for that great day when Jesus will come and carry us through that open door to share eternal joys with him at the throne of the Father.

Christ holds the *Keys of the Kingdom,* such that what he opens no one can close! He has opened the way into the holiest now, and the door cannot be closed. He will open the way into heaven when he comes, and no one will be able to block the ascending church. So then, let us by faith ascend with him into the heavenly places, and sit with him there till all our enemies become his footstool, and we inherit paradise with him for ever.

Oh! How true it is –

> *Everything God did in Christ was in agreement with his eternal purpose, which he has achieved through Christ Jesus our Lord, so that, because of our **union** with Christ and through our **faith** in him, we may now go **boldly** and with all **confidence** into the very **presence** of God!*
> (Ep 3:11-12)

Seventeen:

Exceeding Abundantly

In the entire history of the Church there has not yet been a time when the people of God have truly embraced the promises of answered prayer contained in the Bible. Those promises represent one of the great spiritual mountain peaks still remaining to be climbed by faith.

Among many examples that could be cited, perhaps the most outstanding and the most comprehensive is found in Ephesians 3:20, *"Your God is able to do exceeding abundantly above everything that you might ask, or even imagine, according to the working of the ability that is in you!"* [46]

Based on that verse, I want to tell you three things about God's ability, and four things about your ability.

Three Statements About God

God's Ability

Said Paul, *"Your God is ABLE!"* That is, you cannot think of any situation in life that would tax the resources of heaven. There is no circumstance imaginable that could weary the arm of the Lord. His treasures will never be exhausted, his wisdom never perplexed, his love never outworn, his promise never broken. In the face of every problem, every need, every debt, every sin, every disease, every hurt – YOUR GOD IS ABLE!

---

[46] Paraphrased a little.

The technical name for this attribute of God is *omnipotence*, which means "all-powerful". And the Almighty does indeed possess vastly more strength than he will ever need to do all that he has ever purposed. Yet we do have to place one limit upon the statement that "God is able." It does not mean that God can do anything anyone might ever think of. Rather, it means only that he can do everything that is consistent with his divine nature, holiness, and justice.

So, while no single force, nor any combination of forces, will ever be strong enough to defeat God, and he can do whatever he chooses to do, he cannot choose to act against his own nature or decrees (2 Ti 2:13). This means that God cannot deny his promise, nor violate his holiness, nor act against the law of love, nor break his own laws (Ja 1:17; 1 Pe 1:23-25), whether in the natural realm, or in the spiritual realm.

Therefore, not even God can put the toothpaste back into its tube once it has been used; nor can he put an apple back on the tree once it has been eaten. He cannot actually play a piano or hit a tennis ball – for those are human actions and require human hands to do them properly. But he *can* raise the dead who have gone back into dust, for there is a seed of immortal life in man out of which the former person can be reconstituted (1 Co 15:35-44).

So a life of faith requires the believer to affirm without question that God, consistent with his nature and promise, is ABLE to do whatever he is asked to do.

God's Action

Hence Paul continues: *"Your God is able to DO."* That is an important statement, for while God may indeed have all power, is he willing actually to *use* that power on our behalf? Yes! For Paul asserts that God not only *can*, but he *does*! He is not only *able*, he *will*! He is not like a tyrant who could act, but won't; on the contrary, the Lord God is eager to exert his strength in favour of his people.

So here is a declaration that the God we serve is not like the gods of the heathen (Ps 115:1-8) – our God sees, knows, loves, and WORKS! He **does** things!

So then, when we are told that God has all power, it is not just to tantalise us with an impossible dream, but to encourage us to believe that what the Father has promised, he is both able to do and willing to do.

God's Answer

Piling superlative upon superlative, Paul tries to convey to us the staggering dimensions of God's willingness and ability to answer our prayers –

- your God is ABLE
- your God is able to DO
- your God is able to do what you ASK
- your God is able to do ALL that you ask
- your God is able to do ABOVE all that you ask
- your God is able to do ABUNDANTLY above all that you ask
- your God is able to do EXCEEDING abundantly above all that you ask
- your God is able to do exceeding abundantly above all that you might ask or even THINK!

But, you may say, if that is how God wants to answer prayer, why does he not do so? How rarely do people get even what they ask, let alone far above what they ask, let alone far above what they can even imagine!

Paul shows that the answer lies in us – he says that God's *ability* is tempered by our *ability*. The same Greek word (*dunamis* = ability or power) is used twice in the text, once of God and once of us – *"Your God is <u>able</u> ... according to the <u>able</u>-ness at work within you."*

Or it could just as well read, "Your God has power ... according to the power at work within you."

Paul, then, is saying that God is indeed "able" – but *his* ability is qualified by how we use *our* ability. Or, according to the power at work *in* you so God will work powerfully *for* you. Or, when you do what you alone can do, then God will do what he alone can do. Or, his working is according to the measure of our working. Which leads me to say that there are

Four Things We Must Do

I would like to suggest that *"the power that works in us"* must include these four things –

The Power Of Righteousness

For our sake God made Christ to be sin who knew no sin, so that in him we might become the righteousness of God. ... Let us approach God with a sincere heart in full assurance of faith, and with our hearts sprinkled clean from an evil conscience. (2 Co 5:21; He 10:22)

Because we have become the very righteousness of God himself through Christ, we can approach the throne of God boldly, with full assurance and with bold faith, providing we can shake off an *"evil conscience"*.

What does that mean? How can a conscience be evil? Isn't conscience a good thing? Can't we trust it implicitly? No, for there are times when conscience, far from putting our feet on the right path can mislead us altogether. Your conscience, although it is normally a reliable tool, becomes "evil" when

- it persists in accusing you, even after you have repented and cleansed yourself in the blood of Christ; and
- when you allow it to turn things into sin that are not sin in the eyes of God; and

- when you allow it to impose upon you some law, rule, or regulation as a means of gaining access to the throne of God.

People make a variety of rules to govern their Christian lives – rules about Bible reading, prayer, church going, fasting, witnessing, and the like. Those rules may be good, but they become ruinous if they become a "law" – that is, if you feel righteous and deserving of God's favour when you keep them, but unrighteous and undeserving of his favour when you don't. Turning personal disciplines into a means of purchasing some higher standing in the sight of God, some quality of righteousness or of special favour, is *legalism*, which scripture furiously condemns, for it brings spiritual death.

So shut your ears to the voice of conscience if it becomes "evil" by trying to persuade you that you do not deserve any good thing from God. When conscience refuses to be stilled by the grace of God in Christ, when it robs you of your right to approach the throne of God, then it is no longer a divine voice, but carries rather an accent of hell. The gospel message is plain and forceful. If you have come into union with Christ through faith, then

- the Father looks upon you with the same joy that he has when he sees Jesus; and
- he loves you as he loves Christ, and you stand in his favour as Christ does; and
- if the Father would answer Christ's prayer (if Christ were where you are), then he is equally willing to answer *your* prayer.

I have phrased that last statement carefully. It is wrong to suppose (as many Christians do) that God will do for us whatever he would have done for Jesus when he lived among us. The Father's purpose for Christ was not the same as it is for us; he did things for and through Christ that he will not necessarily do for us, and he will do things for us that he would not have done for Jesus. There was a task for that Man to fulfil, and there is a task for each of us to fulfil; and the manner in which the Lord answers prayer is conditioned by those individual tasks.

Thus there were things that the Father did for and through Jesus, and there are things that he will do for and through my neighbour, that may not be right for me. We are each required to discover for ourselves (through prayer, scripture, wise counsel, and the like) what the Father has planned for us, and to focus prayer on how we may best fulfil that plan. The Lord deals differently with all of us, and it is enough that we find his will and do it (Jn 21:21-22).

Yet we too are "sons", just as Jesus was the Son; so there still remains a sense in which our claim upon the Father is as great as his was. Therefore this is what you should do –

- Imagine that Jesus is where you are, living your life, under the same instructions from God, having your task to do.
- Then ask yourself, "If Jesus were I, what would the Father give him and do for him?"
- The answer will be a good indication of what the Father is willing to give you, or do for you.

Or, look at it this way. We are commanded to stand in the confidence that characterised Jesus' approach to the Father (cp. Jn 11:41,42). When we do this, righteousness becomes a source of power in our prayers, rather than of weakness. The voice of conscience, instead of castigating us as unworthy of any divine favour, will loudly proclaim our absolute merit in Christ and insist that we are deserving of all that the Father's love has promised. Righteousness becomes a "power" in us when we stop trying to build our own, based on good works, and instead abandon ourselves to the righteousness of God in Christ. (Ro 10:1-3)

When we heartily affirm that we are indeed the righteousness of God in Christ (no matter what we are in ourselves), then that righteousness becomes the basis upon which God liberates us from the oppression of sin, silences the accusations of an "evil conscience", enables us to pray with certainty that the Father will welcome and grant our requests. This righteousness is part of *"the power that works in us"*, it depends upon our ability to stand in it firmly, unwavering, and thus clear the way for the Father to do what lies only in his power.

The Power of Choice

The scriptures in numerous places put upon the believer two special responsibilities –

- we should find out what God wants to do for us; and then
- we should set ourselves to have what God wants, never being content to accept less (see De 20:19-20; 1 Co 15:58; 16:13; Ja 1:5-7; etc.)

Which at once raises a question: "How can I discover just what God wants to do for me?

Some answers are – prayer, the word of God, wise counsel, revelation by the Spirit, prophetic messages, dreams, visions, how God is shaping your circumstances, and so on. [47]

But even after we have found a promise that covers our need, can we reasonably expect to have everything the Father has promised to give? The answer is both yes and no. It is certainly reasonable to expect that every promise of God pertaining to this present life will be (or at least can be)

---

(47) For a thorough exploration of the theme of discovering God's will, see my book *Discovery*.

fulfilled before we die. However, it is sometimes difficult to discover what promise is applicable to a particular circumstance. For example –

- there are promises of healing which sometimes have to yield to the need for discipline (1 Co 11:29-32; He 12:5-12); and
- there are promises of prosperity which sometimes have to yield to the demand to endure hardship (2 Ti 1:8; 2:3; 4:5); and
- there are promises that are conditional – that is, they are qualified either by scripture itself, [48] or by circumstances; and
- there are promises whose full realisation cannot happen until after the resurrection; and
- there are promises that are true generally, and can usually be trusted, but they are subject to many exceptions.

In other words, the Bible contains many different promises that apply to many different situations. Which means that so long as the promise you are "claiming" matches the purpose God has for you *at that particular time*, you have every right to expect its abundant fulfilment. Otherwise, you may or may not be able to establish a rightful claim to it.

Here then is an explanation of the frustration and bewilderment that sometimes overwhelms people – perhaps

---

(48) For example, *Proverbs 22:6* is weakened by other scriptures that stress the freedom of choice God has given to everyone; or, consider Psalm 32:10; 34:19-21. A short survey of life will show that things do not always go well for the righteous nor ill for the wicked – that is, the promise may be true in a general sense, but not always in a particular case. Hence, other passages caution against putting too much trust in this world's treasures (Mt 6:19-20; Pr 23:4-5; 1 Ti 6:17), for they can soon be lost.

they are trying to claim a promise that is not applicable to them at that time or in that situation.

We used to sing –

> Every promise in the Book is mine,
> Every chapter, every verse, every line,
> All the blessings of his love divine,
> Every promise in the Book is mine. [49]

The song is of course true, but only in a general sense. In reality, not every promise is accessible on every occasion, but only those that are appropriate to the circumstances in which you find yourself, or to the need that you presently have, and all conditional upon the Father's purpose for you at each step of your pilgrimage. It is like the items on a pharmacist's shelf. They may all belong to him, but they will not all be suitable for him to use at any one time. Or, consider a well-stocked pantry. Each ingredient belongs to the cook, but no sensible chef will try to use them all at once! For every meal there are foods that are fitting, and those that are not.

Wise Christians, therefore, will expend the time and energy necessary to search out the will of God, and to learn which promise(s) they may sensibly claim in each new circumstance. This too is part of *"the power that works in us"*.

The Power of The Word

Every Christian who is weak in the Word will be weak. Spiritual vitality, surging faith, unyielding authority – they all flow out of the Word of God. If you want to be powerful in prayer, then you must work at the Word and let the Word work in you. That means reading your Bible constantly, praying over it, meditating on its words day and night (Ps

---

[49] I have been unable to discover the author of these lyrics.

1:2-3). There, as the psalmist says, is the key to prosperity and to enjoying a divine abundance in   every area of your life.

So here is a vital principle – there is an unbreakable link between effective prayer and constant meditation in the word of God. This is because the scriptures strengthen prayer in three ways –

First, they contain many specific promises, so that we can pray with much boldness if what we are asking is the subject of one of those promises. Knowing that God has already promised to do something should remove all doubt about his willingness to do it, providing the time and place are right. So if you have no reason to question that a promise belongs to you in your present circumstance, then you should seize it boldly and steadfastly expect its fulfilment.

Second, the scriptures also give us a clear picture of who God is, what his nature is, the things he does, and the things he never does. Thus, even when no specific promise can be found in the Bible, believers can still gain a sense of what God is likely or unlikely to give them in answer to prayer.

Third, the scriptures are infused with the life of God, and they alone have power to impart the kind of faith that makes prayer invincible.

Therefore, when we properly work at the Work of God, doing what we alone can do, then we may rightly expect that the Lord will respond by doing what he alone can do. This too is part of the rule that the working of God's ability will be according to the working of our ability.

The Power of The Spirit

The Word and the Spirit belong together. Search the scriptures and you will find there has hardly ever been a person powerful in faith and prayer who was not also full of the Holy Spirit. Especially, search *John*, chapters 14,15,16, and see how firmly Christ links the Pentecostal event with successful prayer.

Read those chapters, meditate on them, and they will teach you more about this aspect of our theme than I could ever say even half as well! So I won't say any more here, except this – once again, this is part of *"the ability (dunamis) that is at work in us"*. Those Ephesians were a people full of the Holy Spirit (Ac 19:6; Ep 1:13; 5:18-20). When they prayed, Paul expected them to do so as a people alive in the Spirit, empowered by the Spirit, actively walking in the Spirit (cp. Ga 5:16-18), stirring up and drawing upon all the resources of the indwelling Spirit (cp. 1 Ti 4:14; 2 Ti 1:6). This lay within *their* ability. When they used it properly, then God would indeed do *"exceeding abundantly above all they could ask or even imagine!"*

Conclusion

Are you rich in the word of God? Are you full of the Spirit? Have you resolved to have all that is God's promise to you? Are you strong in prayer? Is God doing what you ask? Is he doing exceeding abundantly above what you ask? Have you dared to dream what the Father might do for you if you were to ask in faith?

If you can unleash your fourfold ability, and make it work for God, then God will work for you, and you will begin to find him answering prayer beyond what you ever dared to think might happen!

Section Six:

Ministry Gifts

Eighteen:

Finding Your Place In The Church

*The Church is the **body** of Christ, the fulness of him who fills all in all. ... Here is a mystery, that the Gentiles are fellow-heirs with Christ, members of the same **body**, sharing together the promise Christ Jesus brings to them through the gospel. ... There is one **body** and one Spirit, and you have been called to the one hope, which is part of your call ... God gave gifts to equip the saints for the work of ministry, for building up the **body** of Christ ... Christ equips the whole **body** with many joints, which hold it together and enable it, when each part is working properly, to make the **body** grow so that it builds itself up in love. ... We are members of his **body**. (Eph_1:23; 3:6; 4:4,12,; 5:30)*

Introduction

The Church is given a remarkable identity – it is the "body" of Christ on earth, having the Lord himself as its only true Head. This means that churches can worship and witness effectively only if they are rightly structured and truly functioning as a proper "body" should. But at once we face a strange situation – everybody believes what Paul writes in our text, but no one does it!

How can that be true?

First, note this miracle! Across the entire gamut of Christian Churches worldwide, of all persuasions, no one doubts the validity of Paul's analogy. Everyone agrees that likening the church to the human body (one body with many parts) is an apt simile. How rare it is to find such unanimity on any point of doctrine! On a vast number of ideas Christians quarrel incessantly, but on this they all agree! It is wonderful!

But if that sort of unanimity is rare, then, **second**, it is almost rarer to find any church that truly puts the dogma into practice! Instead, churches tend to compel their people to conform to a familiar pattern, or to take on a common task. Driven by the emphasis of the moment, or the current spiritual fad, they urge every member of the congregation to embrace, say, a burden of intercessory prayer, or to be busy in personal evangelism, or to accept a duty of nurturing hurting people, join a cell group, be a diligent Bible student, do street witnessing, go door-knocking – and so on. Consequently, people who lack the skill to succeed in one enterprise or another have to swallow the bitter pill of failure. They lose their zeal, subside back onto the pew, discouraged, and disappointed. They become dully inactive Christians, or perhaps leave the church altogether.

So this demand that everyone do the same thing, or live in the same way, is a sure pathway to failure for many people. Worse, it is a direct denial of Paul's analogy of one body comprised of many diverse members, each with its own special function in the body. We who are members of a local church are not all the same; rather, we each have a particular task to fulfil or office to occupy or ministry to perform. We each have different gifts. We each have our own call in God. We each have only one true duty – find what God wants us to do and to be, and then set ourselves to achieve what God wants. The task of the local church is to help people to do just that, not to bully them into roles for which they are neither gifted nor called.

Thus, wise church leaders set up their people for lively success, not despondent failure, by directing each person into his or her God-given role and away from tasks for which they are ill-suited. Nothing succeeds like success; nothing fails like failure. So make all the people winners by giving them tasks they will enjoy doing, because they are skilled for them and know they will succeed.

From his simile of the church being like a body, Paul draws two great lessons –

Find Your Proper Level

Paul likes the idea of the Church as the body of Christ on earth, and he mentions it in several of his letters, including the following –

> *For by the grace given to me I say to everyone among you not to think of himself more highly than he ought to think, but to think with sober judgment, each according to the measure of faith that God has assigned. For as in one **body** we have many members, and the members do not all have the same function, so we, though many, are one **body** in Christ, and individually members one of another.* (Ro 12:3-5, ESV)

"Think about yourself soberly, not reckoning yourself to be either better or worse than you are," says Paul. A wrong estimate of yourself, whether too high or too low, will surely bring eventual pain. Do not be so foolish. Join those who are wise and come to an honest estimate of yourself. According to Tennyson, the famous Sir Lancelot demonstrated when a young knight praised him over-much - [50]

> Me you call great; mine is the firmer seat,
> The truer lance; but there is many a youth
> Now crescent, who will come to all I am
> And overcome it; and in me there dwells
> No greatness, save it be some far off touch
> Of greatness to know well I am not great.

---

(50) Alfred, Lord Tennyson, Idylls of the King – "Lancelot and Elaine."

Yet how difficult it is to be honest with oneself! People continually wreak havoc either by imagining they are more than they are or less than they are. Both faults are equally heinous, showing both a failure of submission to God and of faith.

Sensible people embrace honestly not only their skills but also their limitations. They know what they can do and what they can't. They avoid the twin follies of attempting the impossible and of falling short of their potential. They are comfortable with their identity, not wishing to be more than they are, nor afraid to be all that they are. Or, to quote Paul again, *"Think about yourself modestly, and measure yourself by the amount of faith God has apportioned you."* Yet I constantly meet people who either demand responsibilities that would destroy them or shirk duties they could well fulfil. Both characters are sinful.

Long ago Rabbi Sirach recognised the folly of aspiring to things too high for one –

> *Do not aspire to be a judge, unless you have the strength to put an end to injustice; for you may be intimidated by a man of rank and so compromise your integrity.* (6:6)

But it is equally wrong to be content with less than God has equipped one to do –

> *The sluggard says, "There is a lion outside! I shall be killed in the streets!" ... The sluggard says, "There is a lion in the road! There is a lion in the streets!"* (Pr 22:13; 26:13)

Paul was even more stern –

> *Since we have different gifts according to the grace that God has given us, <u>make sure that you use them</u>!"* (Ro 12:6)

And Peter is just as emphatic –

> *Each of you as a good manager <u>must use the gift that God has given you</u> to serve others. Whoever speaks must speak God's words. Whoever serves must serve with the strength God supplies so that in every way God receives glory through Jesus Christ. Glory and power belong to Jesus Christ forever and ever! Amen.* (1 Pe 4:10-11, GW)

So let us be humbly honest and honestly humble. Let us not hold back when we should boldly press forward; nor let us press forward when we should discreetly hold back. It is enough to discover just who you are and to be that person, and no other.

Two Young Men

The Bible is realistic about the differences between people, how one may be strong where another is weak, and the reverse. There is an intriguing passage where Paul, knowing that a *"time of trouble"* was about to come upon the church at Corinth, suggests how they should handle it, and gives different counsel to different people (1 Co 7:1-40, especially vs. 26). In particular, Paul takes up the circumstances facing two young men. (vs. 36-38)

One young man who was firm in his resolve and had good control over his desires, was told to remain single and celibate until conditions improved.

Another young man who couldn't keep his hands off his fiancée was told to wed her as soon as he could. Better to marry than burn! (vs. 9)

According to Paul, they both did well, one to marry, the other not to marry, in accordance with their different characters and strengths.

Yet I can imagine what some preachers nowadays would say to the supposedly weaker youth – "You call yourself a Spirit-filled Christian, you lust-riddled, pusillanimous, mewling, contemptible milksop? Rise up like a man, get control of your passions, show yourself a real Christian, and stop making excuses for your lack of self-control. Resolve now to be celibate and pure, like someone who knows how to live godly in Christ!"

Paul was wiser. With deep sensitivity and genuine pragmatism, he shaped his advice to suit each person's capacity and gifting in God. As Martin Luther once said, walking in the Spirit so that one does not fulfil fleshly lusts (Ga 5:16) may sometimes be best fulfilled, not by engaging in strenuous spiritual warfare, but by getting married! [51]

The Measure of Faith

One of the special criteria for discerning each person's position and task in the local church, the body of Christ in its locality, is the statement that we have each been given a role that accords with the particular *"measure of faith"* that God has also given to us. What you *can* do, what you *cannot* do, what you *can* believe for, what you *cannot* believe for, are determined by this measure of faith. Therefore, by faith one person can shut the mouths of lions, while another will be eaten; one can give his body to be burn, while another escapes the flames; one will be reduced to poverty, another will amass wealth. (He 11:32-40) We cannot please God without faith (vs. 6), bt neither can anyone go beyond the boundaries of faith. And God gives each of us just enough faith and just the right kind of faith to do what he requires of us.

When I was a young man, I dreamed of building a huge church. But I could never fix the vision in my mind. Every time I tried to "see" that glorious church, the image would dissolve into fragments. I could neither conjure it up in my

---

(51) See his Commentary on the *Letter to the Galatians* in loc.

mind, nor hold it there. God gave me no faith for it. But then (in 1974) I caught the vision of a worldwide Bible College, and how quickly things changed! I had no trouble visualising this school coming into existence and straddling the globe. Indeed, Alison and I at once coined the motto, which then seemed almost arrogant, *The Whole Word to the Whole World* – under which banner the college still operates.

Because it was a God-given dream, not proud human ambition, the birth of Vision College was inevitable. So long as I did what the Lord told me, nothing could stop it from happening. All the faith I needed, and more, was overflowing in my spirit. I simply had to step out and follow the path set before me. Thus, having received from the Lord the necessary gifts for the task, I was then also given the measure of faith to do it. Yet I had found it (and still find it) impossible to grasp the same kind of faith to build a large church, for God determines the measure of faith each of us receives. Indeed, what do I or any of us have that we did not first receive from God, so that the honour and glory are his alone? (1 Co 4:7)

I might also add, that in the process I learnt another lesson, that almost anything is possible for the person who doesn't care who gets the glory for it (except God). Or, as English priest and theologian Benjamin Jowett said more than a century ago, *"The way to get things done is not to mind who gets the credit for doing them."* So, I dreamed of a worldwide college, coined its motto, began to write books for its curriculum, and launched it as a correspondence Bible School in 1974. But still the dream would have failed if I had not been willing to yield position and authority to people who were more gifted than I in management and leadership, notably Dr Stan DeKoven, along with many other highly gifted men and women. I truly do not mind who gets whatever glory there is to be had in the enterprise, so long as the dream is fulfilled of taking the whole word to the whole world!

Now, on this measure of faith notice that –

- This "measure" differs *for* each one of us from time to time. That is, today it may directed toward one task, but tomorrow toward another, and later toward still another, so that although we once had faith for a certain task we may not always have such faith.
- This measure may change *in* each one of us from time to time. That is, today I may find it easy to believe God for a particular miracle of answered prayer, but later may lack even a flicker of it. I can look back across nearly 60 years of ministry and see many occasions when I was able to believe for some spectacular thing to happen, and it did; yet today I cannot find in myself any faith for any of them! But there are other things today for which I most certainly can and do believe!

Like the manna in the wilderness for ancient Israel, which had to be gathered each new day, otherwise it became rank, so faith must be reborn for each necessity. *"Give us this day,"* Jesus taught us to pray, *"our daily bread!"*

So faith is given us to do the Father's will in each situation, and its measure in us will differ accordingly.

Centuries before Paul urged people to think honestly and soberly about themselves, a motto was carved above the entrance to the Delphic oracle in ancient Greece. It was a warning to those who were too keen to know the gods, and it is a good rule to follow in all walks of life. It said – *"Know thyself!"*

The idea was, if you are wrong about yourself you will almost certainly be equally wrong about God. Self-delusion usually leads to God-delusions – that is, measuring God by themselves, people expect either too much from him or too little, and fail to apprehend his true purpose or his real promise. In the end, you can know *God* only as well as you know *yourself*. Yet there is a delightful reciprocity here – for it is equally true that you will know *yourself* only as well as you know *God*. Here then is wonderful adventure. Let me know more about God and I will know myself better. Let me know more about myself and I will know God better. The quest for that double knowledge should never end in this life.

Find Your Proper Function

Paul lists seven functions, one or more of which belong to every local church member (Ro 12:6-8). There are no exceptions, no unemployed passengers in the barque of Christ, no room for mere spectators; we are all in the arena of faith.

Those seven functions are –

- ***prophesying*** – which brings to the church <u>revelation</u>
- ***ministering*** – which brings to the church <u>souls</u>
- ***teaching*** – which brings to the church <u>maturity</u>
- ***encouraging*** – which brings to the church <u>nurture</u>
- ***contributing*** – which brings to the church <u>sustenance</u>
- ***leadership*** – which brings to the church <u>direction</u>
- ***mercy*** – which brings to the church <u>healing</u>.

Those functions can operate at different levels, both within and outside the local church – that is, a person may be gifted to serve just one department of the church, or the whole church, or a group of churches, and so on. For example, one teacher may be best suited to a house meeting, another to the church pulpit, another to the wider group of churches, and some may be excellent in all three areas.

Those functions are in general not interchangeable, any more than the members of our bodies can be exchanged for one another. Thus Paul is adamant – *"Since we have different gifts according to the grace given to us, if it is prophecy, then prophesy according to your measure of faith; if ministry, then minister; if teaching, then teach; if exhortation, then exhort; if sharing, in simplicity; if leadership, in diligence; if showing mercy, in cheerfulness."* (Ro 12:6-8)

Now if you check that passage in various translations you will find that it is rendered differently in many of them. That is because the Greek text is clipped, as if Paul were speaking with too much passion to allow elegant and lengthened periods. So the translation remains uncertain, and Paul's instruction may be read in any of three ways –

> *"We have gifts that differ according to the grace that is given to us . . . –*
>
> 1. *some have been given the grace of prophecy so that they may prophesy, in proportion to their faith; others have been given the grace of ministry, so that they may minister, . . ."* (and so on)
>
>   – that is, the gift itself is a grace of God.
>
> 2. *if prophecy, then let the prophet prophesy; if ministry, then let that person minister . . ."* – (and so on)
>
>   – that is, let nothing be done to hinder the gift from functioning.
>
> 3. *if prophecy, then the prophet should prophesy; if ministry, then that person should minister, . . ."* (and so on)
>
>   – that is, those who have a gift, must use it.

Any one of those translations would be valid, and perhaps Paul intended his readers to see all of them in his terse instruction. In any case, we may learn three significant lessons –

1. <u>The necessity of grace</u>

Nothing truly useful can be done in the church without or apart from the grace of God. Every gift, calling, function, exists only as an impartation of divine grace, which should rid us of both pride and envy, and cause us to be thankful only to God for whatever grace we have received.

2. *The necessity of service*

Those who have received grace and the gift of God must employ those heavenly boons, for the glory of God and the benefit of the church. They are not given to be admired but **used** (vs. 6). Let none of us emulate the fool who buried his talent, and was justly cast into outer darkness. (Mt 22:13; 25:30)

3. *The necessity of freedom*

The local church must allow and encourage each person to serve God in his or her best way, according to their proper rôle in the body, doing all that it can to create opportunities for such service.

A church thus structured, and with all the people functioning in their proper task and place, has the best chance to be spiritually dynamic, healthy, prosperous, entirely successful in fulfilling the purpose the Father has for it.

Nineteen:

The Ministry Gifts

> *Christ ascended far above all the heavens so that his presence might be everywhere throughout the universe. And he gave to his church apostles, prophets, evangelists, shepherds, and teachers, whose task is to prepare the saints for the work of ministry and to build up the body of Christ.* (Ep 4:10-12)

The usual way to deal with that passage is to focus on each of the five ministry gifts listed by Paul, explaining what each ministry entails, and the place each has in the life and growth of the universal church. I could do the same. However, in this study I plan to approach the matter rather differently. Yet before doing so, let me at least state some basics about these five gifts of ministry – [52]

- The actual gift of Christ to his church are the *people* whom he has equipped to minister in their separate ways – *"He gave to his church (people who are) apostles, prophets, evangelists, shepherds, and teachers."* The *ministers* are the gift of Christ, not the *ministry*.
- Nonetheless, those ministers have an obligation to minister in the gift and calling that God has given to each of them. So there is no room for self-aggrandisement here, nor any kind of swelling hubris, but only a heart of humble and willing service offered

---

(52) More detailed comments on the five ascension-gift ministries can be found in several other books in the Vision College curriculum.

to Christ and to his church. Yet many times across history, possessors of one gift or another have been oppressors of the church rather than its servants. Those who possess a ministry gift should be deeply thankful to God for the privilege, and eager to serve the church in all humility. The church should be grateful to God for its ministers, and eager to honour them, encouraging and assisting them in their ministry.
- All five ministry gifts should still be functioning in the church. There is nowhere in the NT any suggestion that they were ever to cease prior to the return of Christ.
- It is improbable that all five would be present in any single church, but they should certainly be spread among the group of churches.
- **_Apostles_** are people who are gifted by God to plant churches, often with signs and wonders accompanying their ministry.
- **_Prophets_** are people gifted by God to forth-tell and foretell, being able to convey divine revelation to the church – yet always in agreement with scripture, and never presuming to control their hearers. That is, prophets should be heard with respect, but in the end the recipients of the oracles must remain free to choose how or even if they will respond.
- **_Evangelists_** are people who are gifted by God in winning people to faith in Christ, whether singly, in small groups, or in mass evangelism.
- **_Pastors_** are people who are gifted by God with a shepherd's heart, able to gather the congregation together and safely nurture them all the way from earth to glory.
- **_Teachers_** are people gifted by God to expound scripture truthfully, reliably, always keeping to good faith and adhering to sound doctrine. Note: there is some

ambiguity in the Greek text, which leaves open the possibility that *"shepherds and teachers"* may be seen as one ministry, not two. It is certainly true that all good pastors will have some capacity for teaching, and that all good teachers will have something of a pastor's heart. Otherwise, the pastor may be too sentimental, and the teacher too coldly intellectual. Nonetheless, it seems better to see them as separate functions.

Now I want to look at those ideas again, but under a different structure.

We have seen that just as the "members" of our physical bodies have different, distinct, and non-interchangeable functions, so each person in the "body" of Christ has a particular place and task. One way to summarise the various offices and ministries Christ has given to the Church is to place them under four headings – [53]

Evangelists – A Ministry of Witness

These are people who are gifted by God to share the gospel *effectively* with the unsaved. Notice the adverb! Any donkey can bray in a street, but that is not evangelism. People who truly are called by God to be evangelists are *effective* in their witness. That is, they don't merely make a noise, or pester people, or create a nuisance, they actually do *win* men and women to Christ.

So this, like any other, is a *specific* gift. There is no more reason to force every Christian to be an evangelist than there is to make them all apostles, prophets, pastors, teachers,

---

(53) The remainder of this chapter is similar to a chapter in my book *Building the Church God Wants*. I hope you will think that these ideas are worth repeating.

administrators, or anything else for which the Lord has neither chosen nor equipped them.

The local church then, instead of trying to bully everyone into soul-winning, should create opportunities for true evangelists to function at various levels – that is, some will be good at one-on-one evangelism, others at street witnessing, others at pulpit evangelism, some to small groups, others to large crowds. And some people are just not soul-winners in any sense. If they try they will fail, and probably do more harm than good.

I repeat the aphorism – *Nothing wins like winning, and nothing fails like failing!* Give people the sweet taste of success by giving them a task they are good at and they will be filled with zeal. Compel them to toil in fruitless and distasteful endeavour and they will swiftly fall away, disappointed, discouraged, and may lose all zeal for service.

There is, however, one form of witnessing that all Christians should find within their skill – *"Be ready always to give a good answer to anyone who asks you to explain the reasons for the hope that you have in Christ."* (1 Pe 3:15) That is a passive form of evangelism which anyone should be able to fulfil with joy and without embarrassment. But do remember Peter's qualifier – *"Whenever you respond to such questions, do so with gentleness and respect."* (vs. 16)

Shepherds – A Ministry of Nurture

These are people who are gifted by God with special qualities of compassion and empathy, along with a real ability to heal those who are hurting. Once again, not all have this gift, yet some leaders try to impose this task upon every believer. It is foolish. Some people, though not many, have the grace, love, and nurturing skills to welcome others into their homes, counsel them, and heal them. But other Christians have destroyed their families by trying to turn their homes into centres of nurture. Perhaps they themselves, or other members of the family, were unable emotionally, socially, spiritually, or culturally to cope with the pressures that were unavoidably created. Let those who have a shepherd's heart shepherd, and don't demand that people who lack caring skills become unhappy and ineffective nurturers.

Even among people who are gifted shepherds there are three kinds –

- Those who provide ***immediate*** care, but are not very helpful in a more extended relationship. These carers have amazing skills of empathy, being swiftly able to penetrate the camouflage people hide behind and almost at once perceive and enter into their true feelings. How quickly they discover the real (not the imagined) hurt that is destroying the other person! How effectively they begin to apply the healing balm of Christ to each wound! But they may be too invasive or too intense. They learn too much about their counselee too quickly; the people they are helping, though grateful, soon wish to establish some space away from the shepherd, to break the connection, and may even leave the church to do so.
- Those who provide ***short-term*** care, who are good at establishing a quick and deep relationship, who have an array of shepherding and counselling skills, especially those that enable a true rapport to develop between the shepherd and the counselee. A strong connection is established, rich in sympathy and warmly cooperative, that enables the therapist to bring his or her patient toward a full recovery. But these shepherds, too, can eventually inculcate anxiety or embarrassment in their counselees, so that people wish to create some distance between them.
- Those who provide ***long-term*** care, able to establish more or less permanent relationships with their counselees. Often too, these shepherds develop new

friendships slowly, but then the relationship tends to be lasting, deeply and firmly rooted, and able to withstand many shocks and pressures. They are able to apply gentle but effective healing to even stubborn problems, and to do so without trespassing too far into the privacy or personal space of the counselee. This is because the slow development of the relationship leads to the counselees revealing their problems themselves, rather than the shepherd using the more invasive techniques employed by short-term counsellors.

No doubt there are people who can provide all three kinds of shepherding, but in general they are not interchangeable. In any case, the leaders of a local church should be aware that –

- not everyone has a shepherd's heart, and it is foolish to demand that people who are not called or gifted for this function should try to do it.
- those who are called by God to be shepherds should be encouraged to fulfil their role in whichever way is best suited to their particular gifts.
- the local church should include every member in its nurture programme.

Exhorters – A Ministry of Words

These are people who are gifted by God to teach, exhort, reveal, prophesy, or intercede. They are vital to the wellbeing of the church, for *The Great Commission* commands us to make, not just *converts*, but *disciples*.

Like *Elihu* (Jb 32:17-22), exhorters – [54]

- yearn to bring people to maturity, and are never content to leave them undeveloped, falling short of the demands of true discipleship.
- have confidence in the power of words, and are usually reluctant to diminish the impact of their preaching or teaching by having an "altar call". They are seeking a long-term response to their words rather than immediate action. In this they differ from an evangelist, who is intent upon securing an immediate response to the claims of Christ. Evangelists thrive upon prompt decisions – indeed, many evangelists feel their strongest anointing when they embark on an altar call. But a teacher or exhorter prefers to plant the seed and then let time and the Spirit of God bring that seed to fruition. Hence, exhorters
- are satisfied by the act of speaking. Like Elihu, they are driven by a need to *"tell what they know"*. They are *"full of words"* and are compelled to speak them out and not stop until the message is fully conveyed. But having completed their task, they then have a wonderful sense of "relief", and are content to let their words do their work, without any further human interference. But exhorters
- will return to the theme if they do not gain a satisfactory response (33:1-2; 34:1-3; 36:1-2); they are not content to teach in vain, but rather will repeat the theme over and over until the hearers demonstrate that they have understood and will obey the word of the Lord. (2 Pe 1:12-15; 2 Pe 3:1; 1 Ti 4:6)

---

(54) I am not the inventor of the use of Elihu as the model of an exhorter. I first came across the idea some decades ago, but have long since lost all trace of the source.

So here is a ministry of <u>words</u>, which plainly belongs only to those whom the Lord has called and equipped for this task. It is a ministry close to the heart of Christ who was himself the Great Teacher and is and will always be the Logos, the eternal Word of God. To such people the church should give earnest heed.

Servants – A Ministry of Functions

These are people who serve the church in any of several practical rôles, which can be summarised under two kinds (1 Co 12:28) –

Administrators

These are people gifted by God to see the organisational needs of the church, and to devise plans that will enable it to achieve its goals. They may serve the whole church, or just a single department.

This is a vital ministry, which should be better recognised. Indeed, many growing churches have appointed an assistant pastor when what was needed was not someone to compete with the existing pastor, but an administrator. As a consequence, such churches have often lost their momentum or even suffered divisions when the two pastors began to wrestle for their place in the sun.

Helpers

That is, musicians, choir masters, secretaries, treasurers; and so on. These are not inferior roles; their improper use, as many have sadly discovered, can ruin the church. For example: treasurers who use no faith in handling the finances; musicians who merely play, but do not "prophecy" (1 Ch 25:1-8); deacons who lack compassion or sympathy for the people they manage; and so on.

By contrast, says Paul, those who use a servant role well *"acquire a good standing for themselves, along with great boldness in the faith that is in Christ Jesus"*. (1 Ti 3:13)

The importance to the local church of administrators and helpers is shown by the manner in which Paul places them right alongside apostles, prophets, teaches, miracle-workers, and healers! (1 Co 12:28)

Conclusions

These ministry gifts may overlap, although probably each person will be stronger in one function or ministry than any of the others.

They all function at various levels, from ministering to or serving just a handful of people to entire denominations and beyond.

They create a two-fold responsibility –

(1) The responsibility of the individual

Each local church member should know his or her proper place in the body, and have the courage and faith to commit themselves to that role.

(2) The responsibility of the church

Church leaders must believe that the church will function best if each member is released to serve God in his or her own way. Therefore, they should reverse the common practice, which is to decide on what programmes or departments the church needs, and then find people to fill them. Rather, begin with the *people*, and only then create programmes, activities, offices, and the like to match their skills and capacity. And establish any new function or field of service only when the needed personnel become available. *People* first; *programmes* second! Yet how often church leaders turn that about, sometimes with disastrous results.

The success of the church is assured if all of the people function within their own *"anointing"*. Therefore let each of us set ourselves to do just what God has called and gifted us to do, by faith releasing the power of the Holy Spirit into that task.

When all the people of God are set in their proper place in the local church, fulfilling their own calling, dependent upon God, surrendered to his will, trusting in the efficacy of his gifts to them, then that church truly will become the Body of Christ in its community, with Christ himself as its true Head.

Section Seven:

The Bride of Christ

Twenty:

Chosen by The Father

> *Give thanks always and for everything to God the Father in the name of our Lord Jesus Christ, submitting to one another out of reverence for Christ. Wives, submit to your own husbands, as to the Lord. For the husband is the head of the wife even as Christ is the head of the church, his body, and is himself its Saviour. Now as the church submits to Christ, so also wives should submit in everything to their husbands. Husbands, love your wives, as Christ loved the church and gave himself up for her. . . . In the same way husbands should love their wives as their own bodies. He who loves his wife loves himself. For no one ever hated his own flesh, but nourishes and cherishes it, just as Christ does the church, because we are members of his body. "Therefore a man shall leave his father and mother and hold fast to his wife, and the two shall become one flesh." This mystery is profound, and I am saying that it refers to Christ and the church.* (Ep 5:20-32, ESV)

Among the Greeks and Romans in the first century there was a low view of marriage. Wedding contracts were treated carelessly. They could be easily broken, and either party was free to dissolve a marriage at will. Records still exist of Roman women marrying and divorcing as many as 8 or 9 husbands, one after the other.

The Jews had a much higher conception. They saw *Genesis 1:28* as a command, and viewed marriage and procreation as a sacred duty. Thus their approach to marriage differed greatly from ours; for them it was much more a matter of obligation and law than of love. For example, compare with modern ideas this passage from the Mishnah –

> A wife must do the following for her husband: grind flour, bake bread, wash clothes, cook food, give suck to her child, make ready his bed, and work in wool. If she brought him one maidservant (from her father's house), she need not grind, or bake, or wash. If she brought two maidservants, she need not cook or give her child suck. If she brought three maidservants, she need not make ready his bed or work in wool. If four, she may sit all day and do nothing. (However) Rabbi Eliezer says: "Even if she brought one hundred maidservants he should force her to work in wool, for idleness leads to unchastity." (55)

Consider also this passage –

> Our modern concepts of marriage and of dating practices connected with "falling in love" make it difficult for us to comprehend the quite different approach that prevailed among the Israelites. For one thing, the prime mover in marriages in Palestine, whether in 1200 BC or 30 AD, was not a young man freely choosing a girl (and being accepted freely by her), without much reference, if any, to parents on either side. The prime mover was the father of a son of marrying age. Next most important was the father of the young woman. It was the duty of these fathers, and to a lesser extent their wives, to arrange the best possible marriages for their children after they had passed the time of puberty. Marriage was an agreement

---

(55) *Judaism*, edited by Arthur Hertzberg; George Braziller, New York, 1962; section on the "Torah".

between two heads of families, not between two individuals who were "in love". (56)

So, to understand what the Bible means when it talks about the Church as *"the Bride of Christ"*, you need to think, not like we do, but like they did. I will try to keep that primitive perspective, and then use it to explore the spiritual dynamics of our union with Christ.

An Arranged Marriage

The first thing to note is that our union with Christ is like an ancient "arranged marriage".

Remember that marriages in ancient Israel were arranged by parents; young couples seldom had freedom to choose their own spouse –

- See, for example *Matthew 22:2*, which actually means that the king had chosen a bride for his son, set the wedding date, and put on the marriage feast for his son.
- See also *Genesis 24:1-4*; and note that Isaac was 40 at the time, which was unusually old to be married, but it shows the degree of his submission to Abraham, in contrast, say, with Esau, who married a foreigner (Jacob, however, obeyed his parents).

So private courtship, as we understand it, was almost unknown; courting was done rather by the parents than by the prospective bride and groom –

---

(56) *Harper's Encyclopedia of Bible Life*; Harper & Row, NY; ed. by Madeleine S. and T. Lane Miller; 1978; pg. 98. This does not mean, of course, that romantic love was unknown among the Jews. A glance at Canticles will soon show that they were just as capable as we are of heights of adoration and of passion.

- It was thought that young people could not be trusted to make a sensible decision in this matter, so it was the task of parents to select suitable partners for their children.
- Of course, since most people lived in small villages or farming communities, the young people would seldom have been strangers to each other, and presumably parents would try to match a couple who were already known to get on well together.
- Nonetheless, the choice, and the decision, ultimately lay with the parents. (Cp. Ge 24; notice how Laban gave Rebekah to Isaac but also asked her if she were willing to wed him – vs. 51, 57-58).

The typical Israelite family had a restricted social circle, consisting of relatives, neighbours in the town or village, and a few clansmen living at a distance with whom contacts had been kept up. From this small world the father and mother of the prospective bridegroom surveyed the prospects for a fitting wife for their son. Once a likely wife had been identified – perhaps, but not essentially, one actually longed for by the son (e.g. Ge 34:4; Jg 14:2) – a question would be asked of the girl's father or guardian, and if no rebuff was encountered, negotiations were begun. Once the two fathers had agreed to the match, the young woman could do nothing but accept; after all, her father had authority to sell her into slavery if he wished. [57]

The parents no doubt tried to bring young people together who would be stable in their relationship, fruitful in childbearing, honourable in conduct, and who would sustain

---

(57) Miller; op. cit. pg 98,99.

the name and prosperity of their family in Israel. (58) Nor was the idea of romantic love entirely absent from ancient Israel –

- *Canticles* is a series of ballads designed for public performance, and sings the praises of young love and the joys of marriage.
- *Proverbs* tells about the mystery of a man with maid. (30:19)
- Despite his parents' objections, Samson courted Delilah, with whom he was well-pleased (Jg 14:7) – although in his case he would have done better to heed his parents!
- *Psalm 45* is commonly called an epithalamium, that is, an ode composed to be sung in honour of a bridal couple (especially the bride) on their wedding day. The king is said to be enthralled by the beauty of his bride (vs. 11), and the bride and her maidens enter his palace with immense joy and gladness (vs. 14-15). The psalm sparkles with life; it is a delighted celebration of a wedding that all expect to be happy and fruitful.

Other passages could be added, redolent of love, and what we would call romance. Nonetheless, they cannot alter the general pressure of that ancient society upon parents to control whom their children will marry. Thus –

- a father could refuse to give his consent (Ex 22:17).
- Hagar chose Ishmael's wife (Ge 21:21)
- Laban arranged the marriages of his two daughters (Ge 29:14-30; but romance was not altogether absent, for *"Jacob was in love with Rachel"*, vs. 18, 20).

---

(58) No greater shame or disaster could befall a Jewish family than for its name to be dishonoured, or, even worse, for the line to become extinct (cp. De 25:5-6; 29:20; Ps 41:5; 2 Sa 18:18; etc.).

- A wife could be purchased (Ru 4:10; Ho 3:2); or could be given to a man as a reward for some service rendered (Jg 1:12); and so on.

How does all this relate to us? Read on!

The Betrothal Period

The young couple were first betrothed to each other for a stated period, usually a year, and then the actual wedding occurred. [59]

Love was usually expected to grow **after** the couple were betrothed, not **before** they were promised to each other! If that seems too cold, consider this – the disastrous collapse of so many marriages in our society, both inside and outside the church, hardly commends our method above theirs!

Even where fervent love did _precede_ a marriage, as in the case of Jacob and Rachel, the father's will was still paramount. Hence the two young women (Leah and Rachel) had little say in the matter. Presumably many fathers did consider their child's wishes, yet it was not commonly thought important for the couple to "fall in love" with each other – that is, to grow deeply fond of each other, and to become essential to each other's happiness.

"Love" was defined more as an attitude of amiability and good will, displayed by a fear of God, by mutual obedience to his laws respecting married life, and by dwelling together in friendship and co-operation. If you suppose that this is Old Testament stuff, and not New Testament, consider *1 Timothy 5:14*, where Paul describes marriage in quite utilitarian terms. He plainly had scant notion of the romantic ideals

---

(59) For examples of this preliminary betrothal period, see De 20:7; 28:30.

that are so prevalent in our society [60] – or, he chose to ignore them.

Now these things are all a parable of our identity as the Bride of Christ. Too foolish to choose righteously by ourselves, we were drawn to Christ by the will and choice of the Father, against our own natural desire (Jn 6:44,65), and we have begun to love him truly only after our betrothal.

The Bride Price

An Israelite betrothal was established by the payment of a *"bride-price"*. Thus, David betrothed Michal for the price of 100 Philistine foreskins. (2 Sa 3:14) This bride-price was intended to compensate the bride's father for the loss of her services in the household. That is why it could be paid either in work (as Jacob did for Leah and Rachel), or in goods or coin. A common cash price was 50 shekels of silver, perhaps a week's wages.

In our case, the "bride price" was Jesus offering his own life at Calvary, so that by his blood he has bought us for himself.

The Jewish rabbis plucked a strange idea out of the name of Esau's bride, "Machalath" (*"forgiven"*). They argued from it that entrance into the married state would bring divine pardon of sin. [61] Whether or not that lady found grace I cannot say, but she certainly provides another parable for us – our union with Christ as his Bride has assuredly re-named us *Forgiven*, and it guarantees our entrance into his eternal Paradise!

---

(60) The verse, by the way, should probably read as some translations have it, "I want the younger widows to marry, to bear children, and to govern their households well . . ." Apparently Paul never considered the possibility of a young widow being so desolated at the loss of her "lover-husband" that marriage to another man might be unthinkable to her!

(61) Alfred Edersheim, The Life and Times of Jesus the Messiah, pg. 352.

You will realise from the above that a Jewish *betrothal* was more serious, more legally binding, than our *"engagement"* – which makes the courage of Mary even more remarkable. She risked being stoned to death when, despite her betrothal to Joseph, she accepted Gabriel's word and allowed the Infant to be conceived in her womb by the Holy Spirit! (Mt 1:18-19; Lu 1:26-38) Violation of the betrothal contract was treated as adultery and carried the same penalty: both guilty parties were to be stoned to death (De 22:23-24). [62]

The betrothal period had an important purpose – it allowed the couple to begin building their relationship before they were finally married, starting with friendship and (hopefully) advancing to love.

It was easier (though still difficult) to withdraw from a betrothal than from a marriage, so that a couple who disliked each other could, by mutual agreement, dissolve the contract before their union had been consummated. The bride-price would have to be returned, and there were other social stigmas and legal penalties attached to a broken betrothal.

Likewise, we must consider ourselves to be *"betrothed to one husband (Christ)"* (2 Co 11:2) There is in this idea both liberty and law –

- **_Liberty_**, because in this life we actually are free to renounce Christ and to abandon our "engagement" to him – although such a "breach of promise" will eventually incur a heavy penalty; [63] and
- **_Law_**, because although our final "wedding day" has not yet come, Christ is even now our *"husband"*, and

---

[62] Note that a much lesser penalty was exacted where there was no betrothal (vs. 28-29).

[63] Consider, for example, *Hebrews 6:4-6; 10:26-31*.

like all promised spouses, we owe certain duties to each other.

Those betrothal obligations will be taken up in our next two studies.

Twenty-one:

Betrothal Obligations – The Groom

Under the ancient custom, the future bride and groom owed the same duties to each other as in marriage, except the joy of their final union, which of course awaited their wedding day. Otherwise, they treated each other, and were treated by their neighbours, as if they were already married. This was demonstrated at the time of the betrothal, when the bridegroom, either personally or by deputy, handed to the bride a piece of money or a letter. In either case, it was expressly stated that the man thereby espoused the woman. From that moment, both parties were regarded, and treated in law (as to inheritance, adultery, the need of formal divorce, and so on), as a married couple, except that they were not yet permitted to live together. (64)

Toward his bride the groom had two sets of responsibilities: those required by _law_; and those required by _love_ –

Our Groom Fulfils His Debt of _Law_

An Israelite husband was legally bound to provide three things for his wife: *"food, clothing,* and *marital rights"* (65)

In practice, a true and good husband would extend those items to mean –

---

(64) Alfred Edersheim, *The Life and Times of Jesus the Messiah*; MacDonald Publishing Company, Virginia, reprint of the 1886 edition; Vol I, pg. 354.

(65) Exodus 21:10.

- *Nourishment* – not just bodily, but also mental, cultural, social, spiritual.
- *Protection* – not merely covering his wife's nakedness, but protecting her from all peril, guarding her from anything that might harm her.
- *Intimacy* – not just satisfying her physical desire, even less using her solely for his own carnal pleasure, but rather, bringing her close to his heart, making her part of his whole life, sharing all of himself with her.

Nonetheless, physical intimacy was reckoned to be the foundation of all that followed, and its importance was stressed in Jewish families. The rabbis had a very high sense of the necessity for sexual relations in a marriage; they saw in coitus far more than just a concession to the flesh; rather, they called it a symbol of the soul's union with God. Thus Rabbi Nahman wrote –

> The whole world depends on the holiness of the union between man and woman, for the world was created for the sake of God's glory and the essential revelation of his glory comes through the increase of mankind. Man must therefore sanctify himself in order to bring to the world holy people through whom God's glory will be increased . . . In truth all experiences of the Divine Unity and Holiness depend on the union between man and woman, for the ultimate meaning of this act is very lofty . . .

Therefore the rabbis laid down some quaint rules about the matter –

> Disciples of the sages, for purposes of study of the Torah, may stay away from their wives for thirty days without their consent. Labourers (whose work takes them to another city) may stay away for one week without their consent. The marital duty enjoined upon husbands by the Torah is as follows: every day for those who are unemployed; twice a week for labourers; once a week for

donkey-drivers (who lead caravans for short distances); once every thirty days for camel drivers; and once every six months for sailors. [66]

We may safely dispense with the precise demands of those rules, but not with the principal, that happy and continual intimacy is an essential component of a successful marriage.

Yet, for all its importance, no couple should expect too much from sex, for it must always remain a debtor to its promised joy; it must always offer more than it can give – which John Donne (1572?-1631) expressed in his poem *Farewell to Love* (lines 1-4, 16-20) –

> Whilst yet to prove,
> I thought there was some deity in love,
>   So I did reverence, and gave
> Worship ... (but)
>   Being had, enjoying it decays:
>   And thence,
> What before pleased them all, takes but one sense,
>   And that so lamely, as it leaves behind
> A kind of sorrowing dullness to the mind ...

Also, in his poem *Love's Alchemy* (stanza one), Donne wrote –

> Some that have deeper digged love's mine than I,
> Say, where his centric happiness doth lie:
>   I have loved, and got, and told,
> But should I love, get, tell, till I were old,
> I should not find that hidden mystery;
>   Oh, 'tis imposture all: ...
>   So, lovers dream a rich and long delight
> But get a winter-seeming summer's night.

---

(66) Hertzberg, op. cit.

As Philip Stanhope, the 4th earl of Chesterfield, [67] once said: "The pleasure is momentary, the position ridiculous, and the expense damnable!"

Well whatever may be the divine joys or earthy failures of human love-making, we can be absolutely certain of this: Christ will never fail to provide the three things that are incumbent upon every husband – *Nourishment, Protection, Intimacy* – not only in this life, but throughout eternity!

Our Groom Fulfils His Debt of *Love*

Sometimes parents would arrange a marriage at the behest of their son, with a maiden whom he had already come to love deeply. He had wooed and won her to himself, and now their betrothal would be a time of deepening love and growing intimacy, reaching toward the sweet consummation of their wedding day. He yearns after her as any young swain longs for his absent betrothed. He speaks to his parents and hers, and steps are taken toward a betrothal contract. Yet still he must wait.

In his series of love ballads, *Astrophel and Stella*, Sir Philip Sidney (1554-86) tells about a young man who is parted from his sweetheart. He meets a friend who has recently seen her, and on enquiring about her receives a laconic reply, "I left her well of late," upon which the swain protests –

> O God! Think you that satisfies my care?
> I would know whether she did sit or walk;
> How cloth'd; how waited on; sigh'd she, or smiled;
> Whereof, with whom, how often did she talk;
> With what pastimes Time's journey she beguiled;
> If her lips deign'd to sweeten my poor name?

---

(67) English politician, letter writer, and orator (1694-1773).

> Say all, and, all well said, still say the same!
>
> – #92, lines 8-14.

Thus Christ loved the Church, sought the Father's permission to woo and win her, betrothed her to himself, and now he is lavishing upon her the fulness of his love.

Note too that the gospel is always more a matter of God seeking us than of our seeking God. This is one of the first great revelations in the Bible – that when we were lost, ashamed, guilt-ridden, hiding in shadows, the Father came looking for us (Ge 3:8-10).

That is the gospel.

By contrast, "religion" reverses this, for "religion" is built around the idea of people looking for God, and in the process inventing a god (or gods) made in their own human likeness. But scripture insists that we are made in the image of God, who is ever seeking to bring us out of our hiding places and into fellowship with himself. And he does this, mind you, not because *he* needs us, but because *we* need him. Irenaeus (130?-202?) expressed it thus –

> God did not make the first man because he needed company, but because he wanted someone to whom he could show his generosity and love. God did not tell us to follow him because he needed our help but because he knew that serving him would make us whole. Our work for God – our service – adds nothing to his power or his achievements. He does not need anything we can give him, not even our obedience. But that does not mean that our work and service for him is meaningless or without value. God has promised to those who serve and follow him life, immortality, and eternal glory. These rewards

are specifically for servants who actually serve, and followers who actually follow. [68]

The character of the love of Christ for his Church is reflected by Hosea in three powerful *"I wills"* spoken by God to Israel –

> ***I will*** *betroth you to myself forever.* ***I will*** *betroth you to myself legally, in honesty, in steadfast love, and in kindness.* ***I will*** *betroth you to myself in fidelity. And then you will call me your Lord.* (Ho 2:19-20)

Paul, in the passage at the head of this chapter, plainly appropriates that betrothal pact between Yahweh and Israel and applies it to the union between Christ and his Church. Thus we may see in that ancient covenant a picture of what we may now expect from Christ – and they include the three things that are inherent in such a marriage – protection, nourishment, and intimacy.

Every Jewish maiden hoped that the man to whom she was betrothed would so honour her. I suppose, alas, that many of them were disappointed; yet Hosea does nothing more than describe the quality of love every man should have for his wife – honesty, kindness, integrity, and above all, unfailing love. It is a fine portrayal of what every woman has a right to expect from her husband. But whatever may be true in ordinary marriage, the Church may be sure that Christ will never betray her, for (in the words of Hosea) he swears to her a threefold oath –

---

(68) *Against Heresies*, Book IV, ch. 14.1. I am unsure of the source of the translation.

An Eternal Betrothal

"I will betroth you to myself for ever."

Every true bride has a right to the security of knowing that she can depend utterly upon the constancy of her husband, which is an idea that Sir Thomas Wyatt (1503-42) expressed in two of his *Songs (#67, #84)* –

> It is not time that can wear out
> With me that once is firmly set:
> While Nature keeps her course about
> My love from her no man can lett.
> Though never so sore they me threat,
> Yet am I hers, she may be sure,
> And shall be while that life doth dure.
>
> The time doth pass, yet shall not my love:
> Though I be far, always my heart is near.
> Though other change, yet will I not remove;
> Though other care not, yet love I will and fear;
> Though other hate, yet will I love my dear;
> Though other will of lightness say adieu,
> Yet will I be found steadfast and true.

If that is how it should be between a man and his wife, how much more should we trust that through all the vicissitudes of time and change, Christ will remain faithful! Oh! he will be true a thousand times more than even the truest of human love, which despite Shakespeare's fervent avowal often falls short of the ideal –

> Let me not to the marriage of true minds
> Admit impediments. Love is not love
> Which alters when it alteration finds,
> Or bends with the remover to remove.
> Ah, no! it is an ever-fixed mark
> That looks on tempests, and is never shaken;
> It is the star to every wand'ring bark,

> Whose worth's unknown, although his height be taken.
> Love's not Time's fool, though rosy lips and cheeks
> Within his bending sickle's compass come;
> Love alters not with his brief hours and weeks,
> But bears it out even to the edge of doom.
> > If this be error and upon me prov'd,
> > I never writ, nor no man ever lov'd.

What ravaging changes time wreaks upon us all! Face and form wither and shrink. Teeth fall out, eyes dim, hair vanishes, ears grow dull. Death creeps ever closer. Yet love, true love, good love, will remain unchanged despite the alterations wrought by the advancing years.

So too is the love of Christ for his Church. It will indeed bear out to the edge of doom, and beyond, into Paradise! The Church has a Husband whose vow is immutable; he will never change his mind!

A Lawful and Loving Betrothal

"I will betroth you to myself legally and honestly, with love and kindness."

This is *"lawful wedlock"* ("legally and honestly"), satisfying all legal requirements, conveying to the Bride her full share of her Husband's property, wealth, substance, and inheritance.

This is *"tender wedlock"* ("love and kindness"), with the Groom promising to: honour his Bride and treat her gently, patiently, tolerantly, and compassionately.

But here is something noteworthy:– the Hebrew word used by Hosea, translated as "love", is not the romantic term of our usage. Rather, it contains more the idea of an amiable fulfilment of all the obligations inherent in a social relationship – in this case, marriage – and it promises a generous fulfilment of all the terms of a covenant. Used in connection with a marriage contract, it was taken to include a promise never to default from one's word, always to show tender concern for a spouse's needs, along with a promise not to be narrowly confined by legalities, but to behave more like a friend than a mere contractual partner.

That is just how Christ intends to deal with us. He has chosen to betroth us to himself, and he will not default on anything that is inherent in our union with him. For everything that betrothal signifies we can trust him implicitly.

Thus, too, should be the quality of a true Christian marriage.

An Exclusive Betrothal

"I will betroth you to myself in fidelity."

This is to be a union "to the exclusion of all others"; it is a promise "to have and to hold" for ever! The Bride has no cause to fear that her Husband will turn his eye toward another, nor that his love for her will ever diminish in the slightest degree. Rather, she may suppose that throughout the long ages of their union together, their mutual love and joy will wax ever stronger! There is no room here, nor is there ever such room in true love, for unwarranted jealousy, which is indeed a bitterness in the soul –

> O how the pleasant airs of true love be
> Infected by those vapours which arise
> From out the noisome gulf which gaping lies
> Between the jaws of hellish Jealousy!
> A monster, other's harm, self-misery,
> Beauty's plague, Virtue's scourge, succour of lies,
> Who his own joy to his own hurt applies,
> And only cherish doth with injury;
> Who since he hath by Nature's special grace
> So piercing paws as spoil when they embrace,
> So nimble feet as stir still, though on thorns,
> So many eyes aye seeking their own woe,

> So ample ears as never good news know;
> Is it not evil that such a devil wants [69] horns? [70]

Note once again, though, that there is nothing in Hosea's oracle, nor in Paul's remarks on love and marriage, suggesting the kind of sentimental and romantic love that so engrosses popular attention in our time. Scripture (while never disdaining romance) sees marital love mostly in terms of friendship, goodwill, benevolence, integrity, faithfulness, patience, and compassion.

In this sense, the word used by Hosea is akin to the meaning of *agapé*, the word used in the NT to describe the quality of love God has for the world, Christ has for his Church, and the love we should have for each other. It is a love more of the will than of the heart; it rests more upon choice than upon emotion – although it *can* develop into a heart-felt love.

And what does the Groom ask of is Bride in return? Only one thing: *"you shall know the Lord."* That is –

- *"know"* him in the intimate sense of fulfilling her wifely duty of abandoning herself to the incoming presence of her husband; or,
- *"know"* him in the sense of ever more deeply discovering his character, learning his heart, understanding his ways, merging herself with him in mind and spirit, as well as in body.

More of what this means will comprise our next chapter.

---

(69) "Wants" here means "lacks".
(70) Sir Philip Sidney, *Astrophel and Stella*, Sec 78.

Twenty-two:

Betrothal Obligations – The Bride

Having looked at the obligations the Groom fulfils toward his Bride, we now look at the reverse, the Bride's debt to her Groom.

"In Palestine," said a rabbi long ago, "when a man marries they ask him: 'Finds or Founds?' 'Finds,' as it is said, 'He who finds a wife finds something good' (Pr 18:22). 'Found,' as it is said, 'I have found the woman whose heart is snares and nets, and whose hands are fetters more bitter than death' (Ec 7:26)." [71]

When Christ looks upon us, his Church, as his Betrothed Bride, I wonder what he calls us? "Finds" or "Founds"? That depends, I suppose, on how well we are fulfilling our part of the *betrothal contract*. That contract calls for two major qualities in us –

The Inward Quality of Virtue

I am jealous for you with a godly jealousy. I promised you to one husband, to Christ, so that I might present you as a pure virgin to him. But I am afraid that just as Eve was deceived by the serpent's cunning, your minds may somehow be led astray from your sincere and pure devotion to Christ. [72]

---

(71) Hertzberg, op. cit.; pg. 91.
(72) 2 Corinthians 11:2-3, NIV.

The final clause in that passage is an eloquent snippet of poetry, having both rhyme and rhythm. The Greek words for *"sincerity"* (pronounced "haplo-tetos") and *"purity"* (pronounced "hagno-tetos") rhyme exactly, which may have been a deliberate attempt by the apostle to elevate the Corinthians' view of their union with Christ. Adorning it with an aura of wedding poetry gave to this union a higher dignity, a nimbus of sanctity and nobility.

"Sincere . . . pure . . . devout" – those are the words Paul uses to describe the relationship we should have with Christ –

Sincere

The Greek word basically means "single", as something laid out flat, open to every eye, not having any folds or twists, not divided into parts. Perhaps a close English equivalent would be "frank", although this lacks the sense of simplicity that lies in the Greek. This "sincerity" was thought by the Greeks to express itself especially in a simple goodness that gives itself unreservedly in service, is bountiful in generosity, and singleminded in purpose. Thus should a wife think of her husband; thus should the Church serve Christ.

In English, the word "sincere" comes from two Latin words that mean "without decay" – that is, with no hidden rottenness, free of hypocritical pretence. Richard Baxter (1615-1691) caught the idea well in these lines –

> Though God be free, he works by instruments,
> And wisely fitteth them to his intents.
> A proud unhumbled preacher is unmeet
> To lay proud sinners at Christ's feet;
> So are the blind to tell men what God saith,
> And faithless men to propagate the faith:
> The dead are unfit means to raise the dead,
> And enemies to give the children bread;
> And utter strangers to the life to come
> Are not the best conductors to our home.

> They that never learned to live and die,
> Will scarcely teach it others feelingly.

So should be every preacher in the service of the Church; so should the Church be in her service for Christ; so should husbands be in their devotion to their wives, and wives to their husbands.

Pure

The Greek word is actually the noun form (*"a life of purity"*) of the adjective (*"pure"*); hence it is an *active* not a *passive* word; it describes not so much your *state* as your *behaviour*. It expresses the actions of one who is fully content, who seeks no other union, whose words and behaviour alike convey a single message of faithful affiliation, for whom even the thought of harlotry is abominable. So should Christian spouses be utterly true to each other; so should the Church be, in its union with Christ and in the worship it offers him.

Devotion

The Greek word is not related to the *"heart"* (that is, emotions and feelings), but rather to the *mind*. The idea is that every *thought* is made a captive of the Beloved; [73] every ambition is focussed in him; every desire is toward his honour. That, of course is a high ideal, and perhaps not realistic in today's world, where women, with much justice, demand an equal place in the sun with men. Yet in essence it remains a godly principle, and assuredly expresses how the Church should look upon its Master.

Yet we are not as modern as we profess to be. In ancient times, too, there were women who wished to cast off altogether the yokes that marriage placed upon them. They

---

(73) The same word ("thought") is found in *2 Corinthians 10:4-5*.

were so numerous that the Preacher felt obliged to speak about women with bitter cynicism –

> *I have searched diligently, trying to discover the reason for everything. So far my quest has failed. But at least I can say this – one true man in a thousand I have found; but I have not found even one true woman.* (Ec 7:27-28)

Sadly, there are still men today who think of women in the same sour manner. John Donne in the early 18th century put their gall into words –

> Go, and catch a falling star,
>   Get with child a mandrake root,
> Tell me, where all past years are,
>   Or who cleft the Devil's foot,
> Teach me to hear mermaids singing, ...
> Ride ten thousand days and nights,
>   Till age snow white hairs on thee,
> Thou, when thou return'st wilt tell me
> All strange wonders that befell thee,
>   And swear
>   No where
> Lives a woman true, and fair. (74)

Donne, who usually speaks about his ladies rapturously, must have been enduring a bad day when he penned those lines. I agree neither with his cynicism nor that of the Preacher, for there are many women whose virtue is secure and whose honour cannot be impugned. But even if the sneering contempt of the cynics were true, at least let the Church be true to Christ.

---

(74) Parts of stanzas one & two. The poem has a third stanza also, which morosely laments the supposed short-lived constancy of even the best of women.

As his Bride, she surely has no purpose higher than the joy of her Betrothed, no disposition to oppose his will, no affection to bestow elsewhere. She chooses him entirely and exclusively, which is entirely an act of her will, based on her sense of his excellence and merit.

Elizabeth Barrett Browning (1806-1861) beautifully captured this ideal of wifely love in lines that express her devotion to her much-adored husband, the poet Robert Browning –

> How do I love thee? Let me count the ways.
> I love thee to the depth and breadth and height
> My soul can reach, when feeling out of sight
> For the ends of Being and ideal Grace.
> I love thee to the level of every day's
> Most quiet need, by sun and candlelight.
> I love thee freely, as men strive for Right;
> I love thee purely, as they turn from Praise.
> I love thee with the passion put to use
> In my old griefs, and with my childhood's faith.
> I love thee with a love I seemed to lose
> With my lost saints. I love thee with the breath,
> Smiles, tears, of all my life! And if God choose,
> I shall but love thee better after death.

So should the Church, and each Christian, love Christ.

The Outward Quality of Service

Truly there is nothing new under the sun! Generation by generation the wheel goes round, and history repeats itself. So today, the biblical picture of the ideal wife (*Proverbs*

31:10-31) ⁽⁷⁵⁾ is again finding scope for fulfilment. After decades of being hidden behind the walls of a suburban residence, women are now again free to pursue interests outside the home. Like that wife whose price was *"far above rubies"* (KJV), the modern woman can engage in many enterprises both inside and outside the home – marketing, managing, manufacturing, merchandising, and so on. No wonder her husband was able to spend his days sitting with the elders, praising his wife's enterprise. She was making him rich!

Nevertheless, men have seldom known how to treat women, hence their status in society has often changed – equality in the first century, subjugation in the Dark Ages, exalted to Goddess in the Age of Chivalry, equality in the Reformation, fragile jewels in the Regency, suppression in the Victorian era, equality again in our time.

But we should learn from the way Christ views and treats the Church.

Observe again how the *Ideal Wife* in *Proverbs* was actively engaged in

- financial investments (vs. 11-12,18)
- buying and selling real estate (vs. 16)
- merchandising (vs. 13-14,18,24)
- market gardening/farming (vs. 16b-17)
- product development (vs. 13,19,22,24)
- domestic management (vs. 15)

---

(75) The poem is an acrostic built around the 22 letters of the Hebrew alphabet. The demands made by this artificial structure are the reason for the untidy sequence of the ideas it contains. The acrostic pattern was also a way of showing that the author considered this to be a full treatment of the subject; nothing was left out, everything was covered (as we would say) "from A to Z". We might also say, "This is the ABC of a perfect wife!"

- charity (vs. 20).

The Ideal Wife, we are told, will be –

- *thrifty* (vs. 12), but also *generous*, free of the vice of *parsimony* (vs. 21-22), not *harsh* (vs. 20)
- a tireless worker (vs. 15,17,19, 27), who prepares for every exigency, for both good days and evil (vs. 21,27)
- an example of wisdom, both in word and action, to all those around her (vs. 26), and in every way enlarging her husband's honour (vs. 23)
- good-humoured and pleasant, so that all who know her delight in her and praise her remarkable qualities (vs. 28-29).

Hardly surprising, to her family she is far more precious than a barrow-full of priceless jewels! (vs. 10)

Now I doubt that so much as one woman in all history has fully lived up to that ideal, although many have approached it. But it is a goal for which to aim, especially when we apply it to the Church as the Bride of Christ.

Notice, though, how little there is in that passage of the Hollywood ideal of romantic love as the only basis for a happy marriage! Solomon would have scorned such shallow notions –

- a pretty face is no substitute for practical sense (Pr 11:22)
- a shapely figure cannot compensate for a lack of sound discretion (Pr 31:30)
- the strength of this lady is neither earthy charm, nor physical beauty, but *"the fear of the Lord"*; prudence and piety are her chief attractions; these are the foundation of her prosperity and of her happiness
- her reward will be bountiful (vs. 31).

In these things we may discover two valuable ideas –

A Sensible View of Married Joy

Let us be wise enough to temper the unrealistic expectations of marital bliss that are encouraged by many writers of modern romances, as for example in the following passage –

> The pressure of her husband's lips upon hers was not only a rapture and a joy that was indescribable, but was part of everything that was beautiful and divine. She felt as if he gave her the light of Olympus and the glory and the wonder of the gods themselves. There was in his kiss the glowing radiance she had sensed in the sweetest poetry, which now seemed to be translated into something real and living. It drew her very soul from between her lips and made it a part of his. His kiss was so perfect, so sublime, that when he raised his head to look down at her, she gave a little murmur as if she could not bear him to let her go. The splendour and ecstasy of their love was so marvellous that it seemed to blend them together, yet not just with each other but with the infinite charm of heaven. She was utterly ravished by his love. . . . His lips were on hers again and he was kissing her fiercely, passionately, and more insistently than he had before. He felt her quiver against him and now he drew her body closer and closer still . . . To Loriana, it was as if heaven had poured its light upon her so that the sun enveloped her in a golden haze and the glory from it blinded her eyes and swept through her body like a burning flame. Then the light became more intense and the fire of it leaped within them both and carried them together across the starry heavens to the very heart of eternity. [76]

---

[76] The passage comes from no particular book, but is an amalgam taken from several popular novels.

Young people who approach marriage expecting their union always to carry them to such euphoric heights will be sadly disappointed. The reality is, they may never enjoy such transports of ecstasy. Married love is sweetly delightful, touched with spiritual mystery, a lot of fun, and sometimes truly rapturous. But it seldom, if ever, soars to the dazzling splendours that colour the pages of popular fiction.

A Parable of Christ and the Church

The qualities of the *Ideal Wife* and of the *Perfect Bridegroom* comprise a parable of the Church as the Bride of Christ, and of his relationship with her. She should love, honour, and serve him alone, while he loves her enough to give his life for her – not with a love of adoring admiration, but with a love based upon his own choice of her to be his Bride, a love of goodwill and of eternal fidelity, a love that promises for ever to be her Protector, Nourisher, and intimate Friend.

Twenty-three:

United For Ever

> Rabbi Hanilai said: A man who has no wife lives without joy, without blessing, without good. Without *joy*, for it is written, 'you and your household shall rejoice' (De 14:26). Without *blessing*, for it is written, 'that a blessing may rest upon your house' (Ez 44:30). Without *good*, as it is written, 'It is not good for man to be alone' (Ge 2:18) ...
>
> Rabbi Eleazar said: A man who has no wife is not even a man, as it is stated: 'Male and female God created them, and he named *them* "man"' (Ge 5:2) ... 'I will make man a helper to set over against him' (Ge 2:18). If he proves deserving, she will be a helper; if not, she will be against him. [77]

How much of those two passages do you suppose is applicable to the Church? Can it be said that even Christ discovers in his Betrothed, the Church, *"joy, blessing, and good"*? Can we be bold enough to say that Christ is not complete without the Church?

You can probably find an answer to those questions by thinking about what the situation would be in heaven if somehow the Church utterly failed, if the *"wedding day of the Lamb"* were never to come, if heaven were stripped of all its inhabitants save the Deity and the Angels! Would any laughter then be heard among the celestial spheres? [78]

---

(77) Hertzberg, op. cit. pg. 90-91.
(78) Compare Revelation 5:9-12; 19:6-9.

Thus we can glimpse the extraordinary importance the Church has in the plan of God. That importance is highlighted by the analogy of the Church as the Bride of Christ – for the Spirit takes the symbol of the highest possible union on earth to portray the union Christ will enjoy with his Church for ever in heaven.

Which brings us again to the passage that stands at the beginning of this series of studies on the Bride of Christ – Paul's wondrous description of marriage in *Ephesians 5:22-32*. There the apostle refers back to Genesis 2:24, and says that a *"profound mystery"* lies in in the way a man and a woman unite together. That earthly union, he says, is but a taste of the vastly sweeter union that Christ and the Church do and will enjoy (vs. 31-32).

There is enough here for a book! But let us pick up just a few important lessons about marriage, and about the Church –

The Destiny of the Church

Disordered sexual relationships, broken marriages, do great harm to the spiritual life of the Church. We cannot in the end sustain a higher relationship with Christ than we do with our neighbour, and especially with spouse and family. [79] Strong, loving, God-controlled marriages, make a strong church; when earthly unions within the church flourish, so does the union of the whole Church with Christ!

Know this – the spiritual dimension can never be fully eradicated from human sexuality; our sexual identity is ultimately not physical but spiritual. Any attempt to experience sex on a solely carnal level will bring devastating spiritual (if not also physical) consequences. The more deeply sexual relationships within marriage are seen as an

---

(79) Compare *1 John 2:9-11; 3:15-16*; and especially *4:20-21.*

act of worship, and the more fully they are infused with the Spirit of Christ, the sweeter will be the earthly joy, and the higher the spiritual attainment of the loving couple.

So, be done with the silly idea that there is something intrinsically unholy about marital intercourse. Away with the absurd notion that true spirituality is unattainable within marriage, that true holiness requires a hermit's desert solitude! Nothing of such folly exists in scripture. True, the Lord may call some men and women to a single life, [80] but for most people the purpose of God is marriage, and within that call they can reach the highest pinnacles the Lord has appointed.

So there is an inescapable link between strong, godly marriages, and the spiritual vitality of the Church. Illicit sexual behaviour among its people before, after, or outside of marriage, must inevitably harm the church. We are all one Body in Christ. If one part is ill, or suffering, or deficient, then the entire Body will hurt (1 Co 12:26).

The Duty of the Church

Paul expresses the duty of the Church in one word: *submission*. That is also the duty of a wife to her husband – see *Ephesians 5:22,24*.

Probably it is true to say that a husband desires nothing so much from his wife as that she should trust him and love him enough to abandon herself, all of herself, to him. Where true love exists, this is much more than a duty, it becomes the woman's own deepest desire and joy. Robert Browning

---

(80) *1 Corinthians 7:7; Matthew 19:10-11*. I am not saying of course, that marriage is mandatory, only that for most people it is the most desirable, most welcome, and most fruitful state, and that this is the will of God. But there may be times when it is wiser to postpone marriage, or not to marry at all (cp. 1 Co 7:25 ff.).

(whose own marriage to Elizabeth Barrett was idyllic) expressed this idea beautifully in his poem, *A Woman's Last Word*, of which the following are stanzas 6,7,8 – [81]

> Be a god and hold me with a charm!
> Be a man and fold me with thine arm!
> Teach me, only teach, Love! As I ought
> I will speak thy speech, Love, think thy thought –
> Meet, if thou require it, both demands,
> Laying flesh and spirit in thy hands.

Those lines provide a fine analogy of Christ, who is truly both God and Man, who teaches us both the language and deeds of love, and who asks us to abandon ourselves, flesh and spirit, to him.

However, note that Paul sets the submission a wife owes her husband against two backgrounds – **first,** the mutual submission all members of the church owe each other (vs. 21); and **second,** the sacrificial love of her husband. In other words, there is as much submission demanded of the husband to his wife, as of the wife to her husband. Nor can any husband rightly expect submission from his wife unless he too is willing both to submit himself to her, and to die for her!

These ideas raise two questions –

How Should a Man Submit to His Wife?

Think about such passages as *1 Peter 3:7* –

---

[81] This may seem a strange poem for a man to be writing, but perhaps it shows why their union was so successful – Browning had a deep understanding of his wife's aspirations and needs, and strove to fulfil them. She, in her turn, in the frame of her love, saw him as a god as well as a man, and gave herself to him without reserve.

> *You husbands must treat your wives with sympathy and care, showing her honour as the weaker partner. Remember that she is an heir with you of eternal life. If you don't do this, you may find that your prayers are being hindered.*

Consider also how he should uphold her authority over their children; how he should *never* demean her in public; how he should honour her as his own flesh (Ep 5:28-29); and the like; but above all, how he should treat her as Christ treats the Church (Ep 5:25), with compassion, forgiveness, patience, and unfailing kindness and love, even to a willingness to lay down his life for her.

What wife could resist giving her all to a husband who so loves her, and would die for her, as Christ has done for his Church? That grand old 5th century orator, St John Chrysostom, had this to say about it (in a sermon on *Ephesians 5*) –

> You have seen the measure of obedience that your wife should give you, hear now the measure of love you should show her. Would you have your wife always obedient to you, as the Church is to Christ? Take then the same kindly care of her as Christ takes for the Church. Yes, even if it becomes necessary for you to give your life for her, yes, and to be cut into ten thousand pieces, yes, and to accept and endure any suffering whatever – refuse it not . . . (Thus) by affection, by generosity, you will draw her to lay herself at your feet!

How Should a Woman Submit to Her Husband?

Consider such things as honouring him at all times, upholding his spiritual headship in the home, committing herself to his dream (without abandoning her own goals in life), teaching their children to respect and obey him, and the like. But perhaps the two greatest gifts she can give him are these –

- to yield herself utterly to him and to him alone in the whole world; and
- to be his true companion, sister, and friend. [82]

So let me ask you again to think about these things. How can the Church fulfil this "wifely" duty of submission to Christ? How did Christ establish his claim upon her submission? How does he maintain his right to the *continuing* submission of the Church? See *Ephesians 5:25-26*. Apply *verse 33* both to couples within your local church, and to the relationship between Christ and the Church.

How much more there is to say! But I will have to leave this subject here, yet with a closing admonition – let us all love each other as Christ loves us; and let us love Christ as a Bride adores her Husband, waiting for the glorious day of our final union with him at the magnificent wedding feast of the Lamb! (Re 19:7-9)

---

(82) In that lovely paean to married love, *Canticles*, it is notable that on several occasions the young swain refers to his sweetheart first as his "sister" and only after that, as his wife or his love (4:9, 10, 12; 5:1, 2). It suggests that their union was founded mostly upon deep friendship and unshakeable goodwill. Romantic love was certainly there, in plenty, but the true cement of their marriage was the bond of friendship.

Section Eight:

War in Heaven

Twenty-four:

A Declaration of War

Be strong in the Lord and in the power of his might. Put on the whole armour of God. You will then be able to stand against the wiles of the devil. We are not wrestling against flesh and blood, but against rulers, authorities, and the princes of darkness who control this present world – that is, against spiritual forces of evil in the heavenlies. (Ep 6:10-12)

The Conflict Revealed

"We wrestle" says the apostle. Here is a conflict in which we are all engaged. We cannot escape this bitter fight. Even if we have no love for war, even if we cry, "Truce, truce!" our enemy will yet press hard against us.

So fight we must, or else fall shamefully, without striking one blow in our own defence. Our foe will come to no terms. Though we may have little taste for furious warfare, we must continue to struggle until one of the combatants surrenders.

There is no room for indecision, no place for capitulation, no peace can be established except on the basis of the absolute rout of the enemy. We cannot hide away, hoping to wait out the battle and then emerge unscathed. Nor can we play on both sides; we cannot run with both fox and hound. Choose whose side you are on, and then make ready to fight!

In the terrible British Civil War in the 16th century, Robert Pierrepont, the earl of Kingston, tried to play it safe. He divided his sons into two groups, sent one group to fight for parliament and the other for the king, while he went into hiding. He declared, "When I take arms with the King against parliament, or with the parliament against the King, let a cannon-ball divide me between them." His policy failed, but his words came true. He was eventually obliged to take up arms for the king, but was captured by the Roundheads, and put on a small boat to be carried upriver. Royalists on the banks of the Humber fired on the boat, and a cannon ball cut the earl in half.

You must choose a side. Make sure it's the one that is sure to win!

Close Combat

This *"wrestling"* Paul spoke about is not the modern sort, which ends with a (usually) harmless fall, but it is like the ancient gladiatorial contests, which were to the death. With zeal that is unrelenting we must grapple with the foe, striving to throw him to the ground for the death blow; for if we do not destroy him, he will destroy us. Face to face, hard by our hated enemy, we must fight. There is no dodging this combat; we dare not run; to turn aside will only give our opponent his eagerly looked for advantage, and his fiery dart will swiftly strike home.

We have no alternative but to hold our ground courageously in Jesus' name -

> *"Stay on the alert at all times, stand fast in your faith, behave valiantly, be tough!"* (1 Co 16:13).

Continuing Combat

He did not say, *"We have wrestled,"* nor did he say, *"We will wrestle."* No, he used the present continuous tense, which could be translated, *"We are now wrestling."*

Each day the battle is being joined. No quarter can be asked, nor will any be given. Neither can we relax our vigilance. *"Watch!"* is the command; *"Wrestle!"* is the commission. You may have secured a fall against your adversary today, but tomorrow he will rise again, perhaps more fiercely, equipped with a new strategy, determined to secure your humiliation.

There can be no end to this contest until one of the belligerents is routed, all strength exhausted, all power broken. Which one will it be? That is for you to decide, for as we shall see, God has placed in our hands more than sufficient weapons, both of offence and defence, to smash our antagonist.

The Enemy Exposed

Who is this great foe who fights so relentlessly against us, who shows no mercy, who craves no mercy? The apostle describes him first negatively, and then positively -

Negatively – Our Foe is Not Flesh And Blood

In the battle of life that faces us it is easy to turn our attention to the wrong opponent. Who are you fighting? The government? The world? Your neighbour? Yourself? No, says the apostle, *"we are not fighting against flesh and blood"* – that is, not against any human enemy, nor against any merely human power. The danger does not spring from our own flesh, nor from the hands of other people.

"How can that be true?" you may protest. "Every day of my life the things I have to struggle against come either from within myself – from my own sin – or from the trials and troubles that other people force upon me. I don't know any enemy except my own corruption and the wickedness of the world around me!"

Sometimes it certainly does seem that we should mournfully admit that our greatest enemy is ourselves (cp. Ro 7:15,18-25). At other times, when we may be free from internal strife, our trouble seems to arise externally, from people who tempt or oppose us. Either way, we are prone to sigh that "flesh and blood" are surely our mortal foes!

But Paul insists that behind the *"flesh and blood"* peril we see so plainly, there is a stronger ruler, a power more vicious, a foul enemy dedicated to our destruction. Here is the *"thief"* of whom Jesus spoke (Jn 10:10), the vile robber who comes only *"to steal, to kill, and to destroy."*

Behind every visible, apparent, earthly enemy, then, there stands an unearthly one. People may strike us with their fists, they may mock us with their lips, our own bodies may be the instruments of our undoing – yet our struggle is not against these, but against the shadowy foe who stands behind all wickedness, inspiring it and driving it on.

Suppose it is your hand that longs to grasp another's goods, or your tongue that is addicted to deceitful talk, or your eye that is burning to gaze upon forbidden beauty – what shall you do? Do you fight against your own flesh? Should you mutilate your body, cutting off your hand, plucking out your eye? Not at all. Your fury must be directed against the enemy who provokes those lusts. Your remedy is not to tear off your own limbs. Your foe is *spiritual*, therefore *spiritual* surgery is what you need.

Perhaps where you work there is someone who hates you because you are a Christian. Should you return evil for evil? Should you contend with your neighbours, loathing those who despise you? Far from it. How futile to return abuse for abuse, blow for blow! That man or woman is not your real enemy, but the unseen one who is stoking in them the coals of hatred, and constantly fanning the blaze into a fiery inferno. So we learn then –

Positively – Our Foe is Spiritual

Your real antagonist in the battle of life is spiritual, that dark foe Satan, that fearful dragon, that roaring lion, the devil. Therefore your wrestling must be done on the spiritual plane, and your weapons will be spiritual weapons –

> *"The weapons of our warfare are not carnal. They are spiritual and they are mighty. By them, and with God's help, you can tear down every stronghold of the enemy."* (2 Co 10:4)

Now here is an important principle. In military combat a general will reckon himself remarkably fortunate if he can gain accurate information about his enemy's location, strength, resources, and strategy. Any commander who has gained such knowledge will be sure of winning the war, especially if he also knows that –

(1) he is secure in a better stronghold;
(2) he has greater weapons and resources;
(3) his strategy is wiser; and
(4) his weapons are invincible!

That is just the position we are in. Scripture shows us where the enemy is hiding, measures his total strength, and reveals his battle tactics. Then it also declares that–

- the ground upon which we stand is far better placed than that held by the enemy;
- our weapons are infinitely stronger than any possessed by our opponent; and
- we have been given a plan of attack that will unfailingly make us victors.

Why then do we see so many Christians miserably defeated? The cause is this – either they have underestimated the power of the enemy, and have foolishly turned their backs on him; or they have carelessly failed to arm themselves with the strong armour and the powerful weapons given them by the Lord.

To guard against any of us falling into such folly, let us learn just how strong the devil actually is, and how we should arm ourselves to ensure his utter defeat.

Satan the Secessionist

What is a "secessionist"? He is one who renounces his former allegiance, who breaks away from the established government and tries to form a separate state.

Thus, before Adam and Eve broke God's commandment there was a fall of the angels. A third part of the heavenly host, led by Satan, rebelled against God, were cast out of heaven, and set up their rival government on earth. These are now our foes, the implacable enemies of the entire human race, but especially of the Church, which is the one great hindrance to their design of world dominion. Therefore they maintain a dreadful hatred of Christian people, especially those who actively serve the Saviour Christ.

Let us search out the realm of his Satanic Majesty – [83]

The Prince and His Principality

Paul said (Ep 6:12) that *"We wrestle against ..."* –

Principalities

See what a great prince the devil is, how royal his dominion, how vast his sovereignty (cp. Mt 4:8-9). He is a lordly baron, having beneath him many other lesser princes, each master of his own domain, each ruling in pomp and pride, each haughty beyond telling, full of great swelling words and measureless conceit.

---

(83) No one knows (for scripture is silent on the matter) where the devil comes from, or what kind of being he is, but it is usually assumed that he is a fallen angel. The passages in Isaiah 14:12-14 (which refers primarily to the King of Babylon, vs. 4) and Ezekiel 28:13-18 (which refers primarily to the King of Tyre, vs. 2) are too figurative to give any sure answers to the question of Satan's origin and fall.

The subjects over whom mighty Satan reigns are innumerable, both demons and humans. All who are in his kingdom submit to his rule. His sway is undisputed. His multitudinous slaves yield obedience to his every behest. The lusts and pride of humans, the vanity and viciousness of demons – these are all his ready tools, and with them he rages against God and his saints, who alone block the advance of the realm of darkness.

Powers

Tremendous strength resides in the black prince and his vassals. He has even been given power and authority to wage war upon the saints, *and to conquer them*, and to dominate every race, nation, language, and tribe (Re 13:7). Paul summarises the devil's might in the one word of our heading: *"POWERS"*. What weapons, strength, and brutality it suggests! How can mere mortals ever withstand such an onrush of violence and force? (Re 12:12,17) Notice –

(1) His Nature

Satan is probably some kind of *angel*, which makes him vastly superior to any human in intellect and ability. He is *spiritual*, and is therefore not hindered by merely physical limitations. He has no need of sleep; day and night are alike to him; the passing of the years brings no diminishing of his powers.

(2) His Name

He is called – a *"strong man"* (Mt 12:29; Mk 3:27; Lu 11:21); a *"roaring lion"* (1 Pe 5:8); the *"god of this world"* (2 Co 4:4);

a *"murderer"* (Jn 8:44); the *"father of lies"* (Jn 8:44); a *"robber"* and a *"destroyer"* (Jn 10:10). [84]

(3) His Number

Who can tell the thousands who make up the army of the dread Lord of Darkness? Can anyone intercept the fearsome commands called by countless captains as they marshal their immense host for the fray? There are warriors enough in these battalions to wrestle against each godly pilgrim, with numberless reserves to replace the vanquished. How ferociously they beset each saint, with what awful difficulties they strew our way, how impossible it seems that any of us will reach the Heavenly City!

(4) His Nexus

There is a unity and common purpose among the minions of hell (cp. Mk 3:23-26; Lu 11:17-18), a connection between each demon, an interdependence among our individual foes. They are not bound together by love – such a gracious word is never heard on their lips, let alone felt in their hearts – but they cohere around their common hatred of God and their cruel intent to destroy his saints. In this they never waver nor are ever divided. By this they are welded together. Because of this they constantly flee to each other's aid, and counsel together to concoct yet greater wickedness against the Lord and his Church. (Ps 2:1-2)

(5) His Notoriety

Observe the ravages of evil across the ages. How well Satan has aroused the elemental forces of nature! How well he has caused great nations to fall upon each other in constant wars and bloodshed. What rivers of misery! What oceans of

---

(84) You will find a dramatic description of Satan under the guise of "Apollyon" in John Bunyan's Pilgrim's Progress).

despair! Then see what devastation he has wrought in the bodies and minds of people, through disease and famine, flood and fire, and disasters of every kind. [85] But most of all, what havoc he has wrought in the souls of men and women – what degradation, sin, and shame. How many multitudes there are who lie in *"the snare of the devil, and are taken captive by him whenever he pleases!"* (2 Ti 2:26).

Potentates

Satan and his hosts are the actual rulers of this world. Among millions of people his authority is uncontested. At his will and caprice, men and women are taken captive by sin and sickness, suffering and sorrow.

But while that ancient Dragon is indeed called *"the god of this world"* (whom the mass of humankind unwittingly worships), and *"the prince of this world"* (with men and women as his willing, if unknowing vassals), scripture nonetheless limits his control to *"this present dark age"* (Ep 6:12). From this we infer –

(1) Satan's power is limited in strength

Whatever might the devil has comes from God (who turns the Arch Fiend's wrath to his own glory), and his strength is able to stand only so long as the Lord permits. "So far and no further," saith the Lord, "thou mayest go!" (cp. Jb 1:12; 2:6; also Is 54:16-17). That last passage tells how a smith forges iron weapons and says that in the same way God, to fulfil his divine purpose, has created the Waster. But he exists under

---

(85) I do not mean to suggest that every disaster of every kind has a Satanic origin, except in an ultimate sense. Our planet has been disordered by human sin, of which the devil is the originator, so that we are now obliged to suffer many ills. But particular events may have purely natural causes, without any direct intervention by the powers of darkness. Satan can be blamed as the original source of sin and of all the sorrows it has caused. But he is not the immediate cause of every sin, sickness, loss, or hurt.

restraint. Final hurt to the people of God the Waster may not do; his venom cannot ultimately prevail over the saints.)

(2) *Satan's power is limited in time*

His rule will last only so long as this present dark age. With the dissolution of the world at the coming of Christ will come also the end of Satan's dominion.

(3) *Satan's power is limited in place*

His authority holds sway on the earth alone. He no longer has any voice in the heavenly counsels (Lu 10:18); he cannot touch those who have gone beyond this earthly sphere, nor those who walk in heavenly fellowship with Christ – of which I shall say more later.

(4) *Satan's power is limited in condition*

He has no lordship where the light of God prevails, nor where grace and truth reign supreme. The kingdom of the enemy holds sway only where there is darkness; that is, where the darkness of sin and ignorance prevail. Outside those boundaries his strength becomes a rope of sand.

Having said that we wrestle against *"principalities, powers, and potentates of darkness,"* Paul then adds that our warfare is also against the

Preternatural

That is, against *"superhuman forces of wickedness in the heavenlies"*. He means the enormous array of wicked spirits who inhabit the atmosphere, and the spiritual wickedness they provoke. They also wage war in the spiritual dimension. The enemy troops are demons who roam the planet, and they are exceedingly evil, seeking only to do evil and never good.

Because they are spirits, they are also extremely cunning and so gain great advantage over unwary men and women. Should we then fear them? No, for like us they too are finite, limited both in time and space. They share with us the infirmity of being restrained by the boundaries of their own created nature. They cannot escape the atmospheric realm in which they are presently confined by the decree of the Almighty. They cannot transcend the laws of their own being. They cannot escape the confines of the will of God. They can do only what he permits; they cannot do what he forbids.

They are also under the severe sentence of God, waiting with incessant trembling for the hour of judgment, when their iniquity will be sternly punished (Ja 2:19).

Paul adds a further dimension to the nature of our Enemy, when he calls him by a fifth name and talks about *"the fiery darts of the Wicked One"* (Ep 6:16). Notice –

(1) The Evil Character of Satan

The Greek word is *poneros*; it describes someone who is corrupt in character and evil in action; it holds the idea both of moral decay and of vile behaviour. One of my Greek dictionaries sums it up in an old English word, "facinorous", which means "atrociously wicked". Thus in Satan nothing remains that is good or noble. His every action is toward ruin; he intends only to hurt; his influence can bring only harm; whatever he sets his hand to results in calamity for men and women. The belch of this fiery dragon brings only scorching misery; his glittering promises are all lies; his offers of health and happiness are delusions; he can do no other than trade in falsehood and death.

But *poneros* goes beyond a description of what Satan is and what he does; it describes also the evil that is done to him. For in addition to the meanings given above, *poneros* carries the senses of "diseased, guilty, derelict." Which leads on to the idea of –

(2) *The Fatal Weakness of Satan*

Vicious though our enemy is, we observe that a mortal wound is constantly sapping his strength. He is eaten by a foul cancer, wracked by illness, bearing the marks of increasing dereliction.

Do you wonder at that? Look at yourself. What is it that weakens your own spiritual strength and saps your vitality? Is it not sin? If you sow corruption, do you not reap corruption? (Ga 6:8). So it is that the increasing atrocities of Satan, his abounding wickedness, are the very things that are crumbling his might and decaying his strength.

More than this, in his evil the Evil One has made himself the implacable enemy of all godliness. Yet only in righteousness can lasting virility be found. That is why the humblest saint who lives godly in Christ is vastly superior to the kingdom of darkness in strength. In Satan's appalling *wickedness* lies his overwhelming *weakness*.

If the devil is emaciated, what then sustains him? Like a man who exists on drugs, or who is inflamed by alcohol, so Satan is sustained and energised by his insatiable hatred and his terrible wrath (Re 12:12). But only a short time is left to him. For just as the false impulse of a drug swiftly wanes, so the vigour of the devil's anger must soon be exhausted. Soon all his force will be spent, and he will collapse, quivering and despoiled, beneath the justice of God. Great as the devil's anger may be, it is yet surpassed by the inexhaustible fury of the Son of God who will crush him underfoot (Is 63:5) as a wine-treader crushes grapes.

So the indignation of the Almighty burns hot against the Wicked One, and the righteousness of the saints stands invincible against him. Therefore press strongly upon him O ye saints, for soon the God of heaven will sorely bruise him beneath your feet! (Ro 16:20)

However, lest we should become careless, we are reminded that our enemy still has strength enough to hurl his fiery darts against us! This we shall consider in its place; but now let us look at the seat of the devil's dominion –

The Enemy and His Environment

He is located, says Paul, *"in the heavenlies"*, which means –

The Atmospheric Heavens Above Us

The physical location of Satan and his hordes is, at present, the atmosphere of this Earth. The Lake of Fire, the place of his eternal torment, has not yet been prepared by God. (Ep 2:2; Re 12:9-12; 20:10)

The Spiritual Realm Around Us

Mark again that our wrestling is with Satan for heavenly issues, not earthly. We are contending for spiritual victory, not for worldly triumph. The saints may be poor, and hunted, and persecuted, on earth, yet still gloriously victorious in the heavenlies. (Ro 8:36-37; He 10:32-34; 11:35b-39a) The outcome of this conflict is settled in God's heaven, not on this planet. Hence the one all-consuming purpose of our foe is to obstruct our communion with God, to block our fellowship with Christ. The Evil One labours incessantly to break down our spiritual experience, to destroy our heavenly joy, to deface the likeness of Christ in our lives. Whatever means he may use, those are always his wicked ends.

Therefore we must remain continually vigilant (1 Pe 5:8-11), for the way to heaven is laid down through many difficulties and constant opposition. Only such as are God's true heroes will dare to fight, to go forward, and to win. For cowards there remains only the lake of fire (Re 21:8). But for the brave victors the rewards are splendid beyond all telling! (Re 21:1-7; 19:5-9; etc.)

Twenty-five:

The Armour of God

Plutarch tells this story about the young Julius Caesar –

After a short stay in Bithynia, and while he was sailing back to Rome, Julius Caesar was taken prisoner by some pirates. At that time, the pirates had large fleets of ships and countless smaller vessels, and they infested the seas everywhere.

For his ransom, Caesar's captors demanded twenty talents, [86] but he mocked them for not understanding the value of their prisoner, and instead offered to give them fifty talents. Messengers were sent off to several places to raise the money, and Caesar had to wait for their return. In the meantime, he found himself among a set of the most bloodthirsty people in the world, the Cilicians, with only one friend and two servants to attend him. Yet he made so little of the pirates, that when he had a mind to sleep, he would send them an order to make no noise. For thirty-eight days, with all the freedom in the world, he amused himself with joining in their exercises and games, as if they had not been his jailors, but his servants. He wrote verses and speeches, and made them his auditors, and those who did not admire them, he called to their faces illiterate and barbarous, and would often, in raillery, threaten to hang them. They were greatly taken with this, and attributed his free talking to a kind of simplicity and boyish playfulness (he was not yet 25 years

---

(86) That is, in total, about 600 kilograms, or 1400 pounds, of silver.

of age). As soon as his ransom was come from Miletus, he paid it, and was discharged, and proceeded at once to man some ships at the port of Miletus, and went in pursuit of the pirates, whom he surprised with their ships still stationed at the island, and took most of them. Their money he made his prize, and the men he secured in prison until he ordered them to be taken out and crucified. He had indeed often threatened them with that very punishment while he was in their hands, and they little dreamed he was in earnest. [87]

Since he showed such authority, daring, and swift, ruthless action at such a young age, it is not surprising that Caesar went on to become master of Rome and to make himself master of an empire! And while I hope that none of my readers aspire to be tyrants, the young Caesar certainly sets an example of the kind of serenity, assurance in every situation, and courage that should be part of every Christian's character. For, as we have seen, we too are called to shake off our captivity and to wage total war against a horde of pirates –

> *"Our real fight is not with other people, but against ... the superhuman forces of evil in the heavenlies!"* (Ep 6:12)

Among all the statements Paul makes about *"the heavenlies"* that is perhaps the most astonishing. There are *"superhuman forces of evil"* in the heavenlies, against which we must *"wrestle"*! We learn the truth, perhaps not a happy one, that both our *wealth* and our *warfare* are in the heavenlies,

---

(87) Plutarch, *Lives of the Noble Greeks and Romans*, "Caesar". Abbreviated and modified from the translation by John Dryden (17th century). Some ten years later the Romans marshalled a large fleet, attacked every pirate stronghold they could find, and effectively purged the Mediterranean of piracy for the next 400 years.

and if we hope to possess the former, we cannot avoid the latter.

Indeed, here is a fundamental principle: *nothing happens on earth until it first happens in heaven*. It is a law of God – *first* the spiritual, then the natural. [88] Establish victory in the heavenlies, and earthly triumph must follow. Prosperity on earth depends upon how well we are prospering in the heavenlies. (3 Jn 2) For that reason, all the weapons of our warfare are *spiritual* –

> *Put on the whole armour of God so that you will be able to defend yourself against every attack. You must always stand firm, with the belt of truth fastened around you, and wearing the breastplate of righteousness. On your feet put the gospel of peace, so that you will always be able to stand fast. Never let go of the shield of faith, for by it you can extinguish every burning arrow the evil one shoots at you. Put on the helmet of salvation, and firmly grip the sword of the Spirit, which is the word of God.* (Ep 6:13-17)

Here is something rare in scripture – twice in three verses Paul repeats this command, **"Put on the whole armour of God!"** (11,13). This then is no small matter, but something that demands our serious attention. What is this "armour"? How do we "put it on"?

You will notice that five of the pieces of armour are for *defensive* action (the belt, the breastplate, the greaves, the shield, the helmet), and one is for *offensive* action (the sword).

We may here briefly glean two things. **First**, that we should not always be on the defensive, but must set to against the

---

(88) Before you rejoice because you have caught me in an error, I know what Paul says in 1 Co 15:46; but the context is different!

enemy, mounting our own attack against his ramparts. **Second**, much of our effort must nonetheless be devoted to defending ourselves against the adversary's onslaughts.

Notice the emphasis Paul places upon *"standing fast"* against the enemy, and *"quenching"* the burning arrows of the enemy. Both terms are defensive. Thus the main purpose of the armour is to protect each warrior who wears it. Yet neither can we forget that we are protected only to take up the sword safely and to launch an attack upon the enemy. So we are called both to prevent our own defeat and then to ensure the defeat of our satanic opponent.

The Belt of Truth

"Fasten the belt of truth around your waist"

The "belt" was a strong leather strap that was buckled around the soldier's waist. It was worn to brace the body and to bind the warrior's armour together. It enhanced his strength and made his armour secure.

Among orientals, a similar girdle was used to gather up and clasp together their long robes, thus freeing the wearer for more vigorous exertion, such as running or fighting. Hence the Jewish phrase *"gird up your loins"* became a synonym for "get ready for action" (cp. Lu 12:35; 1 Pe 1:13).

It shows that we should never relax our vigilance, but day by day stay girded for battle, ready at a moment's notice to wage war, equipped with the strength and stamina that *"truth"* provides. What is this *"belt of truth"*?

Paul tells us that this is the rôle of the word of God in our daily lives. It binds everything together, it gives us protection, it fits us for battle. Without the belt, the warrior's armour would not only be made ineffective, unable to protect him, but it would actually hinder his freedom of movement, crippling his ability to fight. The belt gave his armour its cohesion and made its strength useful.

So are we. Unless we wrap the word of God around ourselves, reading it regularly, meditating in it, absorbing it, we too will find our defences flapping around uselessly. The enemy will have little difficulty inflicting many wounds, perhaps even one that is fatal. But girt around with the belt of truth, how impenetrable our armour will be, how strong it will make us!

So, heed the psalmist's advice, and meditate in the word of God day and night! (1:1-3). He says that such people will succeed in everything they do! They will prosper and be fruitful! How happy they will be!

About this *"belt of truth"* we may also say that it is built by –

Sincerity of Heart

The silliest thing Satan ever did was to rebel against truth and make himself the father of lies (Jn 8:44b). For that folly he was cast out of heaven; for that stupidity he will be consumed in the lake of fire.

The silliest thing a Christian can do is to suppose that it is possible to defeat the devil while embracing a lie, which makes one an ally of the dark hordes.

Those who would stand against Satan must be girded about with honesty; they must set themselves to act justly, to live uprightly, and to deal fairly with others (Ro 12:17). A sincere, gracious, unfeigned, and trustworthy life has great beauty in the sight heaven and earth, and is garbed with unconquerable strength. But hypocrisy is horrible. Deceit and untruth are detested alike by our good God and by good people. Yet there are many Christians who are not what they seem to be. Outwardly they appear righteous; inwardly they are full of corruption. Feigning to be what they are not, they are vulnerable to the snares of the devil and to the rebuke of the Lord.

How can such people hope for real happiness? They pretend to godliness, but their real character is far removed from the holy way. How can they resist the enemy? They assume an appearance of piety and virtue, but true religion is unknown to them. How can they triumph in life? They have abandoned the way of truth and allowed malice to fill their hearts. Their overthrow is inevitable.

But people whose hearts are sincere, whose life is genuine and free from sham, have a strong guard against sin. Even if temptation should suddenly overwhelm them, being sincere in faith they are ready quickly to repent and to be quickly rescued from their wrongdoing. Then being upright they guide themselves onward with more care, taking pains to avoid another slip.

Thus truthfulness of character is a support and comfort in every trial, a bracing girdle around the soul.

Soundness of Doctrine

We should labour to become established in sound doctrine. Only those who have rightly established what they most firmly believe can withstand the fierce assaults of the enemy. Scripture itself urges us to become fully acquainted with the truth. Again and again we read solemn warnings against false teachers; over and over the perils of wrong doctrine are stated.

Concerning sound doctrine see, for example, *Proverbs 4:1-4; Titus 2:6-8; 2 Timothy 3:14-17*; etc; and concerning false teachers see *Galatians 1:8-9; Colossians 2:8; 1 Timothy 6:3-4; Titus 1:11*; etc.

So a vital part of putting on the full armour of God consists not only of meditating in the word of God, day and night (Ps 1:1-3), but also of thoroughly grasping the great concepts of our faith. There is no substitute for becoming deeply rooted in the truths of the gospel. There can be no hope of lasting victory without at least some grasp of sound doctrine.

An example of poor doctrine in our time is the crazy practice of standing on top of a hill, turning to the various points of the compass, and shouting loud commands against the demons that are thought to rule the land below. The idea is that each district is controlled by a group of territorial spirits, and that we have been commissioned by Christ to exert dominion over them. This is best done by facing north, south, west and east, while demanding that all the demons below yield to the speaker's authority. Only after each territorial demon has been subdued and driven away, so these foolish teachers claim, can there be any hope of the church succeeding in its mission of winning the lost, healing the sick, and building the kingdom of God.

The proponents of this ridiculous practice also claim that it is the best way to wage spiritual warfare. I think it is probably the worst. Where is there any substantive biblical support for such bizarre behaviour? Where does Christ command it? Where did any apostle do any such silly thing? It smacks more of superstition than true faith. I think its practitioners simply make themselves vulnerable to delusion and to possible serious harm. At best it is absurd. At worst it is downright dangerous.

Demons are indeed real, and we are certainly called to wage war against them. But make sure to keep within the boundaries of scripture, of sound doctrine, and of good practice, following the example of Jesus and of the apostles.

The Breastplate of Righteousness

"Put on the breastplate of righteousness."

This was perhaps the most important part of the soldier's defensive armour, for it sheltered the heart and other vital organs, where a wound would be fatal. Thus no Christian can survive the battle without righteousness, for this is our only breastplate. Without it we are vulnerable, standing naked before the enemy's dart. Never doubt that he will cruelly press home his advantage upon the defenceless soul and soon have it lying bleeding at his feet.

About this righteousness, we may say that it is –

Righteousness Imputed

Let us never suppose that we can build any righteousness of our own that will be acceptable to God (cp. Ro 10:2-4). We are either made fully righteous by the gift of God to us in Christ or we shall never be righteous at all (2 Co 5:21; Ga 2:16; Ph 3:8-9). The gospel calls us to abandon all righteousness of our own and to find absolute satisfaction (as God himself does) in the imputed righteousness of Christ (Ro 4:6,11,22-24). Hold firmly to that breastplate, and nothing will be able finally to strip you of your victory. Let go of it, or worse, try to replace with some good work of your own (which at best, as Isaiah said, can be only a tattered rag, far removed from burnished steel), and you will be like a soldier going naked into combat against a fully armed foe.

Nonetheless, having stated our confidence in the work of Christ, I want to focus here on the other side of the coin, the idea expressed by James -

> *Do I hear you saying, "One person chooses faith, but another prefers action"? Here is my reply: "Try to show me this faith-without-action you keep on talking about, and I will at once by my actions demonstrate to you my faith!" ... Do you really have to be told that faith without action is false? How can you be so stupid? Could our father Abraham have been justified in God's sight if he had not shown his faith by offering his son Isaac upon the altar? No! Plainly, his faith was both at work in his action and also perfected by it. ... So then, it is not by faith alone but also by your actions that you will be*

justified; ... for just as a body without any breath in it will be pronounced dead, so too faith separated from action is dead." (2:14-26)

So then, imputed righteousness remains incomplete unless it is also –

Righteousness Outworked

There is no room in Christian life for a merely passive righteousness. Rather, ours must be an aggressive righteousness, full of zeal for God; righteousness that we wear openly; righteousness that makes us fit warriors for God. This is a righteousness that shows itself in godly living, in outward holiness; it is a righteousness that is fastened and held to us by the strong girdle of truth. Without it we are undone. With it we are invincible.

Even Shakespeare recognised this, and made one of his characters say –

> What stronger breastplate than a heart untainted! Thrice is he armed that hath his quarrel just; and he but naked, though locked up in steel, whose conscience with injustice is corrupted. [89]

Let us learn then -

- It is God's design, in giving us Christ, to make us holy, not to provide a licence for sin.
- It is also God's decree that only in holiness shall we be able to stand against the onslaughts of Satan.
- And unless we do stand against the devil in holiness we shall by no means gain heaven, for *"without holiness no one will see the Lord."* (He 12:14)

---

[89] *King Henry VI*, Part II, III, ii, 232.

What is holiness? The basic meaning of the word is "difference" or "separation". We may live *in* the world, but we must always be different *from* the world. We have a different standard, a different goal, a different reward. Our aim is not so much to stand well in the eyes of people but to stand well in the eyes of the angels. If that is your commitment then everything else will naturally fall into its right place in your life.

In all his striving against you, the devil's design is to move you away from righteousness, to make you unholy. Whatever burning javelin he hurls against you, whether temptation, persecution, disease, poverty, trouble at home or work, or any other trial, his real target is always your soul. He aims to cause you, by word or deed, to blaspheme the name of God.

Opposed to this mischief of Satan see the eminent desirability of righteousness, which brings strength in prayer (1 Jn 3:21), and shows that we have an unbreakable grip upon the inheritance of God. Iniquity saps the vitality of the soul; but outworked righteousness makes a believer bold as a lion (Pr 28:1).

All this raises a question – "How can I know if I am wearing the breastplate of righteousness?" You will know that you are clad with this impenetrable armour

- **_If you are striving to avoid even the appearance of sin._**

It is impossible in this life, of course, to be entirely free of all sin (1 Jn 1:8). Nonetheless, every Christian is expected to shake off as much sin as possible. For the rest, it is enough that we be found sincerely and earnestly warring against whatever fault shows itself from time to time.

- ***If you are steadfastly unwilling to capitulate to sin.***

Despite the continuing presence of sin, any true saint yearns to be rid of it all, and is never so glad as when one strong vice or another is finally banished. Do not forget though that our striving, to be effective, must be with a right motive (that we loathe sin because it is hateful to God), and with a right goal (not our praise but the glory of God).

- ***If you are careful not to become proud of your holiness.***

Do you see someone who is vainglorious about some victory over the devil? Then watch for his or her inevitable fall (1 Co 10:12; 15:57; Pr 10:8; 16:18). The true saint is humbly thankful to God for any triumph, great or small, and eager to give glory only to him for every attainment.

- ***If you have a deep love for the Church and the saints.***

Any person truly clad in righteousness will possess also a fervent desire to serve the Church. Those who shun public assemblies of the people of God can hardly claim to be numbered amongst the saints who are keeping faithful station on the battle field (He 10:25). Active participation in a local church and fruitful involvement in its worship, work, and witness, are the most effective ways to wage war for the Lord of the Church against the powers of darkness.

- ***If you are diligent in your secular responsibilities.***

True saints do all things inside and outside the Church as to the Lord (Cl 3:22-24; Ep 6:5-8). If they have a job in the secular world then they render whatever is right and honest to their employers, as if they were working for Christ himself. We must deal equally and fairly with everyone, without respect of person, but out of love for the Lord.

- ***If you are loving, gracious, and considerate at home.***

Who can admire the man who is courteous toward women in general, but rude to his own wife? What shall we say about people whose behaviour in the outside world is beyond reproach, but at home they are harsh, selfish, violent, abusive, and the like? Shall we praise the woman who is tender toward others, but careless and slovenly in her duty to her family? "Charity," the old proverb rightly says, "begins at home." If it is not found there, it has little value anywhere else.

Above all, you will know that you are wearing the breastplate of righteousness if you trust in Christ, and Christ alone, to make you acceptable in the sight of God. You have probably sung, or at least heard, this hymn; but have you ever truly reflected upon what it says –

> My hope is built on nothing less
> Than Jesus' blood and righteousness;
> I dare not trust the sweetest frame,
> But wholly lean on Jesus' name.
> *On Christ, the solid Rock, I stand;*
> *All other ground is sinking sand.* [90]

By the evidence of such things we may know that *"the breastplate of righteousness"* is firmly girded around us, and that we are well-defended against a barrage of satanic barbs.

---

(90) Edward Mote (1797-1874). He was an English Baptist pastor, so well-liked by his congregation, that they offered to give him the church building (so that he could collect its pew rents). He replied, "I do not want the chapel, I only want the pulpit; and when I cease to preach Christ, then turn me out of that."

The Greaves

"Wear on your feet the gospel of peace so that you will always be able to stand firm."

Here Paul refers to an armoured sandal combined with a metal plate, designed to protect both the warrior's feet and his legs below the knees. They were known as "greaves", and they are mentioned in the description of Goliath's armour (1 Sa 17:5-7). Greaves shielded the soldier's feet and legs from the traps and sharpened sticks that were often laid in his path, and they braced his ankles, enabling him to turn swiftly without twisting or spraining them. The sandals were usually made with heavy, rough, cleated soles, to prevent the soldier from slipping on steep or muddy ground. The upper parts could be crafted out of thick leather, or from bronze or copper.

"The gospel of peace," says Paul, fulfils the function of greaves in our spiritual warfare. He means that the gospel provides the only sure footing in this world; it is the one fundamental principle, the one true philosophy, upon which we may build a peaceful life. Only by the gospel can we pick our way safely through the slippery maze of life; upon it alone can we stand unmoved by the buffeting winds of time and chance. Nothing else can ward off the troubling pricks of conscience, nor hold our feet from stumbling upon the wounding snares of sin.

In connection with the greaves, Paul uses two strong words, a *noun* and a *verb* –

Noun – *"Peace"*

He calls the good news *"the gospel of peace"*, which means –

- **_Peace with God_**. (Ro 5:1; Cl 1:20)

Until the day Christ took hold of us and we took hold of Christ we were bitter enemies of God (Ro 5:8-10). All that we did, all that we said, went against the purpose of the Father. But now everything is changed. God is no longer at war with us. By the blood of his Son the wrath of the law against our sin has been placated, righteousness has been vindicated, peace has been declared, and we are now welcomed as the Father's children and friends.

It follows then, if we have peace with God and know that we have it, we will take no fright at war with Satan, for greater is he who is for us than they who are with our foe! Chains of peace that cannot be severed bind us to our God and all his strength is ours.

Let us then spurn any allegiance to sin. Irrevocably change sides,. Take up the weapons of righteousness, and knowing that God is your ally, fall heavily upon your former master, the devil, and rout him in Jesus' name!

- ***Peace with our neighbour***. (Ep 2:14,19; 4:3)

If God has reconciled us to himself in Christ, he has also reconciled us to our neighbours, which means that we cannot truthfully claim to have peace with God if we are quarrelling with those around us (1 Jn 1:6-7; 2:9-11; 4:19-21). Remember how an earlier part of our text declared that we are *"not wrestling against flesh and blood"*. If then we are busy fighting with our fellow Christians then we have been distracted from our true adversary. Be sure that the devil will take full advantage of such folly.

- ***Peace with ourselves***. (Jn 14:27; 16:33)

Here, the most treacherous ground of all, is where we most need to have our feet shod with the gospel of peace. We may guard the precious peace we have with God, never doubting that God has reconciled us to himself by the gospel. We may also sustain good fellowship and cordial relationships with those around us. But our own hearts! How hardly they are controlled! What disturbance and agitation sweeps through the corridors of our souls! How often we are disquieted in spirit! How frequently is our inner security shaken! How easily we can be made to doubt our standing before God! How quickly we question whether we do indeed still stand in his favour and may still expect his bountiful blessing! With false humility we are induced to say that we are not worthy to join with the saints of God, and that we dare not approach the throne of grace, nor expect any great thing from the generous hand of the Lord.

Now those tremors all come because we look to the feelings of our hearts and not to the promise of God. We are not firmly enough established in the gospel of peace, and therefore we do not *"judge ourselves with righteous judgment"* (Jn 7:24). And what harm we cause! For when we are thus troubled within we become ineffective warriors and may then be discomforted even more by the enemy.

Recognising this weakness, Paul adds to his noun a strong

Verb – "*Wrap*"

The Greek text can be rendered as, *"**Wrap** around your feet and ankles the bracing gospel of peace."* Or perhaps, *"Give yourself a firm footing by **wrapping** around your feet and ankles the gospel of peace."*

- ### *Putting on the Gospel*

The Greek word used by Paul means literally to "bind under one's feet". It suggests that by a settled determination, by an act of definite faith, we must daily brace ourselves with the gospel of peace. Like sailors who used to lash themselves to the helm of a gale-tossed ship, to save them from being washed overboard, so we must bind ourselves to the gospel. Christ and his righteousness alone must be the bedrock upon which we stand. We abjure any confidence in our own merits; we renounce any claim based on self-endeavour; we depend for welcome and succour only upon the grace of Christ. Neither will we allow our defeats to build a barrier between ourselves and the mercy of God. If our merits cannot gain us access to the throne neither can our demerits deny us access. It is all by grace. That is the gospel, and there is no other.

Thus Paul calls it the gospel of *"peace"*, because all who so wrap themselves with this gospel will find peace settled in their hearts. No matter how inexplicable the vicissitudes of life may be, people anchored in the gospel will not be able to doubt the Father's love and care. Their peace will not be found in some outer circumstance, but in God himself. No work of the enemy will be able to unsettle them nor move them away from the victory of Christ.

- ### *Prepared by the Gospel*

The Greek word translated as the *"bracing"* gospel of peace has the idea of *"advance preparation"* – such as strengthening something to bear an extra weight; or smoothing a roadway in readiness for the king to use it; or erecting a barrier against an expected peril; or taking a medicine to prevent an attack of sickness; and the like. We might apply it to ourselves in three ways -

– ### *Braced Against Falling*

The gospel, and the gospel alone provides a solid foundation upon which our true peace can stand. For a short time peace may be founded upon other things, but when a howling storm arises they will surely fail, and the house will tumble down (Mt 7:24-27), the ship will founder.

– ### *Braced Against Disease*

The gospel has been especially prepared, or compounded, by God as the one effective medicine for the soul's distemper. The dread sin that sickened us, that fevered our spirit, that sapped our goodness, can be purged by the gospel alone. The gospel is the one preparation that can bring health and soundness to the whole person, body, soul, and spirit (1 Th 5:23-24).

– *__Braced Against Attack__*

The word suggests a state of *"preparation"* (cp. the KJV), and in its context, especially of "preparation for war". If we are not firmly rooted and grounded in the hope of the gospel, prepared to withstand the heaviest shock of the enemy's assault, we shall soon be overthrown (Cl 1:23; 2:6-7; Ep 3:16-17).

In ancient times, soldiers had no choice except to march wherever they had to go. But with these well-made greaves and sandals there was little risk that shredded shoes or injured shins would check the advance of the imperial legions of Rome.

Because of the peace that is dug deep into our souls by the glorious gospel of Christ, we too can walk steadily through life, unhurried, without fear, pressing confidently on toward the prize that is set before us.

The Shield of Faith

"In every circumstance hold up the shield of faith."

Roman shields came in a variety of shapes, but most commonly they consisted of a wooden frame covered with leather. They were oblong, curved, large enough to shelter almost the entire body of the soldier who carried it, and could be turned to ward off a blow from any direction. Often, just before battle, soldiers would soak their shields in water, to tighten the leather, and to make the shield more effective in deflecting or quenching the burning arrows of the enemy.

Our shield and shelter is faith, which we place between ourselves and the enemy, so that try as he may he cannot penetrate our defence nor deliver a mortal wound.

Faith's Shelter

• *Sheltering the Mind*

Satan may attack your mind, perhaps suggesting that if you were truly intelligent you would see at once that the Bible is unreliable. Or by some other whispers, whether wickedly blasphemous, or subtly devious, he may try to wean you away from the Christ. He may attack you directly, by implanting such ideas in your mind, or indirectly, through the voice of some scoffing critic.

But even if your mind reels under those attacks, and you cannot summon any arguments adequate enough to defend the truth, still faith can spring to the fore and powerfully uphold the integrity of scripture. Faith brings its own witness; it has a self-authenticating power possessed by no other faculty – by faith, *"we know"* (cp. He 11:3). Faith once truly fixed on Christ stands serene against all argument, whether human or demonic, and laughs at every satanic bombardment.

Of course, I do not mean that faith is blind, that it refuses to see what is plain, or that it should succumb to mere superstition. No! Faith is reasonable, and rests upon truth; it is sensible and behaves rationally; it abhors falsehood and cannot abide deception. But to faith nothing is so reasonable as to believe in God and nothing is so believable as the word of God. So faith finds an indestructible foundation upon which to stand, and there it stands, able to endure every assault, protecting the mind from every blow, and keeping the soul safe from all lasting harm.

• *Sheltering the Senses*

Perhaps it is some other sense being assailed by the devil: maybe your consciousness of God's presence, or the joy of salvation, or the feeling of peace with God. If he can rob you of your awareness of those things, and others like them, then his mocking voice will cause you to fear and tremble and doubt whether you are indeed saved.

But again, faith raises a bulwark against all hellish deceptions, for we do not rest upon either sight or feeling, but upon the reliability of God's promise, which cannot lie (Ro 8:24; 2 Co 5:7; He 11:1; 1 Pe 1:8).

- ### *Sheltering the Conscience*

The devil may take hold of your conscience, and turn it to a wicked end by forcing it to accuse you falsely. He may twist it to accuse you of things you have not even done; or warp it to condemn you for things of which you have already repented.

If you heed those scathing accusations you will swiftly plunge into a pit of despair. But against every blow, faith provides a shield that is blazoned with the impenetrable heraldry of the gospel. When (as we saw in an earlier chapter) conscience becomes *"evil"* and ceases being trustworthy, then the shield of faith will quench its accusatory voice, and replace those corrupt words with the calming grace of the gospel. (He 10:22-23; Ro 10:9-10).

- ### *Sheltering the Will*

Cunningly and maliciously the enemy may try to subvert your will and turn you into a traitor against God. How often he has incited people to mutiny against the Lord! What multitudes has he provoked into violating the King's holy law, causing them to curse the Name, as Job's wife taunted him to do?

But true faith will have none of it. Secure in the Word of God, enraptured by the vision of Christ, reinforced by a vision of the invisible (2 Co 4:16-18), faith cries "No!" to unrighteousness and "Yes!" to righteousness and presses on in the glad service of the Saviour.

Faith's Supremacy

"***Above all these*** *take up the tough shield of faith,*" says the apostle. What does he mean by *"above all"*?

For a Roman soldier the tough shield was the cover and defence for his other pieces of armour. Similarly, our girdle, our breastplate, our greaves, may become damaged and rent in the course of conflict. That is, our righteousness (say) may fail, and we may slip into sin; our apprehension of the truth may become blurred and uncertain; our peace in the gospel may be somehow sorely disturbed; we may be near to falling under our foe's violent assault; but faith can still stand firm. Against its unyielding barrier the enemy will wear out his strength in vain. Forced to retreat, his weapons blunted, his ammunition exhausted, the devil will finally turn and flee (Ja 4:7).

What we lack in grasp of the truth, or in performance of righteousness, or in possession of the peace of Christ, will be more than compensated for by faith, so long as that divinely wrought shield is held firmly against the arrows of our antagonist.

You may ask: "How shall I know when my armour is damaged? How can I tell when the shield of faith must be taken up and held in place?" By these signs –

- when temptations or afflictions that you thought were broken and for ever banished come flocking back in shattering savagery.
- when you have lost your taste for, and your delight in, Christian duties; when tasks that once were pleasurable now seem dull and difficult.
- when in place of once-abounding blessings your soul has withered, and there is a famine in your spiritual life.

- when your love for God seems to have grown cold, and try as you may it will not warm again.
- when you find that you have grown apathetic toward sin, and can no longer weep over iniquity; when godly sorrow for your own unrighteousness and for that of those around you has abated in your heart.
- when, laid low by temptation, you have fallen into sin, lost your outward experience of God, failed your Lord, broken your testimony, and shamed your soul.

When, despite every effort on your part, those things, whether some or all of them, are happening to you, then you know that you urgently need to grasp the shield of faith to protect you from further harm; and to shelter you while the Holy Spirit mends the damage and makes you whole again (cp. Ps 51:1-4, 10-12).

But mark this: faith does not always bring an immediate remedy. Sometimes it has to continue steadfast through a long night. The Lord does not always heal every hurt speedily. Sometimes he permits us to remain for a time in our darkened state so that we might learn humility and total dependence upon him. Nonetheless, if we hold fast to faith, even the blackest midnight will be followed by a new dawning of his love (cp. Ps 84:5-7,11).

Faith's Success

"You will quench all the fiery arrows of the Evil One."

Paul comprehends Satan's entire armoury under one phrase: *"fiery arrows"*. Of them we may say that they come –

- *Swiftly*

How quickly Satan's temptations and afflictions dart upon us. The scriptures many times warn us to watch carefully, lest we be caught off guard.

- **_Secretly_**

Silent and unseen temptations can creep up and seize us. They may come subtly, from friends and those who are closest to us (cp. Mt 16:23), or from other sources least expected. They may come when we are most engaged in the Lord's work.

- **_Sorely_**

Every satanic dart is designed to kill (Jn 10:10). Each arrow is intended to destroy a servant of God and to nullify his or her salvation, stealing them away from God.

The epithet *"fiery"* may refer to the practice of dipping arrow-heads in poison to pollute the bloodstream of the victim, bringing disease and then death. Paul means that if we allow Satan's darts to strike home they will inflame passion, poison the heart, and infect one's whole life with deadly venom.

- **_Searingly_**

Or *"fiery"* may refer instead to the practice of wrapping a tar-soaked cloth around an arrow and igniting it before the bolt was sped on its way. If so, then Paul is using a flaming arrow as a metaphor for burning temptation. The devil has a quiver-full of them: *"the lust of the flesh ... the lust of the eye ... the pride of life ... unwarranted fears ... an evil conscience ... pride"* — and many others.

How shall we quench these dread darts? How shall we dodge such a barrage of evil? Simply, and fully, by the shield of faith. Paul is emphatic – take up the shield of faith and **_you will_** quench all the fiery arrows of the devil. And note, he does not say merely that you will resist, or repel, those questing, poisoned points, but that you will utterly **_quench_** them! The shield of faith will drain all their venom, extinguish all their flames, absorb all their virulence, and render them harmless.

How does faith perform such feats?

- By showing us the true joys of salvation, and giving us a desire for righteousness, and a happiness in holiness, such that we resolve never to allow anything to snatch those delights from us.
- By showing us that Christ's victory is our victory, and that everything he wrought in triumph at Calvary was done on our behalf. Faith gladly unites with Christ and all the benefits of his completed work, and takes her stand behind Christ, presenting his merits, not her own, both to the enemy and to God, and grandly conquers by those same merits (cp. Ps 115:9; Pr 30:5).
- By showing us those promises in scripture that affirm the perseverance to final salvation of each person who truly makes Jesus Saviour and Lord. Despite all that the enemy may do he cannot finally pluck anyone who is fixed in faith out of the hand of God, nor shift that person from the Rock (Christ) upon which every true believer is well-founded.
- By showing us that despite our many failures, God remains abundantly merciful, ever willing to forgive the contrite soul, and to restore us again to the joy of his salvation. Thus the sting of Satan's dart, even should it strike home, is quickly neutralised, and we are healed again.

The eye of faith always pierces through the gloom, the dust, and the noise of battle, and clearly sees the victory that must surely be won, the spoils of war that will surely be gained!

Paul says that the flaming darts of our enemy can be stopped only by the shield of faith. So let us stir up that faith! Believe God! Believe his promise! Believe, and scorn whatever weapon the enemy hurls against you. Faith overcomes the world! (1 Jn 5:4)

The Helmet of Salvation

"Put on the helmet of salvation."

The meaning of Paul's analogy is found in another place, where he writes, *"Let us put on for a helmet the hope of salvation"* (1 Th 5:8). Anyone who has a clear and shining *"hope of salvation"*, which will be revealed at the coming of the Lord Jesus Christ (1 Pe 1:5-6), will find there a great incentive to ward off every defiling blow of the enemy.

The helmet had three functions –

- it protected the head and neck in battle;
- it was a symbol of rank;
- it signified membership in a particular unit.

Thus the salvation we have found in Christ is a sure bulwark against the threat of sin and judgment; it shows that we are now the children of God, princes by birth and rank; and it marks us as members of God's royal priesthood, possessing the highest rank in heaven and an ineradicable right to stand boldly before God, having all confidence that we are welcome.

Just as a helmet protects one's head, so the hope of receiving full salvation on the day of Christ's return builds in a believer sharpness of vision, clarity of understanding, sensible judgment about the true value of things, good balance in one's walk through life. Further, in times of trial, should the enemy try to pull us into despair, this hope, ever beating strong in the heart, will keep us untroubled and full of joy in the Lord.

The Sword of the Spirit

"Take up the sword of the Spirit."

This is the only offensive item mentioned in the list; all the other pieces are defensive. In the main, too, the other pieces protected the soldier only when he was facing forward. A man who turned and ran away had little protection, and could easily be brought down.

The Roman sword was designed to wound or kill an enemy in close personal combat; it was two-edged and sometimes very ornate.

The sword was also a weapon for defence, but only by an attacking soldier. A retreating warrior would find little use for his sword. So is the word of God to a Christian. By it we toss aside the enemy's blitz; and by it we in turn blitz the enemy, and deliver him a mortal wound.

These things we have seen already, insomuch that the word of God is the fabric and foundation of all the pieces of the Christian's armour.

This only should be added here (as it is by Paul), that the word is the *"sword of the Spirit"*. That is, it was fashioned by the Spirit of God, tempered and sharpened by his own hand; therefore, it cannot be effective and powerful in the fray unless he makes it so. Hence, we must not only bear this sword about with us, but also make sure that we both carry it and wield it under the influence of the Spirit. Hence Paul says in the very next verse (Ep 6:18) that we should *"never stop calling upon God, always guided in prayer by the Spirit, keeping alert, seeking God's help in everything, never giving up, and praying especially for the people of God."*

So there is no substitute in fruitful, prosperous, and victorious Christian life for constantly *reading* and *praying* through your Bible. Christians who are weak in the word will simply be weak. But strength in the word of God immersed in prayer conveys vigour to every part of the believer's being.

Conclusion

"Put on the full armour of God, so that you can stand against the wiles of the devil ... Clothe yourself with

every piece of God's armour, so that when the evil day comes you will be able to withstand the enemy's attacks, and having done all, still to stand your ground" (Ep 6:11,13).

The Evil Day

What is this day? It is perhaps the day when sickness strikes, or when some affliction falls upon us, or persecution begins, or temptation is launched against us. Or it may be one of those days when we are suddenly overwhelmed by the remembrance of sin (Ps 49:4-5). Such days happen to us all. What shall we do? Shall we fear, or fail, or fall? No! Rather, be prepared by daily wearing the full armour of God. Surely it is wisdom to don this heavenly armour. It is also our duty, lest we allow the enemy some advantage and incur heaven's anger by defiling these temples of the Holy Spirit, our bodies (1 Co 3:16-17; 6:19-20).

The Full Armour

We are commanded to take up this armour, and to put it on, all of it, piece by piece, omitting no part of it. One piece without the other will not do. If any piece is missing, our entire defence will be weakened. This is your personal responsibility, as it is mine, carefully and deliberately, having complete confidence in its efficacy, to pick up God's armour and fasten it around yourself. Examine yourself from time to time. Has a piece become damaged, or loose, or perhaps even fallen off? Is the sword still free in its scabbard, the shield firmly on your arm, the helmet safely laced, the breastplate strongly secured, the girdle buckled fast? Are the greaves wrapped tightly around your feet and ankles? Is everything in place, ready for battle?

Before each new fight, or when simply standing guard, a good soldier regularly checks his armour and weapons. Is there any rust, are there any weak spots, does some military skill need improving, is more training or practice required? Here is an injunction to be obeyed: put on the armour, put it on properly, put it on carefully, put it on skilfully, put it all on, and make sure you are ready – ready for any attack or ambush, ready to defend yourself successfully, and ready to crush your foe utterly!

Our Battle Plan is Prayer

"Pray in the Spirit at all times" (vs. 18-20)

In Christian warfare our *strategic* aim is to defeat Satan, and our *tactic* is prayer, without which we are headed for defeat. The Spirit – the Word – Prayer – they are indispensable resources for Christian warriors who are resolved to triumph in Christ.

True prayer is a continuous conversation with God, in a real personal sense, not some formal address to an unknown entity who may or may not be attending.

How should you pray? That is more question than I can answer here. Suffice it to say that there are many different ways to pray, from formally on your knees to chatting with God while, say, you walk down the street or sit at your desk. In my opinion, the most common and perhaps the most important, way to pray is to maintain a more or less continuous conversation with the Lord (Ep 5:20; 6:18).

Prayer provides vital support for an assertion of victory in the spiritual dimension, thus ensuring that you will soon also obtain victory in the natural. It is part of our spiritual warfare. People might wish they could avoid that struggle, but it is inescapable. Once again, whether we like it or not, we are at war with the powers of darkness, and will be throughout our earthly pilgrimage. [91]

Consider the example of Israel. Canaan was a land of milk and honey; but Israel first had to dispossess the enemy, by faith, and only then could they take possession of the land.

The main difference between them and us is that they had to take the earthly land in order to get the heavenly blessing, but we have to win our victory in the heavenly realm in order to enjoy its blessings on earth!

Does this mean that we should ignore practical actions? Hardly. In the economy of God the spiritual and the natural are not in opposition, but should work in synergy together. This is the theme of the next chapter.

---

(91) If you have never read John Bunyan's *Pilgrim's Progress*, this would be a great time to do it! You will never read a more enthralling description of the way and warfare of we who are pilgrims, and of our sure victory in Christ.

Twenty-six:

Playing Your Part

"Stay alert, and never give up" (Ep 6:18)

It has been said that England became mistress of a worldwide empire more by accident than design, which is an ingenuous claim, based upon sublime ignorance of reality. Empires are built and maintained by courage, conquest, and most of all, brutal strength – all of which were displayed in abundance by the explorers and generals, the merchants and warriors, whom Great Britain sent around the globe searching for glory, power, and riches. When I was a boy, the map was peppered with pink, marking the colonies, territories, and nations that were part of "the empire upon which the sun never set". We learned all about the heroism of the British warriors, but nothing was said to us about the tens of thousands of native peoples whose blood was mixed into the foundations of the empire. [92]

Still, there is no denying the heroic deeds of its builders. The brief but savage *Battle of Abu Klea*, fought in the Sudan in 1885, is a dramatic example of many similar conflicts. A

---

(92) As a boy I was at best only vaguely aware that the Australian aborigines had been all but annihilated 150 years earlier by the colonising British.

small British force of 1100 soldiers and officers faced a vast Sudanese army of 12,000, and, astonishingly, prevailed. [93]

The battle inspired a poem, built around the rallying cry of the sporting teams of Clifton College in Bristol, England – "Play up! Play up! And play the game!" In the poem, a cricket game is ending, with the scores closely matched, and only one more wicket to fall. The boy upon whom his team's hopes rest, the last batsman, is encouraged by his coach –

> There's a breathless hush in the Close [94] to-night
> Ten to make and the match to win
> A bumping pitch and a blinding light,
> An hour to play, and the last man in.
> And it's not for the sake of a ribboned coat.
> Or the selfish hope of a season's fame,
> But his captain's hand on his shoulder smote:
> *"Play up! Play up! And play the game!"*
>
> The sand of the desert is sodden red – [95]
> Red with the wreck of a square that broke;
> The Gatling's jammed [96] and the colonel dead, [97]
> And the regiment blind with dust and smoke.

---

(93) Although the British drove back the Sudanese in that skirmish, in the end they were temporarily forced to abandon their rule over the country. They returned fifteen years later, and this time successfully turned Sudan into a British colony, albeit with immense slaughter, caused mainly by the recently invented machine guns, against which the poorly armed Sudanese had no defence. They were cut down in their thousands. Sudan remained under British rule until it gained independence in 1956.

(94) The name of the sporting field at Clifton is "The Close".

(95) The boy is now an officer in the small British regiment at the battle of Abu Klea.

(96) Early in the battle, the only machine gun the British had became clogged with desert sand and inoperable.

(97) Several other senior officers were also killed, and command had to be assumed by an inexperienced intelligence officer.

> The river of death has brimmed its banks,
> And England's far, and Honour a name,
> But the voice of a schoolboy rallies the ranks –
> *"Play up! Play up! And play the game!"* [98]

And play the game they did, and well enough to win. The same spirit was still beating in the British breast decades later, during World War II, when Winston Churchill made his arousing speech –

> We shall not flag or fail. We shall go on to the end, we shall fight in France, we shall fight on the seas and oceans, we shall fight with growing confidence and growing strength in the air, we shall defend our Island, whatever the cost may be, we shall fight on the beaches, we shall fight on the landing grounds, we shall fight in the fields and in the streets, we shall fight in the hills; we shall never surrender! [99]

Shall the warriors of Christ be less doughty? Will our determination pale before theirs? How can we cede to those empire-builders greater courage, tougher zeal, more intrepid bravery? God forbid! Our cry, too, must be, "We will never surrender!"

But this highlights again the principle that what God has promised we must activate by both *faith* and *action*. As James says, *"Faith without works is dead!"* (2:17) The game must be played, and played with courage, and with an unshakable resolve to win! There is a battle to fight, a prize to be gained – but the spoils will never go to the lazy nor to the fearful, nor will the sword prevail if it remains sheathed.

---

(98) *Vitae Lampada* ("The Torch of Life"), by Sir Henry Newbolt (1862-1938); first and second stanzas.

(99) From a speech in the House of Commons, June 4, 1940.

Faith Without Works is "Dead"

Despite the clear warnings of scripture, some people try to adopt an extreme "faith" position. They scorn any use of natural means, or any application of human effort. But how can such an attitude be proper, when God himself has provided the natural world, along with all its skills and wisdom, its remedies and resources? And since we are still creatures of nature, we dare not despise these natural provisions. What God has given we are expected to gather and enjoy (Ps 104:27-28).

Sirach, in connection with illness, long ago recognised this aspect of the life of faith. He was fully aware of the promise and power of God. He well knew that the Lord, without calling upon any natural force, could do whatever he pleased. But he also understood that God seldom does for us what we can do for ourselves, and that we are expected to utilise every resource that has been placed in our hands. Sirach imparted this wisdom to the young men he was training to be rabbis in his "House of Instruction" [100] (51:23) –

> You should honour physicians for what they can do. The Lord created them and gave them their skill in curing sickness. ... The Lord has created medicines from the earth, and a sensible man will not disparage them. ...The Lord has imparted knowledge to men, that by their use of his marvels he may win praise; by using them the doctor relieves pain and from them the pharmacist makes up his mixture. There is no end to the works of the Lord, who spreads health over the whole world. My son, if you have an illness, do not neglect it, but pray to the Lord, and he will heal you. ... Then call in the doctor, for the Lord created him; do not let him leave you, for you need him.

---

(100) Today we would call it a Bible College, or Theological Seminary.

There may come a time when your recovery is in their hands" (38:1-15, NEB).

What a lovely expression the old rabbi uses – *"There is no end to the works of the Lord, who spreads health over the whole world!"* Our glorious God is still spreading health and prosperity throughout his church. He does so in response to believing prayer. But he also works through the use of means. God, as Sirach says, has imparted knowledge to people, and those who are sensible will make full use of those whom the Lord has made skilful.

So the correct rule is this: once you have seized victory in the heavenlies (where all our real spiritual warfare takes place), you are then free to use, and should use, whatever natural resources are appropriate. Thus King Asa was condemned, not (as some think) because he turned to the physicians, but because he failed beforehand to turn to the Lord (2 Ch 16:12,13).

This idea, of using good sense, of maintaining proper balance, can be applied to many areas of life, not just times of sickness. Trust the Lord, but also, do what you can to help yourself. As Sirach says, if you refuse to employ a physician, when one is available, you may find yourself sinning against your Maker! (38:15) – and that rule, of course, can be applied to many different areas of human need.

A Greek Fable

Other cultures have recognised the same principle. For example, around 600 B.C., the Greek story-teller Aesop told his fable, *Hercules and the Waggoner* –

> A Waggoner was once driving a heavy load along a very muddy track. He was forced to stop when the wheels of his wagon sank to their axles in the mire. The more the horses pulled, the deeper sank the wheels. So the Waggoner cast aside his whip, knelt down on the track,

and prayed fervently to Hercules the Strong: "O Hercules, help me in this my hour of distress!" But Hercules appeared to him, and said: "Don't just sprawl there! Get up man, and *put your shoulder to the wheel*. If you will do nothing to help yourself, then you can't expect the gods to care for you."

Moral: heaven helps those who help themselves!

Likewise, Valentine Blacker (1778-1823), an English lieutenant-colonel and Surveyor-General of India, told his soldiers, "Put your trust in God, my boys, but keep your powder dry." [101] And Howell Forgy (1908-1983), an American naval chaplain, during the Japanese attack on Pearl Harbour in 1941, was asked to pray for the naval gunners. Instead, he dropped his Bible, manned one of the gun turrets himself, and began firing at the enemy, crying out, "Praise the Lord, and pass the ammunition!" [102]

In other words, there is, or should be, balance in all things. There is a time to trust God alone for some miracle of answered prayer – not as a last resort, but because you realise that is what he wants. There are other times when it is wiser, and proper in the sight of God, to trust the Lord while also making full use of every available natural resource. What there is *never* a time for (as King Asa discovered), is

---

(101) He was actually quoting an old saying, reputedly first spoken by Oliver Cromwell during his invasion of Ireland.

(102) Another version of the story, and perhaps more likely, has Forgy, in 1941, on board the cruiser New Orleans. "As the Japanese planes roared overhead, it was discovered that the man with the keys to the ammunition locker had gone ashore. A group of crewmen managed to break into the locker, only to face a second obstacle – the power ammunition hoist was out of action. So the men, Forgy among them, formed a human chain, passing the shells from hand to hand up to the gun deck." Forgy encouraged the tiring men, and his words became a catchphrase and the title of a popular war song, written by Frank Loesser in 1942, *Praise the Lord and Pass the Ammunition*.

trusting in human hands alone without any recourse to prayer. Prayer must always undergird and surround *all* that we plan and do.

But sometimes people, eager to stand on faith alone, or unsure about what to do, try to pressure the Lord into action. But you cannot bully God, nor force the Almighty into a corner. Nor can you put God into your debt, nor strike a bargain with him. Rather, we should strive to discover what the Lord wants to do, and how he wants it to be done!

Judith

The Jewish *Book of Judith*, written probably around 200 B.C., warns against the folly of trying to manipulate God. Threatened with an invasion, the Jewish elders begged their enemies for five days' grace, after which they would surrender. In the meantime, they promised themselves that the Lord would come and rescue them by a miracle. But Judith rebuked their temerity. "How dare you tempt the Lord," she cried, "and presume to tell God when he must deliver you!" She then expressed her own certainty that the Lord would indeed save them from defeat, but that he would do it in his own way and in his own time. And so it happened. The Lord gave her a plan that enabled her to cut off the head of the enemy commander, Holofernes, which caused the invading army to flee in dismay! (Judith 8:11-17)

So, out of a synergy of deep faith, fervent prayer, shrewd planning, and human action, arose a glorious victory.

The story is probably fiction, but the lesson it conveys is assuredly true – you should trust the Lord, but *you cannot coerce him!* No one can back God into a trap. No one can hustle him into doing what he has chosen not to do. The Lord has no duty to rescue fools from their folly, and he seldom does so. Yet I have often seen people, say, plunging themselves into debt, sure that God will bail them out. How shocked they are when he allows their creditors to foreclose on them! But those who dig a hole should not complain when they fall into it. And how can those who set snares for their own feet be surprised when they find themselves caught? Rather, we should walk circumspectly and wisely, never trying to put God to the test. [103]

But what if some enemy has dug a hole to catch you, or set a snare to trap you? Then believe God for deliverance! And ask him also if there is anything your own hands can do, some natural skill you can call upon, to facilitate the miracle you need.

Maccabees

Another story from old Israel, this time probably true, tells about a slaughter that occurred around 150 B.C. The Seleucid army invaded Palestine, and soon learned that devout Jews would not fight on the Sabbath day. Inevitably, the invaders launched an attack on the Sabbath and mercilessly cut to pieces the unresisting Jews.

Following that awful disaster, the Jewish leaders said to each other, "If we all do as our brethren have done, and refuse to fight for our lives and for our laws, then the heathen will quickly root us out of the earth!" So they issued a decree – "If

---

(103) Readers who know their Bibles well will sense a paradox here (cp. Ma 3:10; etc). But there is a difference between "proving" God (on the one hand) by taking up, trusting, and acting upon his promises, and (on the other) by rashly acting outside his promise. The one he will honour; the other he will probably scorn. The one is faith; the other is presumption. The one is based upon submission to the Father's will; the other is directed by self-will and self-interest. Jesus understood the difference between those two approaches (Mt 4:6-7; Lu 4:9-12). Jesus was quoting Deuteronomy 6:16, showing that scripture must be interpreted by scripture. Each promise has its own time, place, and manner of fulfilment. Hence, you can trust the Lord to protect you; but if you throw yourself off a high building, then you are on your own! You will hope in vain for an angel to hold you up.

anyone attacks us on the Sabbath day, we will fight against him; we will not let ourselves be murdered like our brethren were!"

They had learned a harsh lesson about the folly of abandoning common sense, and of trying to thrust upon the Lord duties that he expects us to fulfil! (1 Mc 2:32-41)

You may ask anyway, "How could God sit silent in the heavens while men, women, and children who had trusted him to keep them safe were ruthlessly killed? Why didn't he step in and defend them? After all, they were only obeying his own command to keep the Sabbath day holy!"

I don't know the whole answer to such questions. Nor does anyone else. There are times when I do think that the Lord should have acted to prevent unspeakable things from happening. But his hand remained still. Why didn't he stop Herod from murdering the babies in Bethlehem when Jesus was born? The most joyous event in all history has been for ever stained by the wracking cries of those bereaved and inconsolable mothers. Why didn't God turn the Titanic aside when he saw its certain wreck approaching? And one could go on, and on. It is the age old problem of how and why a good God can allow bad things to happen.

We simply don't know. [104] But we can say that tragedies are

---

(104) The common solution to this problem (which is known as theodicy) is to argue that God is working a greater good out of what seems evil. No doubt that is sometimes true. But in the end, it is too trite. Many terrible events – such as torture chambers, overwhelming floods, fires, famines, pestilences, wars, and similar catastrophes – are just too horrible to have any valid redeeming features. The patriarch Job is an example. He could find no justification for the unparalleled series of disasters that struck him down. Nor did God offer him any reason for his pain. The Lord simply silenced Job by showing him a vision of heaven's glory. Likewise, he silences our complaints by showing us Calvary, and then a vision of Paradise to come.

often a product of human ignorance, folly, lack of good sense, or downright wickedness, from which, once again, the Lord has no sworn duty to rescue us. He expects us to learn, to act wisely, to avoid peril when we can, to accept responsibility both for our actions and for our lack of action.

Yet vast mystery remains, for which Calvary alone provides an assuring answer. There the Father himself silently watched his only Son being horribly tortured and brutally murdered. But he knew that the cross was not the end. Rather it was a beginning. Three days later came the resurrection of Christ, followed by his ascension, his enthronement at the Father's right hand (He 1:3; 8:1), and his reign in triumph for ever.

The present benefit is that we have a High Priest in heaven who has himself suffered deeply and terribly, yet prevailed, and so can console, comfort, and heal all who come to him in loving trust and surrender. (He 2:17-18; 4:15; 5:2)

In the meantime, trust God with all your heart, expecting his promises to be fulfilled. And while you wait, let not your hands be idle, but set to and "Play! Play up! And play the game!" Or, to return to a biblical analogy –

Rise Up and Possess the Land

Here is the truth of the matter. We have been made the rightful heirs of a magnificent land called *The Heavenlies* – but an enemy has rushed in and seized it unlawfully. Shall we allow ourselves to be dispossessed? Shall we cravenly yield to hopelessness? Will you permit Satan to trample you down, or will you instead tread him underfoot? I am resolved rather to be like the Israelites of old, who planted their feet on Canaan's soil, and pressed on to capture the Promised Land. Let us all do the same in Christ. Position yourself on the throne with Christ, and fight every battle from the security of that heavenly position, making use of *every* resource, *natural* and *supernatural*, that the Lord has put into your hands.

We face the same choice that Alexander gave to Abdalonymus in the suburbs of Sidon in 332 B.C. The former king of Sidon had been executed. So Alexander com-missioned his friend and general Hephaestion to search through the city and find someone of the blood royal who was fit to rule it –

> (Hephaestion) decided that no one was preferable to a certain Abdalonymus, a man who was indeed distantly connected to the royal family, but who, because of his poverty, was obliged for scanty profit to cultivate a garden in the suburbs.
>
> The reason for his poverty, as is true of many men, was his honesty. In fact, he had been so fully engaged in his daily toil that he knew nothing about the din of arms that had shaken all Asia! So he was much startled when the messengers of Alexander suddenly stood before him, carrying the royal insignia and the king's garments.
>
> They had found him still busily at work, clearing his garden, and plucking out the useless weeds. But Hephaestion hailed him as king, and said: "Abdalonymus, you must change that poor garment of yours for the robes that you see in my hand. Wash yourself, and rid yourself of the stains you carry from the dust and filth of the earth; then take on the spirit of a king, and carry on your self control into the good fortune of which you have shown yourself to be worthy. And when you sit upon the throne, master of the life and death of all the citizens, do not forget the humble condition in which – and, by heaven, because of which – you are now receiving the crown!"
>
> It all seemed to Abdalonymus like a dream. From time to time he kept asking whether these royal courtiers, who seemed to be making fun of him, were altogether sane!

But, while he continued to hesitate, they washed the dirt from his body, and placed upon him a robe adorned with purple and gold, and then confirmed their good faith by many oaths. So, convinced by now that he was truly made king, and attended by the same courtiers, Abdalonymus entered the palace and took his seat upon the throne. [105]

How stirring are the words Hephaestion spoke to Abdalonymus – "Wash yourself, change your filthy garments for a royal robe, and *take on the spirit of a king!*"

We should do the same in Christ. Wash yourself in the blood of the Lamb. Clothe yourself with his spotless robe of righteousness. And above all, take on *the spirit of a king*! You are a member of his royal priesthood. You have priestly rights of unfettered access to the throne of grace. You have kingly rights to speak with authority against sin, sickness, poverty, defeat, and all the works of the enemy. So tread on serpents and scorpions. Take authority over the kingdom of darkness. Know that while you remain in union with Christ nothing can finally hurt you (Lu 10:19).

---

[105] Quintus Curtius Rufus (circa 50 A.D.), *Life of Alexander the Great*, 4.1.19-26

Twenty-seven:

The Rules of Combat

In the ancient Roman arena no gladiator could hope to obtain the victor's prize unless he used the right weapons and fought according to the laws of combat. Each particular contest had its own weapons and its own rules. (106) Similarly, we cannot win the fight against sin and Satan unless we too use the proper weapons in the proper way (2 Ti 2:5). Like wrestlers in a ring, we will be disqualified if we employ foul play. How then should we fight? What rules of combat have been fixed by the King – rules that our enemy too is obliged to obey?

Total War Must Be Declared

Let there be no thought of surrender, no toying with capitulation, no compromise with victory. No terms of peace can ever be signed between us and our foe. This is total war which can end only with the absolute defeat of one combatant or the other.

In 1808 José Palafox was the governor of Saragossa, which was under siege by the French army. The French commander sent in a demand to capitulate. Palafox sent back the curt reply, *"War, even to the knife!"*

---

(106) You might find it useful to obtain a picture of a Roman soldier, and of a gladiator, or refer to an encyclopedia for a description of the gladiatorial combats, and the weapons used.

He meant that he would continue to fight even if all his troops were killed, his gunpowder exhausted, and the people were reduced to defending their city with cutlery. [107]

"War to the knife!" That must be our cry. There can be no half victory. We cannot be content with partially disarming the enemy; we cannot allow him to keep possession over any territory. His entire empire must be yielded to our King.

In 333 B.C, at the Battle of Issus, Alexander the Great inflicted a crushing defeat upon the Persian monarch Darius and captured his mother, wife, and daughters. Darius "wrote Alexander a letter, and sent friends to intercede with him, requesting him to accept as a ransom of his captives the sum of 1000 talents, and offering him in exchange for his amity and alliance all the countries on this side of the river Euphrates, together with one of his daughters in marriage. These propositions he communicated to his friends, [108] and when Parmenio [109] told him that, for his part, if he were Alexander, he should readily embrace them, 'So would I,' said Alexander, 'if I were Parmenio.'" [110]

Alexander, refusing to accept half a victory, went on to make himself lord of the entire Persian empire, and of much more beside. Our cry, too, must be "All! Or nothing!" We cannot capitulate to the devil. Even if he has us flat on our backs, and is terrifying us with jeers that we are abandoned by God, still we will shout back – *"Though I have fallen, I will stand*

---

[107] As it happens, the city fell under the French battering, and Palafox was imprisoned in France for four years. But the Allies finally won the war, Palafox was released, proclaimed a Duke, and elevated to the rank of Grandee of Spain.

[108] That is, Alexander's chief officers.

[109] A close friend, and one of his generals.

[110] From Dryden's translation of Plutarch's *Life of Alexander*.

up again! Though I sit in darkness, I will yet see the light! Though God may be angry with me now, he will raise me up again and vindicate me! Then you, O my enemy, will be crushed by shame and trampled into the mire!" (Mi 7:7-10)

Sin Must Be Overcome

If two swordsmen are fighting it may be said that one man is fighting the other. But the real intention of each duelist is twofold – *first*, to avoid the opponent's rapier; and *second*, to disarm him, and compel him to yield.

The same applies to our duel with the devil. His sword is sin. What savage wounds, some of them mortal, he can inflict with it!

Mark this – the struggle against sin is no game. There is nothing in life more serious than the demand that we overcome iniquity and walk in righteousness. The unholy cannot inherit the kingdom of God (He 12:14; 1 Co 6:9-10; Ga 5:21; Ep 4:22-32; Ph 3:17-19; etc.).

There are some, however, who make a great show of wrestling against one sin while they indulge another. They boast of their stern suppression of such and such a sin; but it is all a sham, intended to hide their addiction to another forbidden delight. By this subterfuge they try to distract conscience and hush its demands that all unrighteousness be uprooted and cast out. But conscience is not deceived. Nor is God.

Rather, let us resolve to ward off each wicked allurement, avoiding the barb of sin, never allowing thrusting temptation to strike home. Then let us break each sin in pieces, banishing it forever from our lives, so that Satan may never again pick it up and wound us with it – yet not by dealing with sins *individually*. God forbid! That is a sure path to disappointment and frustration. Sin must be dealt with as a whole. How can you do that?

Decide to Be Free

Every advance in Christian life begins with a decision. You will be free when you choose to be free. You will serve God and not sin when you choose to serve him (De 30:19; Js 24:15). There is never any excuse for sin (1 Co 10:13). No cloak can disguise it. No rationalising can justify it. If we sin it is because we want to. If we don't sin it is because we don't want to. Two hundred years before Christ, Sirach understood this, and insisted that people could shun sin if they chose to do so. If that was true under the old covenant, which had only the blood of animals to seal it, a thousand-fold more must it be true under the new covenant! Here is what the old rabbi said –

> Don't ever say that the Lord is to blame for your wrongdoing. It is your responsibility to shun what he hates. Nor can you ever blame God for leading you into a fault. Don't you know that he has no liking for sinners? All unrighteousness is disgusting to the Lord. How then can you claim to love him while playing around with iniquity? In the very beginning, when God first made men and women, he gave them freedom to determine their own actions. Therefore, if you choose, you can keep his commands; if you really want to be faithful, then you will find the strength to do it. See how God has put before you fire and water, and says, "Now choose which one it will be!" You and I are offered life or death. The one you choose is the one you will get" (15:11-17).

> So come back to the Lord, and be done with sin once and for all ... Return to the Most High, and renounce all wicked behaviour. ... God always leaves a way open for those who are sorry for their sin. If you turn back to him he will give you strength to endure and to overcome (17:25-26,24).

The Lord is full of compassion and delights in mercy; he is always willing to forgive sin and to deliver his people from trouble. But

- woe to the craven heart and the quavering hand;
- woe to the hypocrite who leads a double life;
- woe to cowardly souls who have no faith, for their hope that God will keep them safe is futile;
- woe to those who have given up the struggle, for where will they hide when the Lord comes in judgment?

But people who revere the Lord do not break his law; those who love him cling to his ways. All who fear God try to do his will; those who delight in him obey his commands (2:11-16).

Dare we, who have a better covenant and a better promise, allow a worse obedience than the old rabbi allowed?

So keep on bravely striking at every fiery weapon of unrighteousness the enemy may hurl against you, fending them off, cleaving them in two, smashing them down, pressing on from victory to victory.

Deal With the Source

Victory should be assured for us because God has given us something that was not available under the old covenant. What is it? A splendid way to deal not just with *outward* behaviour but rather with the *source* of wrongdoing; that is, a way to destroy the very nature of sin within us.

By *faith* we declare ourselves God's new creation in Christ; by *faith* we declare the old nature with all its wicked works is dead; by *faith* we toss aside the old nature, and clothe ourselves with Christ; by *faith* we reckon ourselves dead indeed to sin and alive only to God (Ro 6:11-14; 2 Co 5:17; Ep 4:22-24; Cl 3:1-12; etc.).

Concentrate your eye, then, not upon sin but upon Christ. Don't fight the darkness, just turn on the light! Sin cannot be overcome by plucking off each piece of rotting fruit one by one; rather, put the axe of faith to the diseased tree and cut it all down! Don't try to hold back the tide; instead, just walk off the beach. Don't try to beat out the fire of sin with your hands, simply pour over it the drenching water of the righteousness of Christ. Focus on the positive, not the negative. Set yourself to walk in the Spirit and it will happen that you no longer fulfil the lusts of the flesh (Ga 5:16).

Sir Kenelm Digby was one of the many extraordinary adventurers, scholars, and courtiers of 17th cent. England. By a peculiarity of fate he was born, died, and won a great naval battle at Scanderoon, all on the same date, June 11th. After his death the following epitaph was placed over his grave –

> Under this stone the matchless Digby lies,
> Digby the great, the valiant, and the wise:
> This age's wonder for his noble parts,
> Skill'd in six tongues, and learn'd in all the arts.
> Born on the day he died, th'eleventh of June,
> On which he bravely fought at Scanderoon.
> 'Tis rare that one and the self-same day should be
> His day of birth, of death, and of victory! [111]

The great Digby provides an apt metaphor of a victorious Christian; for, like him, we too are born, die, and made victorious on the one day – that day when we truly yield to the gospel and firmly declare ourselves *born* with Christ into the kingdom of God, *dead* with Christ to all unrighteousness, and *victorious* with Christ over all the power of the enemy!

---

(111) John Aubrey, *Brief Lives*; Folio Society, London, 1975; pg. 116.

Our Motives Must Be Right

Some wrestle against sin, but not because they hate it, nor because they fervently love God. Their aim is selfish. Sin stands in the way of worldly advance, or they are ashamed of being caught, or they fear hell. But if they could prosper and gain heaven despite their misdeeds, if sin carried no penalty, if they thought the Judge would simply overlook their crimes, they would do wrong with an easy conscience. They do not hate sin itself, only its consequences. If the choice were theirs, they would prefer to have unrighteousness and heaven together.

The true saint hates iniquity and loves righteousness for its own sake (cp. He 1:9). Sin remains appalling to him or her whether in secret or in the open, whether observed or unobserved, whether punished or unpunished. Sin itself, not merely its consequences, is loathed by those who love the Lord, and only to them can the victory of Christ be communicated.

Surely the words of *Galatians 5:19-21* are clear enough! If someone who has been brought out of sin and to Christ, then turns around and does despite to the blood of the covenant by indulging in repeated practice of the sins listed there, then they certainly endanger their salvation. Indeed, if they become too hardened in sin to find again a place of repentance, then they will lose all claim upon the kingdom (He 6:4-6; 10:29; 12:17). After all, it is faith that brings us into union with Christ, who alone is Guarantor of eternal life and of all our priestly and royal rights. But faith cannot survive if it is immersed in a vile miasma of perpetual rebellion against God, and where faith is lost (because of wilful and continued sin), then Christ too is lost.

Our Weapons Must Be God-Given

People wrestle against sin, but with weapons other than the scriptures allow, hence they are marked for defeat. The weapons we use, and the battle tactics we follow, must agree with the instructions of our Commander. No other way is acceptable to him.

Some labour to break sin by keeping certain of the commandments of Moses; others seek victory by performing religious penances; others think to surmount the dreadful barrier by grim determination and earnest resolutions; others hope to gain heaven by joining a particular church. None of those ways will do, nor any other that human imagination might conjure. It is God's way, or no way; it must be God's weapons or no weapon. We must overcome lawfully, or be lawfully overcome. Satan has a right to fight us, and, if he can, crush us (Re 13:7).

Something of what this means we have already considered; but let us look at it from the perspective of our text (Ep 6:13-18) -

The Chief Requirement for Victory

> *Put on the full armour of God, then you will be able to **stand** against the enemy in the darkest hour, and, having exerted your utmost strength, still to **stand** your ground. **Stand** fast, I say.*

Three times Paul urges the need to **stand** fast in the name of the Lord, clothed in the armour of God.

(1) *Stand Bravely*

Remember again Sirach's stringent warning –

> Woe to the craven heart and the quavering hand; woe to the hypocrite who leads a double life; woe to cowardly souls who have no faith. How can such people expect God to keep them safe? Woe to you who have given up the

struggle! Where will you hide when the Lord comes in judgment?

Are we cowards? Shall we flee just because the battle is hot? Let the craven flee if they will; let the timid scurry away if they must. As for us, we will stand for our God. We do not fear the foe. We are not daunted by the thought of furious combat. Rather, though we may smart from many wounds ere the fight is finished, our spirits tingle with anticipation of certain triumph. Not for us the chilly tremblings of the fearful; rather, we leap into the fray with hot expectation of laying our enemy in the dust! (Ro 16:20)

(2) Stand Forward

Remember that the armour of a Roman soldier gave no protection to his back. Protection was provided only for the front part of a legionary's body. The soldier who turned his back to fly, committed suicide. The hungry arrow, the lusty sword, the thirsty spear, would quickly find its home in his flesh. If he would live, then he must stand, facing the battle!

Likewise, our only safety lies, not in trying to avoid the conflict, but in boldly resisting the enemy. But then we have this promise: *"resist the devil and he will flee from you!"* (Ja 4:7). Hence Peter also says -

> *Stay alert! Keep a sharp lookout! Like a savage lion your enemy the devil is prowling around looking for a victim to devour. So stand up to him, always unshakeable in faith.* (1 Pe 5:8-9a)

(3) Stand Correctly

It matters little how bravely a soldier fights if he is not where his commanding officer expects him to be. His absence from his appointed place will leave a breach in his general's defences; the battle plan may be disrupted; the enemy may gain an advantage that the soldier's efforts in another place cannot allay.

So for each of us there is a place appointed, a role designated. There we must abide. There we must labour. There we must serve our King and defend his interests. Should we (like Jonah) run away from our place we shall be accounted deserters, and the penalty for abandoning a post must fall upon us. We must go where the Lord sends us; we must stand where the Lord places us; we must wrestle as the Lord commands.

(4) <u>Stand Armed</u>

In ancient times only a fool, or a man determined to die, went into battle unprotected by armour. The cohorts of Greece, the legions of Rome, were all sheltered by their strong armour. Many a brave life was saved by the stout steel; skilful use of the shield warded off many an arrow and spear, and turned aside the blows of many swords.

So too in our Christian warfare: here is our defence, that we put on the armour of God. If by carelessness or indifference we fail to wear this divine protection, we can hardly complain if we are pricked by the darts of the enemy. There are many who bear sore wounds because they did not pay proper heed to their armour.

Notice, too, that this armour is designed not only for defence but also for attack. By it we may secure our own castle; but by it also we may assault and pull down the strongholds of the enemy (2 Co 10:4).

The Standing Warrior

*"Having done all, <u>**stand**</u>!"* said Paul. He means that victory may not always come quickly, nor even seem near; you may even feel that the enemy is winning the day. Yet true believers will still stand, fully armed, and in place, knowing that Christ will plead our cause, that God will fight for us, and that we will surely triumph (2 Ch 20:15).

Or perhaps there is a different caution here. We most need to stand when there seems the least need for it. That is, after some great victory or rich success, just when grace is flowing abundantly into our lives and when we seem to be going from triumph to triumph, fruitful in righteousness, bountiful in answered prayer, then above all we need to stand armed and ready. For it is just at such times, when our defences may be relaxed, that the enemy delights to unleash a barrage of fiery darts (cp. 1 Co 10:12). So there is no time when we may safely lay down our armour, nor relax our vigilance. We dare not forget

- we are under solemn oath of allegiance to God, which we cannot safely break, nor slacken in his service, nor leave it; and
- the enemy is relentless in his pursuit of our souls, and will persevere to the very end in his attempts to destroy us; and
- all our hope of eternal life and glory depend upon us successfully withstanding every assault by the powers of darkness, and of overcoming them in the name of Christ (Re 2:7,11,17,26-29; 3:5,12-13,21-22; etc.)

A priest was sent to console the dying Frederick William I, the king of Prussia (1688-1740), and began to read to him from the book of Job, *"Naked came I out of my mother's womb, and naked shall I return thither."* The king rallied briefly, and protested, "No, not quite naked, for I shall have my uniform on." Those were his last words. A few moments later, he died.

Be sure that when your last call comes, and you are brought before the Commander, you will enter his presence in full uniform, victorious to the end, and worthy of his most splendid prize in Christ!

Bibliography

Aesop's Fables; *Hercules and the Waggoner* (circa 600 BC) The Harvard Classics; Published 1909.

Against Heresies; Irenaeus; Church Fathers; Book IV.

Believer's Bible Commentary; William Macdonald; Thomas Nelson Publishers; 1989.

Bible Background Commentary; Intervarsity Press, Nottingham UK; 1993.

Bible Knowledge Commentary, The; by John Walvoord and Roy Zuck; Cook Communications, Colorado springs, Colorado; 1989.

Book of Common Prayer; *A Collect for Peace;* Church Publishing, United States; 2001.

Brief Lives; John Aubrey; Folio Society, London; 1975.

Calvin's Commentaries; John Calvin (1509-1564).

Church History; Theodoret; (circa 429AD).

College Press NIV Commentary, The; Joplin, Missouri; 1996.

Commentary on Ephesians, A; Charles Hodge (1797-1878).

Commentary on the Bible; Adam Clarke (1715-1832).

Commentary on the Letter to the Galatians; Martin Luther; *Crossway Classic Commentaries* Alister McGrath, J. I. Packer, Edwin Sandys.

Commentary On The Old And New Testaments, A; John Trapp (1601-1669).

Commentary on the Old and New Testaments, A; Robert Jamieson, A. R. Fausset, David Brown; 1871.

Discovery; K. & A. Chant; Vision Publishing; Sydney, Australia; 1991.

Equipped to Serve; K. Chant; Vision Publishing Sydney, Australia; 1995.

Explanatory Notes on the Whole Bible; John Wesley (1703-1791).

Exposition of the Entire Bible; John Gill (1690-1771).

Expositor's Bible Commentary, The; Ed. Frank E. Gaebelein; Zondervan Publishers, Grand Rapids, Michigan.

Expository Commentary; H.A. Ironside (1876-1951).

Great Words of the Gospel; K. Chant; Vision Publishing; Sydney, Australia; 1998.

Harper's Encyclopedia of Bible Life; Ed. by Madeleine S. and T. Lane Miller; Harper & Row, NY; 1978.
History of Rome, The; Livy (B.C 59-A.D 17) Tr. by Rev Canon Roberts; 1905.
Holman New Testament Commentary; Ed. Max Anders; B&H Publishing Group, Nashville, Tennessee; 2004.
Interpreter's Bible, The; Abingdon Press, New York; 1952.
IVP New Testament Commentary Series, The; Intervarsity Press, Nottingham UK.
Jewish New Testament Commentary; David H. Stern; Jewish New Testament Publications, Inc., Clarksville, Maryland; 1982.
Judaism; Ed. by Arthur Hertzberg; George Braziller, New York; Section on the "Torah"; 1962.
Judith – OT Apocrypha
King Henry VI; William Shakespeare; Collins Tudor Shakespeare; Ed. by Professor Peter Alexander; The Heritage Press; Norwalk CT; 1986.
Letter to the Romans; Ignatius; Church Fathers.
Life and Times of Jesus the Messiah, The; Alfred Edersheim; MacDonald Publishing Company, Virginia, reprint of the 1886 edition; Vol I.
Life of Alexander the Great; Quintus Curtius Rufus; (circa 50 AD).
Life of Alexander; Plutarch; Tr by John Dryden (17th Century).
Lives of the Noble Greeks and Romans - *Caesar*; Plutarch; Abbreviated and modified from the translation by John Dryden (17th Century).
Matthew Henry's Commentary; Marshall, Morgan, and Scott, London; 1953.
Matthew Poole's Commentary; 1685.
Nelson's New Illustrated Bible Commentary; Thomas Nelson Inc, New York; 1999.
New Testament Commentary; Baker's Publishing House, Grand Rapids, Michigan; 1987.
Notes on the Bible; Albert Barnes (1798-1870).
People's New Testament Commentary, The; B. W. Johnson; Word Search Corporation, Nashville, Tennessee; 2010.
People's New Testament, The; by B. W. Johnson; 1891.
Pilgrim's Progress, The; John Bunyan; – *"The Second Stage."* Tee Publishing; 2nd edition; 2009.
Poor Man's Commentary On The Whole Bible, The; Robert

Hawker; 1850.
Preacher's Commentary, The; Word Inc; Nashville, Tennessee; 1992.
Preacher's Outline and Sermon Bible; Word Search Corporation, Nashville, Tennessee; 2010.
Pulpit Commentary, The; Ed. Joseph S. Exell, Henry Donald Maurice Spence-Jones; 1881.
Sirach – OT Apocrypha.
Speech in the House of Commons, A; Winston Churchill; June 4th.1940.
The Church; B. Chant; Vision Publishing, Sydney, Australia; 1992.
The Histories; Herodotus; Tr. by G. Macauley; Macmillan, London & New York; 1890.
Throne Rights; K. Chant; Vision Publishing; Sydney, Australia; 1997.
Vincent's Word Studies; Marvin R. Vincent; 1886.
Wiersbe's Expository Outlines; Warren W. Wiersbe; pub. David C. Cook, Colorado Springs, Colorado.
Word Pictures In The New Testament; A. T. Robertson; 1933.

Poetry & Hymns:

Aladdin and the Wonderful Lamp; (Wikipedia)
Golden Treasury, The; Francis Turner Palgrave; Penguin Popular Classics; 1994.
Hymns and Sacred Poems; Charles Wesley; 1742.
Invictus; Henley; (Wikipedia)
Love Sonnets; William Shakespeare; (Wikipedia).
Poems 67 & 84; Sir Thomas Wyatt; (Wikipedia).
Poems of Robert Browning; Selected, edited and introduced by C. Day Lewis; The Heritage Press, Norwalk, CT; 1971.
Silver Poets of the Sixteenth Century; Sir Thomas Wyatt, Henry Howard, Sir Philip Sydney, Sir Walter Raleigh, Sir John Davies; London, J. M. Dent & Sons Ltd. New York, E.P. Dutton & Co. Inc.; 1947.
Songs of Many Seasons; Oliver Wendell Holmes; (1862-1874). This Elibron Classics Title is a reprint of the original edition published by James Osgood and Co. Boston.
Tennyson's Poetry; Lord Alfred Tennyson; *"Idylls of the King"* – *"Lancelot and Elaine."* –*"St Simeon Stylites";* Selected &

Edited by Robert H. Hill Jr.; W.W. Norton & Co. New York & London; 1972.
<u>Torch of Life, The</u>; Sir Henry Newbolt; *Vitae Lampada* - (1862-1938).

Glossary

Abjure – to renounce or repudiate
Admonition – a gentle reproof, a caution
Affirm – to state or assert positively
Alluring – fascinating, charming
Analogy – a partial similarity on which a comparison may be based
Apathetic – having a lack of interest, or showing little emotion
Appropriate – fitting for a particular purpose
Ascription – assigning a quality or character to something
Avowal – affirmation, acknowledge openly
Bountiful – generous
Cajole – to persuade by flattery, wheedle, coax
Castigate – to punish in order to correct
Cavalier – offhand, casual, lacking attention or interest
Cede – yield, surrender
Cohesion – ability to stick together, logical, consistent
Conjure – to call upon or command (a devil or spirit) by incantation or spell, produce as if by magic
Conundrum – a riddle, a difficult problem
Criteria – established rule for testing anything,
Declaim – to speak loudly for effect
Demolition – to overcome, overthrow or pull down
Depredations – to prey upon, plunder or lay waste
Derogatory – belittling, expressing a low opinion of something
Disparage – look down upon
Despot – tyrant or oppressor
Discrete – separate, distinct from others
Dissipate – squander, indulge in extravagant pleasure
Eclipsed – made to appear of no importance or value
Efficacy – skill to produce a desired effect
Emulate – copy, try to equal or excel, to rival with some degree of success

Enervating – weakening
Entice – draw on by exciting hope or desire
Enunciate – pronounce words clearly
Epithalamium – a wedding song or poem
Eponymous – having the same name
Estrangement – alienation of the affections
Ethereal – light, airy
Euphoric – experiencing a high level of elation or wellbeing
Exigency – an emergency that demands action
Exploit – to take advantage of
Facilitate – to make easy or less difficult
Fidelity – faithfulness
Frangibility – fragile, easily broken
Glossolalic church – a church consisting of people who speak in tongues
Heinous – utterly odious or wicked
Heraldry – armorial bearings decorating a shield
Hiatus – a break or gap
Hubris – arrogant pride or presumption
Hyperbole – exaggeration, not meant to be taken literally
Ignoramus – an ignorant person
Illustrious – distinguished, famous
Immutable – unchangeable, cannot be moved
Implacable – cannot be appeased or changed
Impugned – challenged or called into question
Imputed – ascribed, given to a person
Incalculable – that which cannot be reckoned
Incandescent – shining brightly, glowing with heat
Inculcate – urge or impress persistently
Incumbent – as a duty resting on one
Ineradicable – cannot be destroyed or rooted out
Inexorable – relentless
Infrangable – unbreakable, invisible
Intolerable – cannot be endured
Intrinsically – inheritly, belonging
Invincible – cannot be conquered

Inviolable – not to be violated or profaned
Irrefragably – indisputable, unanswerable
Irrevocable – unalterable
Jeopardise – endanger
Magnanimous – nobly generous, not petty in feeling or conduct
Masochistic – deriving gratification from one's own pain
Mewling – crying feebly, whimpering
Minions – a servile dependent, a slave
Monotheism – the doctrine of belief in one God
Munificent – splendidly generous, bountiful
Negate – nullify, invalidate, assert the non existence of
Nexus – a bond, connection between a group or a series
Nimbus – halo, bright cloud surrounding a deity
Nullified – neutralised, made of no account
Otiose – having no effect, unable to function
Paradox – seemingly absurd or contradictory statement
Paramount – supreme
Parsimonious – reluctant to spend or give money
Parsimony – meanness, stinginess
Pharmacist – person trained to prepare and give drugs
Placate – pacify
Prerogative – right or privilege, exclusive to an individual or class
Prescription – written instruction
Presumptuous – overbearingly confident, forward to an excess
Pungent – strong, sharp taste or smell
Pusillanimous – timid, lacking courage
Rancour – bitterness, malignant hate
Redolent – a capacity to bring something to mind
Retaliation – repaying an injury in kind
Rigorous – strict, severe, allowing no deviation
Spurious – not genuine
Stigma – mark of disgrace or discredit
Superlative – of the highest quality or degree

Supernal – heavenly or divine
Supine – flat on his back, offering no resistance
Supplant – dispossess, take the place of, especially by underhanded means
Synergy – combined action
Tantalise – torment, tease, raise and then dash the hopes of anyone
Transcendent – surpassing human experience
Unanimity – all in agreement
Unassailable – unable to be attacked
Unfeigned – genuine, sincere
Unscrupulous – lacking in principles
Usurper – one who seizes a throne or power wrongfully
Utilitarian – designed to be useful, for a purpose
Valid – well grounded, sound, truthful
Vicissitudes – change of circumstances, especially variations of fortune
Vindictive – seeking revenge
Virulent – poisonous
Vitiated – robbed of legal force, made ineffective
Voluntary – acting of your own free will
Wreak – to cause something to happen

www.ingramcontent.com/pod-product-compliance
Lightning Source LLC
Chambersburg PA
CBHW050552170426
43201CB00011B/1667